To the residents of Plush mills

[signature]

UNDER THE TOWERING TREE

A Daughter's Memoir

ANNABEL ANNUO LIU

ISBN-13: 978-1503369313
ISBN-10: 1503369315

UNDER THE TOWERING TREE

A Daughter's Memoir

Also by Annabel Annuo Liu
(劉安諾)

My Years as Chang Tsen: Two Wars, One Childhood

哈囉，希兒薇亞！

乘著微笑的翅膀

風流與幽默

愛情的獵人

浮世情懷

人間多幽默

笑語人生

一杯半咖啡

for

Andrea, Doug, Clif, Tracy
&
Sylvia and Julia

CONTENTS

CONTENTS

Part Two: The New World

PROLOGUE

If one of my granddaughters asked me how I happened to marry her grandfather, I would admit, a bit sheepishly, "I did a naughty thing. His girlfriend snubbed me, and I gave him a sweet smile out of spite."

"Then what happened?"

"He talked about grasshoppers."

Two small, mundane moments that irrevocably changed our lives. They were turning points, one precipitating the other, pivotal only in retrospect.

What actually happened is, of course, a great deal more complicated than that, and it is a story within a story.

Freud said that six people are found in every marriage bed— husband, wife, and their respective parents. In mine, my father and my mother-in-law took up so much space that there was hardly any room for the rest of us.

Writing this memoir in my old age, I have come to appreciate the full import of Freud's statement, and its connection with a secret so assiduously hidden from me for thirty long years.

All of us were once small and vulnerable, at the mercy of the circumstances into which we were born—our parents, the time period of our births, and social mores of that era. We are fully-grown when we come to our marriage beds, but with disparate vulnerabilities already ingrained in us.

This is a book I have tried all my life *not* to write.

Like a child burned by hot coals, I was afraid to go near the fire.

I didn't know the extent, the nature of the conflagration, or that I had already been consumed by it.

Some say every life is a story; my life has been a mystery story. Most of the time I was in the dark about the so-called *five w's and h* that I had learned back in journalism school. I didn't know *who* did *what* to *whom*, *when*, *where*, *how*—or most importantly, *why*.

By poking around in the ashes and writing this memoir, I hope I'll come to a better and deeper understanding of the mystery.

It feels as though it has taken only a blink of an eye to live through nearly six decades in this country, to evolve from expectant youth suffused with possibilities, to decrepit old age, ruminating about the past in a small apartment.

The secret that had been hidden from me for three decades and that I then guarded for another two is more than half a century old. Perhaps it's time for it to be told.

I have lived my life merely reacting to circumstances. I have even written about it in bits and pieces in two languages, without pausing to examine it as a whole. I have never seriously reflected upon my life, including my marriage. Now, in order to do so, I must summon my courage and face the two forces of nature that shaped this marriage and so much of my life: my mother-in-law, and above all, my father.

Part One:
The Old World

My father in his early twenties, a modern young man.

Chapter 1

AN INFALLIBLE MAN

My father was an infallible man. He knew it, and we all knew it. As a child in a far corner of our house, I thanked my ancestors for having such a great man as a father.

He had so many wonderful qualities, so much to be proud of.

He was charismatic, as if the word had been invented just for him. It didn't hurt that he was born into a wealthy family and lived in luxury until the second Sino-Japanese War. He was reputed to be "the most handsome man from Yangzhou." He was eloquent, able to "talk a dead man to life," as my mother put it. And he had a great sense of humor. He commanded the center of attention at any gathering.

Everyone and everything seemed to do his bidding—even nature.

I always marveled at, for example, his ability to take catnaps. His daily regimen was cramped with work and social demands. However, whenever he needed rest and only had a few minutes to spare, he would simply declare, "I'll have a little snooze," and instantly begin snoring in an easy chair. Five minutes later, he would open his eyes, refreshed and ready to tackle anything required of him.

How I wished I could have inherited that precious ability! A lifelong insomniac, my affliction is worse when I am especially tired and under time constraints.

Even when things did not go his way, my father ensured that they did. One winter afternoon he went to call on his fiancée, my mother. He found her and her best friend, a nurse from the same medical school my mother attended, eating slices of fresh watermelon. He was appalled, as it was commonly believed that raw and cold foods like watermelon would cause digestive problems, especially in cold weather. He asked them to stop, but the two willful young ladies simply laughed at him. In desperation, he spit on each piece and put a swift and decisive end to their "dangerous binge."

Throughout his life, however, there was something over which he had no control—his tear ducts. Understandably, he was rather embarrassed by it.

He told us once about going to a movie with my mother and her best friend, the nurse. He sat between the two, and the movie was, unfortunately, a tearjerker. When the lights came back on, he was still sobbing and gasping for air. Both young ladies were dry-eyed and composed.

Regrettably, I'm the same way. A passage in a book or a scene in a film can bring me to tears. Once I even started crying when I read a mundane article in the "Home and Family" page of a Chinese newspaper. The article was about the writer, who, as a child, had to take a bus to and from school. It was dark in the winter when her bus arrived at the stop a few blocks away from home. Her father was always there. The warmth of his large, thick, calloused hand in his coat pocket enveloping hers…I never read the rest, for my vision was hopelessly blurred.

Yet, when *my* father died, I never shed a tear. Not at the hospital, or funeral, or after. Ever.

The funeral parlor did a great job. In death, he looked much healthier than he had when alive, though a bit artificial. His sparse, white hair was neatly combed, his cheeks plump and pink; he appeared to have just dozed off with his glasses on. Benign and peaceful in his eternal rest, he was not the gaunt, wax-like figure on the hospital bed I had seen a few hours after his death.

My mother broke down completely—my stoic mother of all people! For the first time in my sixty years I witnessed her lose her composure. With my brother and me holding fast to her arms, she struggled to break free and climb into the coffin, wailing, "Why didn't you take me with you?" More embarrassingly, she even tried to hug him one last time.

I was in shock. In spite of decades of his put-downs, in spite of their constant bickering and her bitterness at his refusal to let her practice medicine, she *still* loved him. But where had her love gotten her those last sixty-three years?

How do you sort out the relationship between your parents when you don't even understand your own feelings about them?

§

My father was from Yangzhou in Jiansu province, a city with 2,500 years of history, where Marco Polo had once served as a municipal official.

Historically one of the wealthiest cities in China, Yangzhou was a political, business, and transportation hub until the advent of the railroad. It was also the country's southern capital at one point. Located 150 miles northeast of Shanghai, at the junction of the Yangtze River, the Grand Canal, and the Huai River, it was called *Jiangdu*, or "River Capital." During the Qing Dynasty (1644-1911), the emperors Kangxi and Qianlong both visited.

Over the centuries, Yangzhou's rich cultural life drew renowned poets and scholars. The famous "Eight Eccentrics of Yangzhou," a group of extremely impoverished and unorthodox painters, each with a distinct style of his own, further contributed to the city's cultural heritage at the beginning of the Qing Dynasty.

Lastly, Huaiyang Cuisine, one of the four best-known regional cuisines of China, originated from Yangzhou.

My father happened to be a great connoisseur of food as well as a firm believer of Confucius' teachings, including *gentlemen should stay away from the kitchen*. In his eighty-seven years of life, he had the good fortune of never having eaten a morsel of food that he had cooked himself.

His lack of experience didn't prevent him from being a self-appointed authority on the subject of proper food preparation. When I was growing up, I often heard him speak at length about the proper preparation of the famous Yangzhou dish, *shizitou*

(Lion's Head)—large meatballs resting on a bed of napa cabbage.

To make this dish properly, my father emphasized, you must never, ever use ground pork. Rather, you take a quarter pound of lean pork and chop until pulverized. Then add three-quarter pound of pork fat, cut into small cubes about the size of the first section of your pinkie. When mixed, the two should look like fishnet. Stir in the usual seasonings—wine, soy sauce, chopped green onions, and minced fresh ginger. Add a lot of water and a little cornstarch, so that the "fishnet" almost collapses.

While stirring the meat mixture, you must do it only in one direction, clockwise or counter-clockwise, never both.

Line a clay pot with leaves of napa cabbage. Beat a couple of eggs well, coat your hands with the beaten egg, and scoop up one quarter of the meat mixture. Form into a large meatball and set it down gently on top of the cabbage leaves in one corner. Repeat the process to make four in the pot. Cover and simmer on low heat for at least five hours, preferably overnight.

Shizitou made from this *correct* process should melt in your mouth, like those made by the family cooks successively trained by my mother. And they were absolutely delectable every time.

I still remember my father's great abhorrence of the wrong preparation, in which the meatballs were fried first. Once fried, they became so durable that when "tossed from one side of the city wall to the other, they would still land intact." The ultimate, inexcusable failure of a dish!

Years after my father's lecture, I had the temerity to make *shizitou*—without either parent's knowledge, of course. My husband Sam and our two children (unfamiliar with the finer things in life, as my father would say) liked them.

In addition to the unforgivable offense of using ground pork, I took a few other liberties. I never forgot to add plenty of water, however, and wouldn't dream of frying them, ever.

Chapter 2

HEAD OF THE HOUSE

My father was born in imperial China in 1907 during the final years of the last dynasty, the Qing Dynasty. When he was four years old, a much called-for revolution overthrew the corrupt and impotent dynasty. During this monumental historical event, five thousand years of imperial rule gave way to the founding of the Republic of China, a democracy built on shaky ground. While upheavals continued in the country, my father enjoyed a peaceful childhood in Yangzhou until his father died when he was eight years old.

The loss of a parent in childhood is always traumatic, but for

my father, the consequences were much more drastic than for any of his siblings. The moment my grandfather left the world, my father became head of the house.

According to Chinese culture, specifically Confucius' *three rules of obedience*, a woman had to *obey her father at home, her husband in marriage, and her son after her husband's death*. My grandmother, the widow, had been brought up in a traditional family. She had bound feet, and, as dictated by Confucius, was totally illiterate.

My grandfather

For centuries, *all* Chinese women were listed in genealogy books by their fathers' last name only, with no identities of their own. My grandmother, identified in our family genealogy book simply as "Deng woman," gave birth to five surviving children—three sons and two daughters. When her husband died, her eldest son, a prodigious student who had earned a medical degree at age eighteen, was studying in France and was unable to come home to attend the funeral. So my grandmother had to obey her second eldest son, my father.

At eight years old, my father was in charge of the household; whatever he said became law. He didn't just decide which or how many guests to invite for family events, or what to do when servants didn't get along or stole rice. He also had to run his late father's business.

My grandfather was a salt merchant. In Yangzhou, salt was an extremely important and lucrative business, and my grandfather was very successful. So successful that he had branched out and founded four more companies, including a couple of textile companies and a paper factory. My father became chairman of the board of all these companies.

His wet nurse (a wet nurse typically stayed in the family for the rest of her life to take care of her charge) would dress him in full regalia—vest, long gown, and watermelon skin hat (pieces of fabric sewn together, rendering the shape of half of a watermelon)—and he would be carried in a four-man sedan chair to preside at the board meetings and make decisions.

All those dignified, long-bearded men hugging their water smoking pipes, almost as tall sitting as he was standing, addressed him either as *Qiye* or Chairman. *Qi* means seven, his number in the extended family birth order, and *ye*, a deferential term for father or grandfather. While such respectful treatment flattered his childish ego, it did nothing to help his understanding of the issues. In these meetings he did the only thing he could—he simply agreed to all their suggestions.

In short order, my father lost his four companies and the salt business. Luckily, the family owned a lot of land and lived by selling one piece after another. By the time the Sino-Japanese War came in 1937, the family, although still living in the same luxurious style, was on its last legs financially.

In all other aspects, my father's childhood and early adulthood were unremarkable. He enjoyed whiling away his days playing mahjongg with his mother, sisters, and assorted relatives. He attended Yangzhou Eighth High School, where he was an average student, showing none of the brilliance or academic promise of his elder brother, Yong-Choen.

Meanwhile, Yong-Choen had received his doctorate in bacteriology from the University of Lyon in France. The family had supported him for more than seven years at great expense and was looking forward to his return. In those days, studying abroad was called *dujin*, "gold gilding." Simply attending a foreign institution of learning for a year or two meant that the student could expect a much better social and financial position upon his return to China, even if he failed to earn a degree.

But my uncle shocked and dismayed his family by taking a job at a hospital in Strasbourg, showing no intention of returning. Worse, they found out that he had fallen in love and was living with a young French woman of German descent named Mimi.

His behavior was inexcusable, but not because he was a married man. He had married early—as arranged by his family—and was a father of two when he left for France. In the eyes of the Chinese, a married man could take as many concubines as he wished as long as he could afford them financially. (The first spouse, married in a proper ceremony, was wife, the rest, numbered according to the time they joined the family, were concubines.) But Mimi was a foreigner, and he was staying in France on account of her. In essence, he was abandoning his family who had spent a fortune on his education, an investment from which glory and great financial returns were expected. Now all was for naught.

It was incumbent upon my father, as head of the house, to solve the problem. He was fifteen years old, ten years his brother's junior, an insignificant "little squirt" when Yong-Choen left home. What this little squirt did was unexpectedly brazen and ruthless. He sent a telegram: "Mother critically ill." The Chinese were extremely superstitious; it was unthinkable to lie about your mother being on her deathbed. My uncle fell for the ruse and rushed home.

When he saw it was a lie, he couldn't very well turn around immediately and go back to his lover in France. My father did everything possible to detain him: ordering the cook to make his brother's favorite dishes (food he hadn't had for seven years) and getting Yong-Choen's friends to come and visit. He tried to cater to Yong-Choen's every wish.

My father even went to the store and bought the most elegant white enamel chamber pot (this being the early 1920s, their home had no modern bathrooms) for Yong-Choen's exclusive use and ordered the servants to clean it well *each time* immediately following its use.

Yong-Choen had arranged to have letters sent through an intermediary in Shanghai, but my father intercepted the mail. Mimi became distraught when months went by without a word. One day a telegram arrived bearing the news: *Mimi mort.* She had taken her own life.

Half a century later when my father told me the story, he was quite proud of himself and pronounced the two fateful French words without a trace of remorse. As my brother Charley put it, "For someone who despised the Communists all his life, he certainly practiced what *they* preached—the end justifies the means." But for my father it was black and white: family came first. I found it rather chilling. After all, between the two telegrams were a young woman's life and his brother's one true love.

Yong-Choen was number three in the extended family birth order; we called him Third Uncle. He married in his early teens at the order of his father. His wife, illiterate and with inevitably bound feet, was content with raising children and playing mahjongg. There obviously wasn't much communication between them. Now, in addition to his guilt and grief over Mimi, he was stuck in a miserable marriage for the rest of his life. Not the least of his sufferings was to bear alone and quietly the profound humiliation of having been outmaneuvered by a fifteen-year-old, his own younger brother, that little squirt. I don't think he ever forgave my father.

After graduating from high school and serving a brief stint in college, my father moved to Shanghai and attended Dongwu

University, majoring in law. For a while he entertained the idea of pursuing graduate studies at the University of Michigan with his friends, but Yong-Choen's years in France had depleted the family finances. More importantly, he met my mother.

Yong-Choen never mentioned going back to France again. He left our ancestral home with his wife and two children and moved to Shanghai. Eventually he became the associate director of the renowned Pasteur Institute in Shanghai and was appointed director after the Japanese occupied Shanghai in 1937 at the beginning of the second Sino-Japanese War. Three children were born after his return from France.

The war went on for eight years, and in the last six my father was away fighting the Japanese. In those six years, the two families—my mother, my siblings and I, and Yong-Choen and his family—both lived in the small French Concession in Japanese-occupied Shanghai.

I remember one day when my mother took us to visit *Nainai*, my paternal grandmother. The war had driven *Nainai* out of our ancestral home to live with Yong-Choen, her eldest son.

Yong-Choen, as the director of the Pasteur Institute, lived in a huge and imposing mansion on Qiqi Road, with a driveway paved with large slabs of smooth dark green limestone. It was Easter time, and the three floors seemed to be chock full of exotic and splendid objects. It was unlike any home I had ever seen.

What I admired and coveted the most were the chocolate eggs, chickens, and bunnies, some of which were wrapped with bright, colorful foil.

We were not invited to stay for dinner and not given a chocolate egg or any goodies to take home—both calculated gestures of rudeness. Our uncle took pains to show us we were unwelcome, and I have no memories of seeing him during our visit.

Yong-Choen was a prodigious scientist. In his early twenties he wrote and published a book entitled *Bacteriology* while pursuing doctoral studies in France. In China, he became *the* pioneer of tuberculosis and rabies vaccines and published more than forty research papers. For his work with a colleague at the University of Strasbourg, a disease, the Barré-Lieou syndrome, was named after the two of them. He was also awarded the Order of the Black Star

Knighthood Medal by the French government.

However, after the Sino-Japanese War, he was considered an enemy collaborator because he had served as the director of the Pasteur Institute during the Japanese occupation. He had to seek the protection of my father, who had been the only one among all our relatives to fight against the Japanese and was in a position to shield him.

While my father relished being the benefactor, those few months spent hiding at our house without his family must have been especially humiliating and galling for my uncle. He kept entirely to himself. I don't remember ever exchanging a word with him. At forty-eight years of age, with swollen legs and diabetes, he seemed inordinately old and tired of life.

For all his contributions to medical science, Yong-Choen's illustrious career was over. In ordinary times, someone like him would at least have been allowed to continue his research in an obscure laboratory corner, but those were not ordinary times.

After the Communists took over the mainland in 1949, Yong-Choen's previous association with the Pasteur Institute, classified as an *evil imperialist* organization by the new regime, made him a prominent target.

One of the Chinese Communists' ways of punishing *imperial running dogs* and intellectuals was to exile them to the countryside for hard labor. Yong-Choen was assigned to the Korean war front as a military physician. Given his age, poor health, the harsh climate in North Korea, and the perilous and humiliating work of binding wounds at the front lines, this assignment was tantamount to a death sentence.

For thirty years after the Communists took power, they maintained a so-called *Bamboo Curtain*—equivalent to the Soviet Iron Curtain—preventing all contact between the Chinese mainland and Taiwan. Having escaped to Taiwan in 1949, we only learned years later that Yong-Choen had died in his home in Shanghai in January 1953, on the eve of his designated departure for North Korea. The timing suggested that he had taken his own life, as Mimi had done decades before him. He was fifty-five years old.

My father never let known his feelings about his brother's death. In fact, all I knew was that he had been the director of the Shanghai Pasteur Institute until my father in his old age told me how he had lured his brother home.

§

In the fall of 1960, I had just finished all requirements for my master's degree and was on my way to New York to find a job. My older brother Charley, a doctoral student at Iowa State University, had supported me for three years with his research assistantship. Our father, who had been living in Taiwan, wrote to tell both of us that our uncle's three younger children had escaped from Shanghai to Hong Kong and were in dire need of help. He had sent them money and pledged to provide full support, including covering their educational expenses.

Charley and I were aghast—where would the money come from?

We knew our father was profligate. He had always lived beyond his means, treating money like dirt. The Chinese way of identifying a spendthrift is to hold up his hand with thumb and fingers pressed close together. If a lot of light appears between the fingers, it means that money leaves his hand as water passes through a sieve. I never examined my father's hand, and I didn't need to. From the way he spent money, his hand had to be like a fishing net.

In fact, the American expression, "Money burns a hole in his pocket" could not apply to my father, who spent money that was not, and would never be, *in* his pocket.

Our cousins' needs couldn't have come at a more inopportune time. The salary from my father's government job was meager to say the least. Charley tried to support the two of us with his assistantship and still squeeze every penny possible to send home.

While I had been attending graduate school at the University of Missouri, I had worked full-time in the summers and part-time during the school year. I couldn't afford to buy textbooks. They were on reserve at the library reference section but were always checked out every time I went there.

To save money, I typed my own thesis, the original and seven carbon copies. For each typing mistake, I had to correct eight times, and my fingers became stained with the dark blue of the carbon paper and whiteout liquid.

After I secured a job in New York, I sent most of my salary home every month, leaving barely enough for essentials. The strong winter gusts in city streets, pouncing on the sides of skyscrapers and bouncing back, were icy and bone-piercing. Shivering in the shabby car coat my brother had bought for me from Montgomery Ward, I didn't have money to buy a proper winter coat.

My father probably harbored some guilt about his brother. His generosity to his school-aged nephews and niece, recent refugees in Hong Kong with no one to turn to, earned a great deal of gratitude from them. But sometimes I suspect an additional reason—he simply couldn't resist the opportunity of assuming the mantle of head of the house once again.

It seems to me that the eight-year-old head of house was forever lurking inside my father. His needs always came first, and everyone else had to look up to *him*. He could not allow his wife to practice medicine. He did not nurture his children, perhaps because *he* had not been nurtured. He spent money as if there was always another piece of family land he could sell.

At times I catch myself harboring conflicting emotions about my father. Over the years his decisions have hurt me grievously, yet I cannot ignore the cultural forces that shaped him. Sometimes my heart goes out to that lost, lonely eight-year-old, trying so hard to perpetuate the deadly serious charade of being *Qiye* or Chairman. Those responsibilities were thrust upon him simply because he was male. Throughout his life, he may have feared deep in his heart that he had failed and might fail again. For this reason and for this reason alone, I'm forever ambivalent about my father.

Chapter 3

WHAT WILL YOU EAT IF YOU DON'T HAVE A HUSBAND?

*W*hen I was a little girl, a friend of mine saw my mother for the first time and exclaimed right afterward, "Good heavens, your mother is so beautiful!" Before I had a chance to gloat, she added, "Too bad you don't look like your mother."

Similar incidents happened so often that eventually I could beat the person to the punch—"Too bad I don't look like my mother"—and derive some satisfaction from her startled, you-took-the-words-right-out-of my-mouth look.

I've told this story to quite a few friends since then. My American friends were invariably horrified. One went as far as asking, "How can your friends be so cruel?" But nature is cruel. It makes some people gorgeous, leaving others in the dust. Why hide that fact? Indeed, how can you hide it?

None of my Chinese friends were shocked. They understood that those who made the brutally frank remark felt they owed it to me to share their true feelings. I happen to agree.

My mother was born in 1907, just three days before my father. Her family lived in the city of Hefei in Anhui province, approximately 250 miles southwest of Shanghai.

My grandfather held the regional dealership of indigo dye, the color of the ubiquitous dark blue cloth worn by the working class. My grandmother gave birth to six boys and four girls.

My mother's birth caught my grandparents by surprise, for it happened after a long hiatus when my grandmother probably thought she was done with childbearing. For this reason, my mother was affectionately called *old girl*, or girl born of aged parents. Her parents were probably only in their early thirties, but that was considered an already venerable age at the time.

After *old girl* was born, my grandmother went into surprisingly high gear again and produced another daughter and three more sons. When my mother became a big sister, she was promoted to the status of *big old girl*, while her younger sister became *little old girl*.

To be born during that time and in that culture was to be imbued at birth with the concept for which the Chinese have an important rule: men are superior to women. Aristotle held the same view, but in China, Confucius took it a step further. Both sages were of the opinion that women were physically, morally, and intellectually inferior to men—fit only for serving men's needs. Confucius was more explicit than Aristotle. In addition to his *three rules of obedience*, women must follow his *four rules of virtue*: morality, physical charm, propriety in speech, and proficiency in housework.

A female baby learned her subservient role viscerally, imbibing it at her mother's breast, drop by drop, absorbing it into every cell of her body. A daughter was a waste of resources. Her parents were just spending money on some other family's future daughter-in-law. There was a time-honored Chinese axiom little boys loved to chant: *A married daughter is like water you throw outside your door.*

While my father's childhood trauma was losing his father (ironically making him the most powerful person in the family long before he was ready), my mother's childhood traumas were foot binding and enforced illiteracy. The inequalities ingrained in their early lives foretold the unfortunate dynamics of their marital relationship.

Foot binding was a Chinese tradition more than a thousand years old, and an estimated four billion girls underwent the process during that time.

For centuries, Chinese poets wrote lyrically in praise of the dainty *three-inch golden lotus* that was a lady's bound foot. Nobody mentioned the fact that the procedure began when girls were three to twelve years of age, most likely five or six years old.

Foot binding required breaking the bones of eight toes—four on each foot—and folding them under to achieve the crescent or new-moon shape. Sometimes other implements were employed when tight binding alone wouldn't do. The arch had to be broken too. The feet were literally folded in half, with a cleft deep enough to hold a couple of coins.

For the rest of their lives the victims had to walk on their heels, necessitating the mincing gait so admired as the most quintessential of feminine charms.

Infection was almost a given, and gangrene was not uncommon. One out of ten girls—an estimated 400 million—died from the process, their only crime having been born female.

Stories vary as to how the custom started. One involves an empress with a clubfoot. To show solidarity, courtesans started to bind their feet. Another story identifies a favorite concubine of a Tang Dynasty emperor, who bound her feet to achieve the pointed-toe effect in her dance.

None of these stories really succeeds in explaining how this custom originated and achieved such widespread practice for a thousand years. The groundwork was laid centuries ago by Confucius, whose ideas of social stability involved relegating woman to serve as the property, breeding machine, and plaything of men.

It gradually led to a societal consciousness that allowed for the evolution of a custom that subjected "the inferior half" to lifelong suffering. Women were deformed, debilitated, and enslaved for a senseless masculine fetish, thereby enforcing the rule of men.

The Chinese do have a sense of humor, however. When a person goes on and on and doesn't know when to stop talking, someone will quietly interject, "Mama Wang's foot-binding cloth," and everyone will laugh. They know the implication: *long and stinky*.

Typically ten feet long and two inches wide, the tight-woven cotton used for binding was white for wealthy families and black or dark blue for the poor, in anticipation of it being caked with pus and blood. No matter what the color, the cloth inevitably reeked with the stench of rotting flesh. When the feet were tightly bound with layers and layers of cloth sewn together, and then squeezed into tiny shoes for good measure, circulation was cut off. Sometimes the toe bones eventually fused to the ball of the foot. Other times the toes simply rotted away.

The pain was excruciating.

To prevent her feet from expanding after they were bound, a girl had to attempt sleep with her tight shoes on overnight. Her feet felt as if they were on fire. The next day, she had to walk on her broken toes "to get used to it." Every few days, her feet were squeezed into slightly smaller shoes, until the ideal length—three inches, at most four—was achieved. In all seasons, in addition to the stinky binding cloth, she wore two pairs of shoes during the day: the outer shoes and the inner shoes. At night she wore only the inner shoes.

The Chinese have a saying, as they do for every situation—*a pair of feet, a tub of tears.*

The pain usually subsided after three to six years. After that, only discomfort remained. The maimed feet required continuous care, making it necessary for the girl to be confined at home, giving her more time to make her special shoes and embroider them with flowers and birds. Her bound, deformed feet also caused falls, especially later in life.

Though breastfeeding in public was generally accepted, a woman's bare feet required the utmost privacy. Even a husband, especially a husband, was not allowed to see them for the simple reason that a glimpse of the naked feet would repulse anyone.

After the Sino-Japanese War, both my paternal and maternal grandmothers came to live with us. They were in their seventies, and both had bound feet. I never saw their naked feet, as baring their feet would have been more unthinkable than undressing in public.

Sometimes I wonder how a people capable of such cruelty as foot binding—not to mention various extreme tortures for prisoners—could also produce great pieces of art. I don't mean the elaborately embroidered three-inch shoes. Even before I learned about the foot binding process, I had never found them beautiful.

What I admire are the simple harmony and graceful lines found in certain works of art that seem to aspire to or express a profound human yearning for being at one with nature.

After all, what is *beautiful*? It should be inherent, like a sunrise or a wild flower in bloom, fleeting and defying improvement. But human nature can't seem to leave a good thing alone, or let an ugly thing be. So throughout history we have socially constructed *beauty*, and foot binding is just one example.

It flourished precisely because it fit hand in glove with the function of a patriarchal society. As in most cases of history, women regrettably played their indispensable part by aiding and abetting men in this shared collusion.

The mother was usually the one who presided over—if not performed—the procedure. In order to make the child cooperate and to justify inflicting such horrific torture on her, the mother rationalized it with one reason and one reason only: *No man would want a girl with big feet. And if you don't have a husband, how will you live? What will you eat?* Women had no way of making a living short of being a prostitute or a servant girl.

On many an occasion, the mother would end up weeping alongside her daughter.

§

My mother was four when the Qing Dynasty was overthrown and the Republic of China established. One of the new government's first acts was to outlaw foot binding.

Unfortunately, the government decree had little influence over the general population. Foot binding was a deep-rooted custom, and men still preferred girls with tiny feet, whatever the new government decided. What could parents do—bring their daughters up to be rejected by prospective husbands?

My mother had two sisters who were much older than she. Like my grandmother, they both had bound feet and were unable even to read their own names, thus perfectly fulfilling Confucius' much quoted and always practiced teaching: *it is a virtue for women to be without talent.*

My aunts' "virtues" ensured success in finding husbands for them. They were married young and had miserable marriages.

One sister had a husband who smoked opium. I don't know the circumstances of the other, but I do know that both sisters were both unhappy and died young.

Their experiences should have served as strong arguments against repeating the nasty practice on my mother. Besides, it was now illegal. But my grandfather was not about to challenge tradition.

My mother was about five or six when she underwent the process, but she was a bright and willful child—not easily given to submission. After a month of incessant crying and pleading, she achieved an unimaginable victory: she succeeded in persuading my grandfather to relent.

Being allowed to stop foot binding was a hard-won victory. Unbinding proved to be even more painful, but my mother endured it without complaining. Unfortunately, her feet had already been permanently damaged. For the rest of her life she had to wear custom-made shoes. Like other women who'd had their feet bound, she suffered many falls. The last one broke her hip, landing her in a wheelchair at a nursing home where she died.

Chapter 4

BREAKING THE BONDS OF ILLITERACY

Nowadays, Hefei is a booming metropolis and an important scientific hub. It boasts three national research laboratories and nine universities, including the acclaimed University of Science and Technology of China. However, when my mother was a child, Hefei was a backwater town. It was unthinkable for my very traditional grandfather to allow his daughter to set foot in a school.

Like other girls of that era, my mother was confined to the house, learning to cook, to sew, to embroider, and to knit. Once she set her mind to a task she excelled, but what she really desired was to learn to read. Her family had a tutor to teach her brothers, but the girls were not allowed near the study. My mother must have heard through relatives about schools for girls, and she set her heart on attending one.

She was her father's favorite. One way he showed his affection was to wake her at night to share his midnight snack after he came home from work. None of her nine siblings ever got to enjoy the privilege.

My mother was not a woman given to sentimentality, and she didn't like to talk about herself. On rare occasions when she reminisced about her midnight snacks with her father, however, an air of nostalgia would come over her, as if she were back in the days when she was small, loved, and hopeful that everything was possible.

Of the many so-called midnight snacks, she mentioned, in

particular, the *jicai* meatballs and *shizitou,* or lion's head.

Although called by the same name as my father's Yangzhou *shizitou,* lion's head in Hefei consisted simply of small folded buns deep-fried to a golden brown. They were eaten with a bowl of luscious, thick soup made by stewing a whole hen slowly to perfection.

Jicai meatballs were something truly special—and labor intensive. *Jicai,* a small green leafy vegetable whose taste and texture know no equal, grew wild in the Southern countryside. After the war, when my maternal grandmother and her oldest son—we called him Big Uncle—came to live with us in Hangzhou, he used to make them. Even now, just thinking about those meatballs is enough to start my mouth watering.

I still remember digging for *jicai* in the spring with my grandmother. I had hoped I might get to know her better, but she was even more laconic than my mother.

Recently I was surprised to find *jicai* is called shepherd's purse in this country. It is classified as a common weed of the cruciferous order and is also an herbal remedy sold in capsule or extract form to stop heavy bleeding.

But I remember it as a vegetable chopped fresh and added to finely chopped pork, mushrooms, dried shrimp, bamboo shoots, and seasonings, formed into balls the size of a child's fist, and deep fried until they turned a golden brown. They were crunchy on the outside and indescribably scrumptious inside.

I'm always amazed that food can be so intimately linked with our memories and experiences that it imperceptibly bonds with our lives and becomes an integral part of us.

My mother never trained any of our cooks to make that dish, or any other food she savored during those midnight snacks with her father. One reason could be that my father had not been brought up with the same specialties and wouldn't care for them. She might have also avoided them to stave off painful memories of her father who died unexpectedly after a brief illness. We were in the hinterlands of Guizhou, and by the time the news reached her it was too late. Due to the war and her pregnancy with my sister, my mother never made it to his funeral.

The most profound regret of my mother's life was failing to live up to her promise to her father. For all the faith he had in her, she never practiced medicine. In her late stage of Alzheimer's, she complained of being stupid. "My mind doesn't work anymore; I don't seem to know anything."

I hastened to reassure her. "No, you're not stupid. You saved all our lives during the war, and you had a medical degree."

At that, she started trembling; her sparse white hair shook, and tears rolled down her cheeks. "I let my father down. I let him down…"

§

It's sad how much my mother's personality was shaped by the upbringing Chinese culture dictated. I've always known her as an unusually quiet, taciturn woman. Only later I found that this was due more to nurture than nature. A woman was not supposed to have a mind, let alone speak her mind. Constantly exhorted to keep quiet as a girl, my mother told me, "The more I was told not to speak, the less I could speak. My mouth seemed to grow stupid from disuse."

Then she married my father, a man known for his eloquence and charisma, who, had been expected to speak with confidence and power from a very young age. In the end, there was simply no room for her to say anything.

In spite of her disadvantage, she did exhibit rare flashes of humor—mostly when my father was not around. Once I was helping her unpack after she arrived from Taiwan to visit us. Eyeing her sundry stylish sweaters, I was moved to utter, "*Muma*, you're so fashionable!"

Her comeback was instantaneous. "When was your *Muma* not fashionable?"

Her desire to go to school was so fervent that she must have mustered all her limited verbal capacities to beg, to beseech, to implore her father to allow her to attempt the unthinkable. She did this day after day at midnight snack time until he finally consented.

She thus became the first girl miles around to be given a chance to break out of the bonds of illiteracy. How many years had it taken her to get the nod? Six? Since the day the binding cloth came off her feet?

She was twelve, twice the age of her classmates in first grade. Like them, she couldn't read a single word, not even the simplest "one," "two," or "three." But unlike them, she was determined to learn and she was a quick learner, an excellent student. She easily won the honor of being first in class and jumped a grade each year.

Rain or snow, she would get up at the crack of dawn, eat a hearty breakfast—her family believed in hearty meals and would never send her off on an empty stomach—and trudge to school. It took nearly an hour each way.

When she graduated from elementary school in a record three years, my grandfather couldn't help but be impressed and proud. Even though he was still firmly entrenched in the traditional concepts of patriarchal society, he raised no more objections to her furthering her education.

At a Methodist missionary girls' high school in the city, my mother maintained her record of being first in class and jumping grades. My grandfather even bought her a piano for her lessons. Photos of her at that time showed her wearing long pleated skirts and sporting the era's fashionable hairstyle, a "horizontal S bun" at the back of her head. She was quite the stylish and elegant young lady.

She probably acquired her English name Catherine while attending high school, but she never became a Christian. Although Buddhism had been the dominant religion in China for many years, Christian missionaries were making significant inroads by that time.

With her oldest brother (my Big Uncle) in business in Shanghai, my grandfather permitted my mother to attend Dongnan Medical School. The Chinese system then did not require an undergraduate degree to study law or medicine. Students attended five years of medical school or four years of law school directly after high school. She specialized in internal medicine.

With *big old girl* blazing the trail, my mother's sister, *little old girl*, had a much easier time—no foot binding or need to beg or plead to attend school. *Little old girl* followed her older sister's footsteps all the way to Shanghai and graduated with a degree in accounting from Fudan University. My mother's two surviving younger brothers also graduated from college. It was too late for her older brothers. They had studied with private tutors at home.

While we may applaud my mother's success in breaking the formidable twin chains of foot binding and illiteracy, we should not forget the luck of her timing. If she had been born only ten years earlier, all her intelligence, spunk, hard work, and determination would have gotten her nowhere. On the other hand, she was not lucky enough to be born later and perhaps marry a man who could tolerate his wife working as a physician.

In the medical school dormitory, the lights went out promptly at 10 p.m. While everyone else was asleep, my mother would still be memorizing the names of bones in the dark by handling and feeling their different shapes, real bones that once belonged to real people.

I thought I would be afraid to handle dead people's bones, but the autopsy classes were even worse. My mother was undaunted by the gruesome dead bodies they had to dissect, which made other students—male and female—grow faint.

Refrigeration was nonexistent, so the bodies were preserved in plenty of formaldehyde. The pungent odor of the preservative got into every pore of her body, as well as her hair and clothes. No matter how many times she scrubbed her hands after class, they reeked of formaldehyde.

My mother mentioned these experiences rather matter-of-factly, but they made me shudder. I simply couldn't get the image of those rotting body parts out of my mind... I must admit my mother was made of sterner stuff than I. Hardships never seemed to deter her and she worked hard to justify her father's confidence in her. He had taken a monumental leap of faith. No woman he had ever known in his life had defied convention, and he took pride in her ability to do so. On her part, she resolved never, ever to let him down. In the highly competitive environment of medical school, she continued to excel.

Neither of them foresaw the looming obstacle that was about to challenge both his faith and her resolve.

It was a thing called love.

Chapter 5

A Match Made in Heaven

It was love at first sight, at least on my father's part. It was winter, and he wore a quilted gown, the Chinese equivalent of the Western suit and tie. In the living room of my mother's distant cousin, she thought he looked like a country bumpkin just arrived in Shanghai, bashful and inarticulate.

She was dead wrong, of course.

My usually reticent mother told me this story for the first and only time in 1988, nearly sixty years later. The occasion still seemed a bit surreal to me. My mother had flown from Taiwan following a serious rift with my father and was staying at my sister's apartment. I had taken off from work to fly to Arlington, Virginia to be with her. She was bitter and seemed slightly confused about numbers but was otherwise her normal self. My siblings and I had no inkling that she was in the early stage of Alzheimer's, which seemed to render her more talkative than usual.

I knew very little of my parents' early history, certainly nothing about how they met. Given my natural curiosity, I would have asked eagerly, "Then what happened?" By then I had worked for ten years as a freelance journalist, and I should have taken advantage of this golden opportunity.

However, whenever I was with my parents, suddenly I was reduced to a child again, obedient and inhibited, tongue tied, incapable of functioning as an adult on equal footing. Questions seemed to shrivel and die like leaves on the vine in late autumn. By the same token, I was incapable of consoling my mother or offering advice when she was pouring her heart out. I could only sit and listen. Like being spoon fed, if you will.

Her grievances were not new. In a six-decade marriage, grievances can accumulate and harden like layers of snow and ice in a long, cold winter, and my parents' union was far from ideal. I was sympathetic. I wracked my brain and came up with one thing I could think of to console her: "At least he has been faithful when many other successful men are not…"

My mother was not impressed. "When we were in Hangzhou," she began, "Ni Feijun called me one day from a hotel and wanted to see me. I told her I didn't want to see her, and I had nothing to say to her."

Ni Feijun? My mother's best friend, the nurse at her medical school. I had not heard her name mentioned for years.

"In the last few months when I was carrying you and was too big to dance, Ni Feijun used to go dancing with your father. She asked him to go to Nanjing with her."

Did he take her up on it? Probably not, but he must have been tempted…and I was the unwitting accomplice in this sad tale. If he had not been tempted at all, my mother would not have sounded so bitter.

Pablo Neruda was right, "Love is so short, forgetting is so long." In the case of my mother, forgetting love's transgressions was pretty long, too.

§

My parents' story began, like most couples' during that time, with an arranged meeting. My mother's cousin, on the faculty at my father's university, did a sort of matchmaking. When my father expressed further interest, the cousin arranged another meeting. It's my conjecture that sometime soon after, my father and mother went out together—most likely to a movie. In that era and culture, love as the basis for marriage was new and extraordinarily rare. Once they had gone on a date, they were considered a couple.

It must have been easy for my father to win her over. He was an attractive and eloquent fellow with a sense of humor; he shone in every social gathering. People couldn't stop commenting on what a beautiful couple they made.

It's uncanny that in English, people often say a couple's union is a match made in heaven. The Chinese saying is *tian zuo zi he*, meaning exactly the same thing. I have always been uncomfortable when people use this cliché. How would anyone know whether two people are a good match? Most of the time, even the couple doesn't know until much later. None of us live in heaven. Even if we felt as though we did for a while, gravity would soon pull us down to earth.

At the time, however, neither of my parents was free. Both had been engaged to others since they were children, arrangements made by their respective families.

In my father's case, getting out of his betrothal was easy. Head of the house since he was a child, he was used to having his wishes obeyed without any fuss. However, abrogating an engagement meant rejection and humiliation for his fiancée. Usually jewelry and money offered at the time of betrothal would be forfeited, and an additional sum, called literally a "shame cover-up fee," would be paid. I'm sure my father took care of the problem rather expeditiously.

In the case of my mother, my father did have to make a solemn promise to her and her father that he would allow her to practice medicine, a promise he later broke with no apologies. Once my father made his promise, my maternal grandfather agreed to rescind my mother's engagement.

§

In a traditional Chinese wedding, the bride wears an exceedingly heavy, bejeweled headdress called the "phoenix crown," and she is literally blindfolded by a heavy red veil. She is attired entirely in bright red, the color symbolizing happiness and blessings. She is carried in a *huajiao*, a "flower sedan," meant for the bride only, and followed by her dowry in a procession to the groom's home, where she kowtows to ancestors, elders, and rest of the groom's family.

Being utterly modern, my parents rejected the old format.

Given the fact that my mother's home was hundreds of miles away in a different province, it wasn't even feasible.

They chose not to have a Western-style wedding either, although it was available then in Shanghai. (Despite the fact that white is the color for funerals in China, it was surprising how many people went for it simply because it was fashionable.)

Instead, they did something rather daring: they held a very simple wedding, in Shanghai, with no family or guests present. I suspect my mother had a hand in this, for she always hated making a fuss—especially about herself. She was stylish and elegant, but she preferred the kind of elegance that was simple and understated.

They were married on the morning of September 6, 1931 and immediately boarded a train for Hangzhou—best known for its beautiful *Xihu*, or West Lake—for their honeymoon. My father's younger brother was instructed to mail their wedding announcement to friends and relatives after the train took off. It was a thoroughly modern wedding for a thoroughly modern couple.

They were young and idealistic, eager to stand at the forefront of society and very much in love, ready to defy anything that might stand in the way of their happiness—a hopeful beginning if there ever was one.

After the honeymoon, they returned to their respective schools to finish their degrees. They each still had a year to go. Upon graduation, my father began to practice law as an attorney in the French Concession, an enclave in Shanghai owned and operated by the French. He also taught law part-time at his alma mater, Dongwu University.

In contrast, my mother was pregnant with Charley when she took her final exams. She graduated at the top of the class. Her professors found her levelheaded and calm in crises and had high expectations that she would make an outstanding physician. But she had to adjust to married life and coming motherhood.

It must have been exciting being married to my father, who was gregarious, prodigiously generous, a born leader with a large circle of friends. Furthermore, as an attorney in the French Concession, he made 800 *yuan* a month at a time when one *yuan* would fetch a whole bushel of rice.

Young and rich, residing in the most fashionable area of cosmopolitan Shanghai, my parents were inundated with social activities. Despite her deformed feet, my mother learned to dance; she also started to play mahjongg and socialize with my father's pleasure-seeking friends.

Charley was born amid this social whirl in 1932, a little more than a year after they were married. Shortly after, my mother found out that she was pregnant again.

Although she had domestic help, being saddled with too many babies certainly was not conducive to her career. But unlike her mother a generation before her, she had an option—abortion—which she chose despite the opposition of my father. Abortion was illegal, but my mother's medical school professor performed it as a minor surgical procedure in her operating room.

A year later, my mother was expecting yet again. She was ready to go through the same procedure when my father, unnerved by the previous experience, deterred her. That was how I came to the world in early 1935.

From that point on, as far as I know, my mother, a stoic, strong-willed woman, who strove so hard for so long to acquire a medical degree with the specific goal of practicing medicine, was never able to go against her husband's wishes. In a battle of wills, she was no match.

The honeymoon was over.

Chapter 6

ONE MAN, TWO SISTERS

If a demanding social life, two babies, and an abortion—in three-and-a-half years—were not challenging enough for my mother, war also loomed around the corner, the eight-year Sino-Japanese war.

Long before the war began in 1937, the Japanese government's ambitions to conquer China were clear. The country's Imperial Army had invaded Manchuria in 1931 and had established a puppet regime there. Frequent incursions, euphemistically called "incidents" by the Japanese, continued into other parts of our country. A war with Japan was inevitable. But the Chinese government was frantically trying to move crucial industrial equipment from the southeastern coast to the interior. The government was also in dire need of young men to join preparations for the coming military confrontation.

Meanwhile, my father was enjoying the good life in Shanghai. He was, as his elder brother the distinguished scholar—with more than a little contempt—put it, "just a playboy."

Yong-Choen was right; my father *was* a playboy. He loved good food and was in the habit of drinking his buddies under the table. He was proud of his capacity for liquor and could down a whole bottle of *mao tai*—the much fabled and most potent of Chinese liquors, which President Nixon was feted with decades later on his historical visit to China—with no untoward effect. He loved to dance and play mahjongg, was always surrounded by a lot of friends, and spent money like water.

I have no idea under what circumstances my father met

the governor of Guizhou Province, Wu Zhongxing. I do know Governor Wu was from Anhui—the same province as my mother—and had previously served as governor there. He was well known as an early revolutionary who, together with the founding father of the Republic, Dr. Sun Yat-sen, and President Chiang Kai-shek, had toppled the Qing Dynasty.

My father's meeting with Governor Wu apparently went well because when it was over, he was offered the job of serving as the governor's personal secretary. It was early 1935, two years before the war.

Before he went to Guizhou, he had no idea how long he would stay. Domestic help for childcare was cheap and readily available; my mother could have remained in Shanghai and begun her practice. But when the chips were down, both behaved in the most traditional Chinese manner—he went off to Guizhou and arranged to have us live with *his* family in Yangzhou.

My mother again acquiesced. She soon found herself with a toddler and a new baby in a strange city, living in a huge, traditional, unkempt house with three less-than-friendly women and sundry servants and children. Practicing medicine was out of the question—promise or no promise—and their glamorous life in Shanghai an ephemeral dream.

She began her life in Yangzhou with several strikes against her. From my grandmother's perspective, her son had rejected a perfectly suitable girl his father had picked for him and married a woman of his own choosing. Then they had married in Shanghai instead of at his home, and there had been no parents presiding over the ceremony. This was sacrilegious. Moreover, the interloper came from a different province, spoke a different dialect, and dressed in the Shanghai fashion, too modern for anyone's tastes. The fact that she had gone to school and even received a degree certainly didn't endear her to anyone, least of all her mother-in-law.

Hanging ominously in the background was the traditional horror between mother-in-law and daughter-in-law.

In the eyes of a son-in-law—unlike in the Western world—the Chinese mother-in-law was a benevolent figure. They typically had minimal contact (a brief annual obligatory visit to one's wife's house), and she exercised no power over him.

But the relationship between a mother-in-law and her daughter-in-law was just the opposite. The daughter-in-law lived under the thumb of her mother-in-law, who had total, absolute power over her. Stories of this mostly calamitous relationship were replete in Chinese literature, folklore, and everyone's general consciousness.

This had been true for thousands of years and was still true when my mother presented herself back in the mid 1930s. (Even with the changes brought by the subsequent wars and even thirty years later in America, a Chinese mother-in-law could still be a formidable force to contend with.)

My grandmother's cold-shoulder attitude was clear from the moment my mother arrived. Though my mother wasn't expected to wait on my grandmother, she was treated as an unwelcome relation to be ignored; one might say my mother suffered malignant neglect. There were also the cold shoulders of her two sisters-in-law. My mother addressed them as my brother Charley and I would: Fifth Aunt and Ninth Aunt. Both women were married and lived at home, a highly unusual situation.

Fifth Aunt, my father's older sister, had been engaged before she was born. It was common practice for two good friends to point at the bulging bellies of their expectant wives and promise that the babies, if of opposite sex, would marry. Fifth Aunt was engaged this way to the son of my grandfather's best friend when she was still in the womb.

Unfortunately, by the time those babies became old enough to marry, my grandfather had been long dead, and his best friend, a Chinese herb medicine doctor, had suffered a reversal of fortune. His practice had somehow dwindled, and he had apprenticed his son to a fabric shop in Shanghai.

My paternal grandfather was an unusually progressive man. He had allowed my Fifth Aunt to study with private tutors at home, and she became well-versed in poetry and skilled in calligraphy. What was more, she turned out to be quite a beauty.

As the wedding date drew near, the prospect of marrying a fabric shop apprentice plunged her into depression, and she fell into fits of crying. Confucius' teaching—*it's a virtue for women to be without talent*—was meant to keep women content with their lot. But Fifth Aunt had learned to read and write and thus thought she was too good for her future husband.

Nevertheless, a promise—especially a dead father's promise—was a promise, and she couldn't be allowed to get out of it.

To prevent her from taking extreme measures—hanging or swallowing gold were two popular ways for women to commit suicide—my father, as head of the house, negotiated a compromise with the groom's family. Since the groom would be spending most of his time in Shanghai, she would marry him but not live at his house as custom required. She would stay at her own home "to provide for the continued comfort of her widowed mother."

This proposal flew straight against the prevailing custom, amounting to a slap in the face for the groom's family. However, when two parties with unequal strengths negotiate, it's unsurprising how often the stronger party gets his way. In this case, my father, being the wealthier of the two, won. In a short span of five years, Fifth Aunt bore her husband three children but saw very little of him otherwise.

With Yong-Choen in Shanghai, my father in Guizhou, and Small Uncle, the youngest son, also in Shanghai studying pharmacology, my grandmother ran out of sons to obey. Fifth Aunt being literate and living at home, became the *de facto* head of the house and assumed all the responsibilities my father used to shoulder.

My only visual memory of Fifth Aunt is from Hangzhou after the war, when my grandmother *Nainai* died at the end of the two years she stayed with us. Fifth Aunt attended the funeral. She was approaching fifty, a mother of five by then, two from her second marriage. For mourning she wore a sky blue *qipao*, a Mandarin style dress, and sat quietly twisting a handkerchief in her hands.

I was thirteen. Descriptions of the classic Chinese beauty in the romance novels I had been reading at the time seemed to come alive in her. I was most taken by her luminous complexion.

In comparison, her unfortunate younger sister Ninth Aunt was considered homely, not very bright, and not very tactful. My mother never said so, but I had the impression that Ninth Aunt was not my father's favorite sibling. To marry her off, my father chose a schoolmate at Dongwu University, an orphan with no family of his own. Since a family precedent already existed, and Ninth Aunt's husband was satisfied with paying conjugal visits during holidays only, it seemed natural that she continued to live at home as well.

The two sisters had nothing to do all day. Fifth Aunt's head-of-house duties were minimal. A cook and other servants took care of the housework, and four personal nursemaids—one for each child—were responsible for Fifth Aunt's three children and Ninth Aunt's daughter, who was my age. (Even when Fifth Aunt's son, Paul, was nine years old, he still had a nursemaid following him with every step he took, pleading all the while, "Little Master, do be careful lest you fall.") The young mothers' only pastime was to keep their mother company by playing mahjongg.

It took four to play, but the three women always had enough people to join them in the time-consuming game. Daily, relatives would arrive in the morning and stay until late at night to fill two or three tables of mahjongg.

In this cozy environment, both sisters, married with absentee husbands, fell in love with the same man, Zhang Lao San, the younger brother of their sister-in-law, Yong-Choen's wife. A college student in name only, he obviously enjoyed the attentions of the two young ladies—especially the older and prettier one. His daily presence engendered a less than harmonious atmosphere in the household.

By the time my mother, brother, and I joined the household, Fifth Aunt had given her middle child, a daughter, to her childless paternal uncle and aunt in Shanghai for adoption. Only her firstborn Paul and her third child, Cecilia (called by their Chinese names in those days) were at home with their mother.

Fifth Aunt was the one who held the family purse strings, and she chose not to hire a maid for my mother to help take care of my brother and me. As luck would have it, Charley and I both caught Cecilia's measles. I had a worse case than Charley, constantly crying and crawling all over the bed from itch and fever, adding to my mother's miseries.

There was also the issue of food. Years later my mother would still recall with a shudder their cook's way of boiling fresh green leafy vegetables until they were yellow and mushy.

After two years of being cooped up with two small children in a house not her own, in the constant company of three unfriendly women who had nothing in common with her, my mother developed a bleeding ulcer. Against my father's long-distance objections, she took us back to Shanghai by way of her own home in Hefei. I was two when we left.

My mother was resilient to have endured two years in that environment. Thanks to her strong will, we left Yangzhou in the spring, before the eight-year Sino-Japanese War began that summer.

Shortly after we left, Fifth Aunt's husband died of tuberculosis in Shanghai. When the war came, she fled to Shanghai with her two children and married her lover, Zhang Lao San. It was quite a scandal for a widow at her wedding to be carrying a near-term baby in her womb.

Ninth Aunt was left at home, heartbroken, but the worse was yet to come. Her husband, Ninth Uncle, somehow got wind of the whole sordid affair in Shanghai, and suddenly showed up stone-faced in Yangzhou one day. He wanted the story from her mouth.

Was she her usual tactless self? My mother didn't know. He left at dawn the next morning, never to return, but continued to support her. Even after the Communists took over the mainland and he moved to Hong Kong, he managed to send money to her every month. Years later he died of a heart attack at his desk in his office, leaving a will to continue support.

Remarkably, he remained friends with my father throughout his life. It was he who alerted my father to a note nailed to a telephone pole by our three cousins, Yong-Choen's younger children. (At the time, Hong Kong was flooded with refugees. Desperate to get in touch with lost family members and without money for personal ads, they often posted notes on telephone poles.)

Ninth Aunt was left in Yangzhou with her daughter; she never saw any of her family again. In the 1990s, my father learned that she had become a grandmother but, mentally confused in her old age, had wandered away from home and died in a ditch. That was the only time my father mentioned her.

Sometimes I can't help but wonder at the discrepancy in my father's attitude toward his two sisters. They were equally guilty of causing him a great deal of shame. As far as I know, my father never lifted a finger to help Ninth Aunt and never kept in touch with her. Perhaps there was some family dynamics involved that even my mother didn't know.

I have never seen a photo of Ninth Aunt. When I was growing up, I heard remarks that I resembled her but didn't understand the significance. Neither did I know that what had transpired between my two aunts would have a connection with my own life.

Chapter 7

HERE COMES THE WAR

In the spring of 1937 we left my father's ancestral home in Yangzhou for Shanghai, stopping briefly at my mother's home in Hefei. The Chinese were bracing themselves for war, a war they knew would come, but not when or where—and definitely not how quickly. On July 7, it began, igniting like wild fire at Luguoqiao, also known as Marco Polo Bridge, near Beijing, the most important

My mother, me, and Charley on the eve of the Battle of Shanghai, 1937

city in the north. A little more than a month later, August 13, it reached Shanghai, the most important city in the South and in all of China.

Well prepared with overwhelming military might, the Japanese calculated that their Imperial Army would conquer China in three months. In actuality, it took them three months and thirteen days just to conquer Shanghai.

Among the twenty-two "major battles" (involving 100,000 troops or more) during the eight-year war, the Battle of Shanghai was the first, the largest, and the most desperately fought. A staggering total of one million soldiers were engaged in action. As one Chinese poet put it, *yicun heshan yichun xue*, an inch of blood for every inch of soil.

Before the battle, we had already returned to Shanghai, exactly where my father didn't wish us to be.

Hindsight tells us that my mother's decision to leave Yangzhou actually saved us. It would have been far worse if we had stayed since the war didn't spare Yangzhou. Leaving when we did, we were able to travel in the remaining days of peace and settle in the area we had lived in before—the French Concession, one of only two enclaves in Shanghai that was protected from that battle. (The other was the International Settlement, joint concessions of the United Kingdom, the United States, and Japan.)

War was raging all around us; it was literally blocks away. We could hear it, smell it, feel it, and even see it. My aunt (my mother's younger sister, *little old girl*, who had married my father's classmate and best friend) also lived in the French Concession. From their balcony, my five-year-old brother Charley watched the Boy Scouts—those not yet old enough to fight and not much older than himself—crawling in the streets, dodging bullets, and bringing supplies to the front lines. Those images were forever seared in his mind.

The hospital in the French Concession was overrun with the wounded and people donating blood. I only learned recently from Charley that our mother volunteered at the hospital during that time. It turned out to be the only chance she had to practice medicine in her life.

Charley and me

The Japanese were furious to have lost 70,000 of their troops in the Battle of Shanghai. Although it was merely one-third of the military deaths the Chinese had suffered—200,000—it was ten times higher than Japan expected. They hadn't anticipated such stiff resistance and consequently, were bent on revenge. After Shanghai, they quickly conquered Nanjing, the capital of China, which was the equivalent of taking New York City then Washington, D. C.

Nanjing went down in history as the city that suffered another type of beastly brutality. The Rape of Nanjing, also known as the Massacre of Nanjing, claimed 300,000 victims. Soldiers of the Japanese Imperial Army received explicit orders to rape; from children to the elderly, no one was spared. Male civilians were ordered to dig large deep holes and be buried alive, to save the Japanese soldiers the trouble of shooting them. The proud perpetrators recorded their horrific deeds in photos and film footage that still exist today.

The Japanese thought at this point that China would certainly surrender. While all the Western powers stood by doing nothing, President Chiang Kai-shek vowed to continue the fight. He retreated to the interior, established Chongqing in Sichuan province as the war capital, and carried on the war from there.

After Shanghai fell, we immediately traveled to Guizhou to reunite with our father. (Too remote and unimportant, it was never occupied by the Japanese.) More than two years had passed since we had last seen him, and he had just had an emergency appendectomy.

To hear him tell it, he relished the experience. He elaborated upon how he had to travel by bus from Pingpa to the hospital in Guiyang (capital of the province) for the surgery; how he gave the go-ahead despite the doctor's apparent reluctance; how it was performed during a Japanese air raid, with the operating room shaking, dust falling, and objects flying all over; and how he came through it all with flying colors, even though the doctor had been badly shaken by the experience. My father always ended his story with a satisfied smile—"I love surgery."

§

In my father's old age, he told me that his work as an attorney defending petty criminals in the French Concession, though lucrative, had been boring, and he was not proud of his decadent life in Shanghai. I thought there might be another reason he took the job of personal secretary to Governor Wu in Guizhou—he was flattered to have the opportunity to work for one of the founding fathers of the Chinese republic, and to be recruited for the lofty purpose of making a contribution to the country. The whole idea was compatible with his head-of-house mentality.

However, it did mean that at twenty-eight years old, he gave up his indulgent life of mahjongg, dancing, movies, and horse-racing. He also relinquished his fabulous 800 *yuan* a month for a pitiful salary to serve in the impoverished province of Guizhou, the true hinterlands of China. He spent a total of four years there. After serving as the personal secretary of Governor Wu Zhongxing, he was appointed by Wu's successor as the magistrate of Pingpa County.

By the time we reached Guizhou, my father seemed to have undergone a transformation more drastic than a removed appendix. Once he set foot in the barren and primitive province, he probably found it strangely captivating. He realized that whatever he could achieve there would be far more meaningful than anything he had accomplished in Shanghai. The fact that he chose to stay after Governor Wu departed tells me he was not the same young man who had set out for the hinterland two years earlier.

Upon my father's arrival at Pingba County, he was apparently appalled by the stark poverty and resolved to eradicate it. He never told us, but at one point—at least according to the memoir of his new superior Wu Dingchang—my father risked the ire of the governor and the Central Government's Military Committee to protect the farmers. I believe that if not for

Our family in Guizhou. Back row (from left): My father, Yongchio Liu, and my mother, Shangying Dai. Front row: Me, my father's deputy's son, and Charley

the war, he would have continued in his post as magistrate of Pingba.

The full-scale Japanese invasion began two years after my father left Shanghai for Guizhou. By the time my mother arrived with us, Shanghai and Nanjing were lost, and the war news from more than a thousand miles away became increasingly dire. It appeared that in a matter of months, if not weeks, our proud country of five thousand years would be no more. Two words, wang guo, meaning perished country, began to weigh heavily on the mind of many. The previously unthinkable abyss

Last family photo before heading back to Shanghai in the Japanese-occupied zone. Back row: Ninth Uncle (husband of Ninth Aunt), my father, and my mother holding Lining. Front row: Charley and me

was now a distinct possibility. And to be taken over by none other than what the Chinese contemptuously called "little Japan"! No task, no matter how important, could be compared with the war and its urgency.

My father, with his head-of-house mindset, always felt it was incumbent upon him to set things right. In this case, he had to go where he was needed the most—the war. He resigned from his magistrate post and enlisted in the resistance forces. We left Pingba with him.

By then we were a family of five. Because it was impossible for my mother to obtain a surgical abortion in Guizhou, my sister Lining was born in early 1939, one month after my fourth birthday.

§

I suspect that what had prevented my mother from joining my father in Guizhou four years earlier was not the lack of amenities such as electricity and water, but the attendant unavailability of modern medicine, specifically medical abortion. For her, trained as a doctor, anything other than a surgical abortion to end a pregnancy was unthinkable. After the war, when we lived in Hangzhou, she had to go to Shanghai for that purpose at least once. She had two abortions in Taiwan. After the second, she was laid up for days.

Later in the States, whenever I saw people yell *BABY KILLER* on television, I would think of my mother, and I would be overwhelmed with sympathy for her. She strove so hard, so long, and so tenaciously, to practice medicine. To justify her father's faith in her. The abortions, which freed her from having one baby after another, were probably her way of keeping her dream alive.

I will add, however, that once she had us she never shirked her duties as a mother. On our way back from Guizhou, for example, while stepping off the bus with my sister in her arms, she lost her balance and fell, probably because of her deformed feet. In order to protect the baby, she used her own head to break the fall and suffered a serious head wound and concussion, which may have contributed to her developing Alzheimer's disease in old age.

Since we had to take a detour through Hanoi, Vietnam on account of the war, it took us several months to return to Shanghai from Guizhou. By then my maternal grandfather had died, and my grandmother and the rest of her family had scattered because of the war. My mother never went home again.

As soon as we arrived in Shanghai, my father left to join the resistance forces organized by the government in the northern part of Jiangsu province. This area saw intense fighting between the Japanese and the Nationalists. There, he endured the most grisly and terrifying experiences of his life.

When he left, neither he nor my mother knew how long he would be away or whether they would see each other again. As it turned out, his volunteer tour lasted six years—until the end of the eight-year war. During most of that time, my mother had no way of knowing whether my father was dead or alive or wounded in a trench somewhere. While those thoughts must have haunted her day and night, the most pressing problem was to provide for her three children, ranging in age from not quite one to seven.

When my father left, he took all the money they had with him and told her to borrow money when needed. This may sound unrealistic, and it was. But my

My kindergarten registration photo

grandfather in his day and later my father were both accustomed to lending money to relatives and friends in need; they had just never been on the receiving end.

My mother's first try—asking her sister *little old girl* for a loan—taught her the necessity of being self-supporting. *Little old girl's* husband, my father's close friend whom we called simply "Uncle," let my mother know, firmly and tactfully, that there would not be a second loan.

My mother found a job manning the medical office at the elementary school my brother and I were attending, in a sort of glorified nurse capacity. It paid barely enough for us to get by. Still, for a while everything seemed fine.

Until one night there came a loud pounding on the door that changed our lives.

Chapter 8

OUR YEARS IN HIDING

I t was December 1941; the Japanese had attacked Pearl Harbor just days earlier. "The Empire of the Sun" was at the apex of its power, with a million soldiers on the Chinese mainland alone. That night, the Japanese had seized the list of those working for the Resistance (and their families) and were on their way to arrest us.

The pounding at our door was from a woman who had been sent to warn us to flee. My nine-year-old brother Charley heard the pounding and understood why. The next thing he remembered was standing on his bed and our maid hurriedly buttoning his winter gown. She couldn't stop trembling. My mother was in bed with a broken ankle from a recent fall on the stairs. I'll never know how she managed to whisk the three of us away, one step ahead of the Japanese military police.

I was six years old. In a real sense, my childhood ended that winter night. I had attended my first-grade classes that day and gone to bed as usual, but the next thing I knew my whole world had vanished. I was left with strangers for six months, and Charley later told me that at some point I was moved to another place with different strangers.

I can only imagine what must have happened—finding myself in a strange house in the dark of night with not a familiar face in sight. The only thing I recognized was the clothes on my back. Did I cry for my mother, brother, and sister? How did I survive? My memory of that night is a complete blank, and to this day, more than seventy years later, that night and the next six months have remained a blank. To this day, tears come rushing out of my eyes whenever I confront that blank.

It must have been spring when my mother paid me a brief surprise visit, bringing me two new dresses. That was the only part of those six months I remember; I even remember one of the dresses was a red and dark blue tartan.

Her visit was like a dream. Since my birthday is shortly after Chinese New Year's Day, I must have turned seven before she came. Prior to her visit I had not known whether she or any of my family was dead or alive. After she left, I didn't know if I would ever see her again.

My mother never explained why she left me, nor did she ask me how I had been treated. During and after the war years, we were forbidden to talk about our war experiences or ask questions.

Now that our parents have been dead for years, Charley feels that what happened in our childhood is water under the bridge. His experience—staying with the in-laws of our father's good friend—was so different from mine that he tends to think, "I got over it. Why can't you?"

For me, it does no good to simply pretend that the past is past. For the past has a way of becoming present in an instant, like a sleeping monster that suddenly awakens.

§

Later Charley and I figured that we were farmed out to separate places because it took my mother that long—limping with a broken ankle in the beginning—to find a new job, earn some money, rent a safe place, and secure fake ID cards for the whole family. She accomplished all this under the imminent danger of being arrested by the Japanese.

My mother found work as a saleswoman for CBC Pharmaceuticals, going from office to office to peddle new medicines to physicians. While she was probably hired on the strength of her medical background, it must have been highly humiliating for her to be a saleswoman instead of a doctor.

She found a second-floor apartment, again in the French

Concession, in a three-story building kitty-corner from—of all places—the Japanese Military Police headquarters. A bold decision. Perhaps she believed that the most exposed places are the least suspected and therefore the safest. Perhaps that was the only apartment she could find.

Our landlords, an old "White Russian" couple, refugees from the 1917 Russian revolution, lived downstairs. We were the only Chinese tenants—an added security measure. My mother chose a loyal and capable woman for a maid, who stayed with us through thick and thin until we left for Taiwan seven years later.

Just as she was ready to bring Charley and me back to our new home, my father showed up. He had been gone for almost two years and suddenly materialized in the dead of night. His clothes were tattered, and he didn't have his eyeglasses, watch, or fountain pen. Although he could only stay for a few days, his arrival must have put my mother in a celebratory mood, for she bought me a red dress for my homecoming.

The day of my homecoming was surreal, disorienting. Like a light turning on, my memory switched on that day from a total blank to normal. Suddenly I was in a different apartment. My brother Charley was there, and shortly afterward, two-year-old Lining was brought through the door. She eagerly asked for our cousins since Charley and I were strangers to her after our six-month separation. Years later we deduced that, for the duration, my mother and sister had probably stayed with our cousins' mother, our aunt, *little old girl*.

Ah, that red dress. For the Chinese, red is the color that symbolizes luck, happiness, and festivity. Unfortunately I have never liked the traditional Chinese orange-hued red, and I didn't know why I had been abandoned and how long I would be with my family this time—for a day, or for good? Without knowing what my parents had just gone through, *I* was bitter. I felt betrayed.

"I hate red!" The words were out before I realized what I was saying. I was rewarded instantly with two hard slaps across my face, administered by my father—my father, who, by that time, had been absent for more than two-thirds of my life.

He was a stranger to me, until the two burning slaps on my

face—and the words, *your mother bought you a new dress. How dare you say you don't like the color!*

As the Chinese saying goes, *gaiguan dinglun*—you can judge a person *only* after the lid is shut on his coffin. But many parents tend to form opinions about their children early, and chances are that those opinions will persist until the parents themselves are dead. That incident probably informed my father that I was selfish and spoiled, with no consideration for others. And as the director of the bureau of military law in the war zone, he was quick to judge me guilty.

In hindsight, what I needed was for my mother to explain to me why she had sent me away. Unfortunately, she probably thought I was too young to understand about the war, too young to feel hurt.

According to our forged identification cards, we were now the Changs, and our father was a businessman. After he went away "on business," the Chang family began a new life in the new neighborhood. Charley and I went to a new school with new names, and I entered second grade.

We were under strict orders never to divulge our real names.

My ID card with fake name in Chinese on one side ...

... and French on the other

Our relatives and friends were not told our new address so that if they were ever questioned, they could honestly say they didn't know.

Despite the constant danger of discovery (an arrest would lead to a swift execution), the frequent checking of ID cards in the streets during the day, and Japanese military police barging into our home at night, my mother remained calm and nurturing and proved to be a very successful saleswoman.

Although the load my mother had to carry was enormous, she managed to never neglect her social obligations with our relatives on both sides. Bearing gifts, we would call on our *Nainai*, uncles, aunts, and cousins on Chinese New Year Days as well as their birthdays.

§

A month after I started fourth grade, my father came home again. We hadn't seen him for almost three years. In the six years he had gone away to fight in the Resistance, this was the second and last time he had come back. Again he arrived in the dead of night, wearing tattered clothes, without eyeglasses, watch, or fountain pen. He looked like one of the many war refugees roaming the city, and indeed he was.

Traveling from the front lines in northern Jiansu province to Shanghai took days and involved braving numerous Japanese patrol lines and checkpoints. He didn't come back for the frivolous reason of visiting us; he came home because he had no other place to go.

He and his colleagues had suffered another serious setback, dealt not by the Japanese, but by the Chinese Communists. Instead of escaping to the north where the Communists held sway, as some of his colleagues did, my father opted to come south to Shanghai.

Unfortunately, I had gotten sick a couple of days before. I had developed a severe sore throat and stayed home from school. The trauma I had suffered from being abandoned to strangers when I was six years old seemed to have turned me inward, transforming me from a carefree and healthy child to a melancholic and sickly one.

When my father showed up, we knew how dangerous it was for him as well as for us. To avoid suspicion, my mother went to work as usual, and, in the meantime, surreptitiously outfitted my father for the road. Thus occupied, she didn't get around to examining my throat until a few days later when she diagnosed my illness as diphtheria.

The seriousness of the disease put my parents in a quandary. Unsure of my mother's diagnosis, my father used his "common sense approach" and argued that I couldn't be very sick since I was quiet and well-behaved. I had stopped complaining about my sore throat. My mother, on the other hand, insisted that I needed immediate medical attention.

But how? Taking me to the hospital could endanger the whole family. Finally my mother took me to Fifth Aunt, my father's older sister, who lived nearest to us (although she didn't know it) and asked her to take me to the children's hospital.

While frantically trying to find a suitable vein in my arms to administer gamma globulin (an antibody) to fight the diphtheria, the emergency room doctor admonished my aunt: "Why did you bring her in so late? I'm not even sure I can save her." I was quickly admitted to the hospital.

I was alone in a strange place again. This time, however, I was nine—three years older than I had been last time. This time I knew where I was and why, and I was too sick to care.

As I got better and more aware of my surroundings, I became desperately lonely, especially as I watched my roommate, a six-year-old boy with typhoid fever, being showered with so much attention from his large family. His doting grandmother never left his side, administering to his demands during the day and sleeping on a cot inches away from him at night.

Days would pass, but my mother would drop by for only a few minutes. She never had time to sit down. How I envied that little boy!

One night I woke up to loud crying; the boy had died a few feet away from my bed. His grandmother had fed him a little porridge, not knowing it would kill him.

Our beds were perpendicular to each other, with no curtain or screen in between. The boy appeared to have shriveled a bit and was totally still. He had been alive when I had gone to sleep. Now he was a corpse, the first corpse I had ever seen in my life, so close I could almost reach out and touch him.

Thoroughly frightened, I turned my face to the wall, but could not avoid coming face to face with thoughts of mortality—my own mortality. I imagined what it would be like to be shut inside a coffin with nothing but absolute darkness and silence surrounding me for all eternity. That unbearable thought, exacerbated by the fear from all the ghost stories I had heard, haunted me through many terrifying nights in my remaining stay in the hospital.

This second traumatic event gradually receded over time, until it, too, became a distant memory, only to resurface decades later in the form of severe anxiety and panic attacks. I came to realize that my childhood experiences and their attendant loneliness and helplessness had long become an integral part of my emotional makeup.

My troubles were not over after I returned home from the hospital. I was bedridden from the aftermath of diphtheria and was not permitted to go back to school. At the time, I had no idea that the complications brought on by delayed medical attention were to plague me for the rest of my life.

The only reason I was allowed to get out of bed many months later in February 1945 was to leave Shanghai with my family as a refugee of American bombing. I had lost the use of my legs from the long months in bed and had to learn to walk again.

America had been at war with Japan since Pearl Harbor. In July 1944, American aircraft appeared over Shanghai, the prized possession of Japan and a prominent target. Major air raids began in November. When the bombing of Shanghai grew intense, my father sent someone under him to escort us out of the city to unoccupied territory.

In order not to arouse suspicion from the Japanese, we stuck to the countryside and avoided public transportation. For four months, mostly on foot, my mother led us from Shanghai through bombed-out roads and bridges, mountains, and streams to Jiangxi province in the unoccupied zone. My father arrived shortly after, bringing my cousin Paul, the seventeen-year-old son of Fifth Aunt.

In September 1945, a short two months after our family was reunited, the war finally, officially ended. My parents were thirty-eight years old. They had lost their youths during the war, survived the most perilous and terrifying time of their lives, and proved their mettle, albeit in different capacities.

The end of the war set my father in pursuit of a new livelihood but put my mother's aspirations of medical practice on permanent hold. For the rest of her life, she served in the capacity my father wanted her—his loyal helpmate and gracious hostess.

The war also put an end to their "modern" phase. Being modern, like a fashionable hat tried on in a moment of frivolity, was unceremoniously discarded and forgotten while they attended to the business of day-to-day living.

In retrospect, those six years hiding from the Japanese military police were no doubt the worst times of my mother's life. But they were the only time that she had the freedom and independence to carry out what her circumstances required of her, and she did so with courage and intelligence. In that sense, ironically, those six years were also the best times of her life.

Chapter 9

A Much-Needed Respite

In 1945 the war ended, the country was in ruins, and twenty-two million Chinese had perished. China desperately needed to recover and rebuild, but tragically, that was not to be. The civil war between the Communists and the Nationalists began immediately, with even more calamitous consequences.

For my family, however, the end of the first war did provide a small, much needed respite, as my father did not fight in the civil war, and we were not in the immediate area of military conflicts.

We lost no time leaving Jiangxi and settling down in Hangzhou, 100 miles from Shanghai. This time, we traveled by public transportation. It took a mere two weeks, a far cry from the four-month arduous journey by foot we had made a few months before.

At the beginning of the first war, we had witnessed the bloody Battle of Shanghai. After two years in Guizhou, the six following years back in Shanghai had been tense but relatively quiet—our mother went to work during the day, came home in the evening, and we had no visitors at any time. No one knew where we lived. During my father's two cameo appearances in that period, he had been quiet and withdrawn, afraid to answer the door, not even daring to be near a window lest someone should spot him.

Now we were reunited with our father as master of the house. Our mother, the only parent we knew and our pillar, was no longer in charge. Instead, she turned all her attention to the requirements of our father.

Our home became chaotic, teeming with our father's wartime

55

colleagues and their wives, strangers whom we addressed as uncles and aunts. Relatives, scattered because of the war and now reconnected, either came to visit or to stay with us. At mealtimes we never knew whether we would get to sit at the table or have to wait patiently for leftovers.

My mother was busy supervising the logistics and taking care of the constant stream of friends and relatives. Sometimes, however, she would be laid up in bed for days with pericarditis, an inflammation of the inner membrane of the heart, which, according to her doctor, had been caused by the stress of the war years. Whenever she was well, she would accompany my father to social gatherings or on trips to Shanghai where my father had started his salt business. Other times he would go to Shanghai by himself for weeks and come back with his entourage.

I was lonely when they were away—and lonelier still amid the hustle and bustle when they were home. Occasionally when they were out, I would go into their bedroom and go through my mother's closet, touching and admiring her array of *qipao*. I have never managed to be stylish or elegant in my life, but oh, how I wished then that I could grow up soon and wear her *qipao*, that I could be just like her.

Charley was thirteen at the end of the war. Mingling easily with adults, he apparently didn't have my social problems. My father became worried that being too much of an extrovert at a young age might lead him astray. I overheard him remark to my mother that Charley needed to be reined in; he was sent off to a boarding school.

Decades later, when my father and Charley were having many conflicts, my mother told me that she failed to understand why they just couldn't get along. As a toddler, she said, Charley had adored his father. As soon as he heard his father's footsteps coming to the door, he would scurry to fetch his slippers, newspapers, and ashtray, but my father paid him little mind. If he happened to be in a good mood, he would give Charley a pat or two on the head.

At ten, I was the quiet, docile one—not because I had been born that way, but because I knew my place in the family as a middle child. As a girl unable to carry the bloodline or family name, I was not as important as Charley. I was also convinced that I wasn't as smart as Charley, for I could see he always knew more than I did.

Our younger sister Lining was six, the undisputed darling of the family; even the servants adored her. I remember one particular lunch during the early years in Shanghai before we had to flee from the Japanese military police. My father was away at the front lines and my mother at work. We three children were under the care of a maid who served us a dumpling dish with shredded pork and bok choy.

Instead of adding the batter to boiling broth in spoonfuls like Westerners make dumplings, the Chinese use a chopstick to push the batter in, one thin strip at a time. Our maid, an unhappy woman with a temper, was probably especially surly that day. Her thin strips became thicker and thicker, until the rest of the batter was dumped in all at once—a big fat lump.

Finding the dumplings tasteless, I grumbled and refused to eat, while Lining happily exclaimed in her childish high voice, "I *love* big dumplings! Jiaojie's big dumplings taste *the best!*" She was two years old. She was to retain her cute baby voice in adulthood, and we nicknamed her "high octave." She was so much younger than we were that neither Charley nor I took her seriously.

When the war was over, our father had missed most of her first six years of life and was determined to make up for lost time. Charley and I have a stubborn streak; Lining was subtle, just like our father. He pampered her, calling her *naibaozi*—breast-hugging baby in Yangzhou dialect—and holding her on his lap every chance he had.

My father was charismatic in the fullest sense of the word. Forever surrounded by admiring friends and relatives, he was like the moon worshiped by a crowd of stars, to use a Chinese expression. This powerful, awe-inspiring father, always on display, was tender, content, and relaxed to the tips of his eyebrows when he held my sister on his lap.

To me, my father *was* the moon, high in the sky, totally unapproachable, unaware of my existence. The impossible distance between us instilled in me a sense of inadequacy, of unworthiness.

And I learned to console myself whenever I wanted something I couldn't have: "That's all right. I don't need it; it doesn't matter if I have it or not." It became my default attitude.

§

Because of the war and complications from diphtheria, my elementary school education essentially ended after my third grade. I was never taught fourth-, fifth-, or sixth-grade math, which put me at a considerable disadvantage after the war when I took the entrance examination for a prestigious missionary girls' high school in Hangzhou.

Despite my math deficiency, I passed the exam, probably because I was good in language and I read every chance I had. I had always had a voracious appetite for books, but my exposure was spotty. We had few books in the house, and I didn't know of any libraries. I simply read whatever I could get my hands on.

Back in Shanghai, Charley would let me read many of the *kungfu* novels he rented from a corner shack. After I entered junior high at Hungdao Girls' School, I borrowed books from fellow classmates who were mostly interested in romance novels. I read so many serial *kungfu* and romance novels in those early years that I've stayed clear of them ever since.

Occasionally there were some classics and translations of foreign novels available from my classmates. Whatever the subject matter, I read them with total absorption. Having little interaction with my family, I used books for my escape, my ticket to a different world.

I didn't do well in algebra, but had no trouble with other classes. Once in a while, my teacher would read one of my essays aloud to the class. I also began to write some stories and poems in secret but was disappointed to find that what often came out were mere clichés.

Summers seemed interminable. When school was out, I was confined at home and unable to borrow books from classmates. However, in my third and last summer in Hangzhou, I learned to play Chinese chess from my cousin Li.

When I was twelve, both of my grandmothers came to live

In front of our house in Hangzhou. Back row: Cousin Li, my mother, my father, Small Uncle (my father's younger brother), and Cousin Paul. Middle row: Me, Lining, and Charley. Front row: My maternal grandmother and my paternal grandmother (Nainai)

with us. *Nainai*, the matriarch who had given my mother the cold shoulder back in Yangzhou, arrived first. Shortly after, my maternal grandmother came with her son Big Uncle, and her grandson Li, who turned out to be a Chinese chess champion at school. He was a strict but kind teacher, and I relished my progress in the game until midsummer when *Nainai* took sick and died.

I came down with a fever after her death, and the aftermath of my diphtheria came back to haunt me. My doctor decided I should stay home from school for a year. As it happened, however, I wouldn't have attended school anyway, because the civil war finally reached us that fall.

Incredibly, the Nationalists, who were supposedly in power, lost battle after battle. It became clear by the fall of 1948 that the Communists would soon take over the country. At thirteen, I understood nothing about the political situation but could clearly sense the panic and indecision that permeated the air. Many in the country had to make the most crucial decision of their lives: to leave or to stay? If leave, where to and how?

In the end, more than two million people fled to Taiwan, including my family. There was never any indecision on my father's part. He was certain that his past in the Resistance meant he would not survive under the Communists.

He was right. His colleagues who stayed behind were all rounded up and killed. But my father didn't predict everything correctly. Our house in Hangzhou was left in the care of our trusted maid in the hopes we might soon return. Several of his boats loaded with salt had to be abandoned hundreds of miles from Shanghai. But we were able to leave. The five of us traveled with three suitcases. We were refugees once again.

Chapter 10

UP CLOSE AND PERSONAL

We left Hangzhou in the morning to board the train for Shanghai. The station was unbelievably chaotic. Frantic crowds, with suitcases and bundles, jostled to get on the train so that when it finally started, hours behind schedule, every inch of space seemed to be packed. A sense of foreboding hung heavy in the air. The clinking and clanking of the train seemed to echo the thoughts on everyone's mind: *what's next? what's next? what's next?*

We were lucky to have tickets that guaranteed seats, and we knew we were going to Taiwan. But I, too, started to worry. What was in Taiwan? From all I knew, it was far away, in the middle of the ocean, and not a nice place at all. Seventh Uncle, my mother's cousin, had been there and hated it. He only stayed three days. Even our maid refused to venture to that never-heard-of island. Without her, would we have to live like Robinson Crusoe?

Bedlam repeated at every stop, and a normally four-hour ride took all day. We stayed overnight in Shanghai and left before dawn, flying over the Taiwan Strait, holding on to our flimsy canvas chairs in a military cargo plane.

When our family of five emerged from the plane into the subtropical sunshine of Taipei in January 1949, we could hardly wait to shed our winter coats and cardigans. We had arrived in a different world—and not only in terms of climate. Taiwan had been occupied by Japan for fifty years before it was finally returned to China in 1945. Our first impression of the island was that of an impoverished, miniature Japan.

We moved into a tiny Japanese-style house, with one bedroom, one bathroom, and incredibly, no kitchen. Doors were made of translucent white paper, and we slept on floors made of thick straw mats that the Japanese call *tatami*. Not a stick of furniture and no servants to help.

Up to now, we had always had at least a maid. When we made our four-month journey from Shanghai to Jiangxi on foot, our trusted maid was with us. My mother, who hadn't cooked a meal for as long as I could remember, now had to go to the market herself. There, she communicated by simple gesturing and somehow managed to buy a small coal stove and a few essentials to cook our meals in the hallway adjacent to the living room.

Language had never been my mother's forte, and it was more of a challenge for her in Taiwan. Since the majority of the early settlers came from Fujian (a province on the southeast coast of the Chinese mainland) and the rest from the province of Canton, the Taiwanese dialect is a combination of Fujian and Cantonese Hakka dialects—totally alien to my mother. For almost a year she bought our daily food but never learned the language. (In fact, in her forty years in Taiwan, she only learned two words in Taiwanese: "I" and "eat.")

Our toilet was a shocking hole in the floor. Someone would come monthly to collect our accumulated contributions, to cart away to fertilize their crops. The stench was so impressive that it still makes me shudder every time I think of it.

The house was in *Machangding*, "horse field district," where the Japanese had once executed their prisoners. Later I heard plenty of ghost stories about that area, but we never encountered anything paranormal there.

Despite these less-than-ideal circumstances, my mother soon turned out some pretty decent meals. We had never before heard of rice noodles, an important element of Fujianese cuisine that had come to Taiwan with the early settlers. To celebrate the Chinese New Year, my mother served us stir-fried rice noodles with chopped beef, tomatoes, and onions. They were delicious.

For the first time in our lives, our father was home every day. He ate every meal with us, sitting on the *tatami*, shifting his legs awkwardly—just like the rest of us.

Every morning he would saunter off to visit his friend, Han Deqin, the former governor of Jiangsu province and former commander of the Shandong and Jiangsu War Zone (part of the most important Third War Zone). For six years, his forces had fought the Japanese at one end and the Communists at the other, in crucial skirmishes where both Han and my father nearly lost their lives.

As staunch foes of the Communists, both Han and my father knew they could not risk falling into enemy hands. Han and his family had come to Taipei before our family. He helped secure our much-coveted seats on the plane, found us our house, and even lent us money to get settled. Han and my father remained lifelong friends, though they never worked together again after the war.

These months were the only time my father was not surrounded by friends, relatives, and assorted people—his entourage. To pass the time during the day, he taught us bridge and poker on the *tatami*. He also taught Charley *weiqi*, an ancient Chinese board game with a history of more than 2,500 years. The Japanese called it "Go." *Weiqi*, "surrounding game," requires two players to alternately place black and white "stones" on a wooden board painted with a black grid. The winner must maneuver his stones to encircle a decidedly larger area on the board than his opponent. I wasn't interested in this game, for it involved strategy and planning ahead, both of which were definitely my father's forte, not mine.

The war wasn't going well. We had left the mainland in January; Shanghai was lost—or as the Communists would say, *liberated*—in May. Lining became my father's sole comfort. Whenever he returned home from Uncle Han's house with discouraging news about the war, he didn't need to call, "Where's my *naibaozi*?" She would always be there and cling to his welcoming breast. *Naibaozi* was the endearment he bestowed on her and no other, and *he* was the only one who had the privilege of addressing her as such. By then, however, Lining was no longer a baby; she had turned ten and grown tall that spring. With our powerful father as her willing and ever-ready protector, the world was her oyster.

I used to stand as far away as possible in a corner of that tiny house, watching and thinking that this was right, the way it should be. The fact that I was not jealous doesn't prove my good nature; rather, it attests to the success of my upbringing.

Growing up, I only knew my mother's standards. Overnight, my mother faded into the background, and my father dominated. I never doubted his judgment. Years later, I still catch myself judging everything, including myself, according to his standards.

Admittedly, my sister possessed attributes I didn't have and could never have hoped to obtain. In addition to being younger and adorable, she knew how to *zuoren*. To this day, I can still hear the words *zuoren* in Yangzhou dialect in the back of my mind.

In Chinese, *zuoren* literally means making a human being of yourself. Its first layer means to toe the line and not make waves. I had no problems with that; I was good at it. I failed miserably (while my sister excelled) at the second and more crucial layer of meaning: to know and do what pleases others, whether you feel like it or not. The social fabric of the Chinese system absolutely demanded *zuoren*.

In this I probably resembled my Ninth Aunt. It is just not in my nature to know how to please or flatter.

Our mother was not sentimental or demonstrative; she treated us in a matter-of-fact manner, and it was hard to tell which one of us she favored. Our father was the opposite, and his preference carried all the weight in the world. Perhaps his favoritism was innate and inexplicable, like one's penchant for chocolate ice cream over vanilla. However, when I became a mother of two, I tried to be scrupulously even-handed, or so I thought. When they both reached college age, each accused me of having favored the other. I guess I just lost on both ends.

§

In early September 1949, less than one month before the total capitulation of the Nationalists and the establishment of the Communist regime known as the People's Republic of China, a devastating fire broke out in Chongqing, the nation's capital at the time and the home of my father's younger brother, Small Uncle.

The fire started in the waterfront and banking district, burned for eighteen hours, killed close to 3,000 people, and injured 10,000. Today, it is still recognized as one of the world's worst fires.

Small Uncle, who had originally resisted my father's urgings to leave, became so frightened that he left his pharmaceutical factory behind and joined us in Taiwan with his wife and our cousins Paul and Cecilia (Fifth Aunt's children). Suddenly there were people everywhere in our small house. The crowding problem became more acute at night, since everyone needed floor space to sleep.

In the meantime, my father landed a job as the director of the Fisheries Bureau of an American organization in Jilong, a seaport near Taipei. He was paid a generous American salary, and a jeep would come and pick him up to drive him to work every day. Soon all nine of us moved into a bigger Japanese-style house, in a better district of Taipei.

Our lives changed again.

Chapter 11

The House of My Adolescence

W henever I think about my adolescent years, memories start to churn and bubble up as if from a deep, turbulent well. A dense fog with an overwhelming sense of loneliness permeates all, and I look at those years with sadness rather than nostalgia.

I was fourteen when we moved from the tiny house to the larger one (with a kitchen!), and we lived there until I was nineteen. Since most of my adolescence—certainly the longest and most important segment—was spent in that particular house, I have always associated one with the other.

We were barely settled in the larger house when we acquired four more residents. Two of my maternal uncles— first Big Uncle, my mother's oldest brother, then Fourth Uncle, with his wife and five-year-old daughter—showed up and stayed with us. These two uncles, unbeknownst to each other, had escaped to Hong Kong and found us in Taipei, one after the other.

Our home became a small refugee camp. It accommodated relatives from both sides of the family and was packed far beyond its capacity. The two sides of the family had never met before, because of the war with the Japanese. Now they had to live together cheek by jowl, because of another war. For years we were all crammed into a modest three-bedroom Japanese-style house with one kitchen, all fifteen of us, including a cook and a maid. In the interim, a baby was born to Small Uncle and Small Aunt. The house had two tiny "bathrooms," one with a hole on the floor, the other accommodated a small Japanese-style bathtub to sit in.

The cook slept in the kitchen, and the maid on the floor of the room that Cecilia, Lining, and I shared (the three of us in the same bed). For a while Charley slept on top of a trunk in a small foyer with Big Uncle, but later he made his bed at night on the living room floor.

At the same time, my father was reconnecting with more and more of his friends who had found their way to Taiwan. As if the house was not crowded enough, my father also began bringing colleagues from his new job and various hangers-on home to dinner. He always preferred to be surrounded by people, the more the merrier. As a result, our house in those days was rife with talk—often tense, unsettling, and intriguing talk.

Our quiet life in the tiny house was gone forever. Our parents had even less time for us than they did in the Hangzhou years. My father never had much to say to Charley, the one who was going to carry on the bloodline. His words to Charley were always the same: "Why, your face looks sallow today. Are you taking care of yourself?"

My sister continued to be his breast-hugging baby long after her limbs stuck out all over his lap.

I remained the quiet, sulky, and ignored middle child, feeling alienated and hemmed in by the people around me. Months often went by without my exchanging a word with either of my parents. With so many people bustling about, it was difficult for me to find an opportunity to ask either one a quick question.

§

With only two years of elementary school and two years of junior high education, I approached the entrance examination to Taipei First Girls' High School (reputed to be the best in Taiwan) with much trepidation. I used to be an indifferent student, but aware of being a refugee on a remote island, I ceased to take the opportunity of school for granted. There was talk of marrying me off if I failed to get in. My parents were half joking, but it was enough to strike terror in my heart.

When I passed the entrance examination and entered my third

year of junior high, I began to take my studies seriously, ranking first in my class both semesters. A year quickly passed, and I soon had to jump the hurdle of another entrance examination for high school. When that was done, I heaved a huge sigh of relief—I wouldn't have to worry about passing an entrance exam for the next three years.

Perhaps it was that sense of relief that led me to enter an island-wide essay contest during my first year of high school.

Our family subscribed to two morning papers and an evening one, *Dahua* (Big China) *Evening News.* My father was assiduous about reading the morning papers. Nobody was allowed to touch them until he was done. But he was so busy with his social life after work that he rarely glanced at the evening one.

Taiwan was under martial law at the time, and each newspaper was allowed to print only four pages. By tradition, Chinese newspapers always had a daily literary page, and *Dahua Evening News* was no exception. Unlike an editorial page, the literary page runs only literary essays, fiction, and poetry. (Historically, the literary essay is an important tradition in Chinese literature, as important as poetry. Fiction didn't exist until late in the penultimate dynasty, the Ming Dynasty.)

An annual essay competition sponsored by the paper had been announced on its literary page for weeks. I was tempted and thought, *why not?* I entered the competition in secret, not wishing to brave family ridicule.

As a student since elementary school, I had always written an essay in class every week, with topics assigned by a teacher. I had never had the freedom to choose a theme on my own. Neither had I ever read anything humorous. If there were translations of Mark Twain or Charles Dickens, I wasn't aware of them then. I don't know what prompted me to write a humor essay with a mundane title "My Nose," except that I had been suffering from severe allergies, manifested by perpetual sneezing and a runny nose. I didn't know about allergies; I just knew I had this annoying problem that made me desperately self-conscious. Perhaps I simply wished to get even with my situation by making fun of it. In any case, I enjoyed writing that piece; I felt light and free.

When my essay won second prize, I was very surprised and elated by the fact that the prize carried a cash award of fifty *yuan*. The exchange rate at the time was forty *yuan* to a dollar, so fifty *yuan* was one dollar and twenty-five cents. It wasn't a lot of money even in 1951 Taiwan, but it did mean wonderful riches to me.

My school was very strict about uniforms: black cotton jacket, dark green cotton blouse, black cotton skirt, and black socks and shoes. My one and only black skirt had turned grey and shrunk above my knees—another source of embarrassment. I eagerly looked forward to buying fabric for a new skirt with the prize money.

After the first-prize essay (written by an old man nostalgic about the mainland, the most popular topic in those days) was published in the paper, "My Nose" was printed. In my excitement, I threw caution to the wind and showed it to my father.

I had chosen a *nom de plume* for the piece, *ziruo*. *Zi* means "self"; *ruo* taken from the right side of the ideogram of my given name, means "at peace." My father waited until his friends and relatives were all there to declare my pen name should have been *ziku. Ku* means "pain, suffering." Instead of having the stroke veer slightly to the left in *ruo*, bringing the same stroke straight down turns the character into *ku*. Voila! "Self at peace" becomes "self-torture."

His brilliant pun brought down the house.

I remember blaming myself: I should have known better. Why did I show him the piece and risk humiliation?

Still, I watched the paper every day for information about how to claim the prize money. Had I forgotten to include my name and address? I didn't know how to inquire at the newspaper, and I knew better than to ask my father for help.

I never received a penny.

If my father had wished to nip my writing ambition in the bud, he certainly succeeded. I didn't write anything of my own for another twenty years, and not another humor piece for more than three decades. I never used a pen name again.

Through all those years, I puzzled over his reaction: why did he punish me like this? Perhaps he felt I was out of bounds, doing something without his knowledge or permission. Whatever his reason, what cut me to the quick that evening was his expression, his smile that clearly showed he was embarrassed for me and the words it expressed unspoken—*who do you think you are?*

§

During my adolescence, I also became acutely aware of my physical shortcomings. First of all, I had a pair of questionable eyebrows—thick and set too closely together. In Chinese thinking, this type of eyebrows meant someone was *xiangbukai*: single-minded and incapable of sensible thinking. As a result, comments were often made about these characteristics that I supposedly possessed. Even Charley, a kind, gentle, and caring brother, would chide, "Here you go again, single-minded and can't think straight."

Later in life I found that the famous Mexican artist Frida Kahlo had eyebrows even thicker and closer together than mine. Hers almost met in the middle. Unfortunately, that discovery came too late. In my twenties in Missouri, two fellow female graduate students (there were only three of us) had already plucked and taken care of mine.

In addition to bad eyebrows, my lips were too thick, and my nose too small—denoting stinginess. Both my parents' families were blessed with big noses and were proud of it. In China, noses were prized for their height. Those in my father's family tended to be tall and straight, lending the face a sort of noble quality, while noses in my mother's family were deemed somewhat inferior but still in the "lion's nose" category. My mother's nose was an exception among her kin. It was tall and straight and measured up to stringent standards. Apparently mine did not.

No criticism was ever leveled at my eyes, but they were getting smaller and smaller behind increasingly stronger corrective lenses. My chin seemed to have stopped growing before it reached a desirable length, and my legs were too thick compared to those of my sister and cousin Cecilia, the indisputable beauty of the family. My mother also said my teeth needed braces, but unfortunately we couldn't afford them.

To top it all off, I was too short. In high school, I came home every day to calcium shots, administered by my mother in the hopes that they would make me grow taller. I don't remember for how long those shots continued (probably months), but she finally gave up when I didn't gain a millimeter.

Fourth Uncle told me about a new surgery that involved cutting off both legs at the calf and employing bone grafting that could somehow make the person two inches taller. It might have been just idle talk on his part, but it reinforced my already well-developed inferiority complex—"Am I so terribly short that I need to resort to such drastic measures?"

§

Although my father was too busy to bother with me, he definitely set the parameters of what I could or couldn't do. In general, we girls were forbidden to go out after school. For instance, I was not allowed to go to my high school classmate's house on a Sunday afternoon to listen to her classical music records.

I felt I really needed a bicycle. I took the city bus to school. The buses were extremely crowded, and people never bothered to stand in line to get on the bus. Sometimes I waited for bus after bus and couldn't manage to squeeze on board.

The vast majority of students rode bicycles, and after school, my friends would let me push one of their bikes while they walked me home. At my request for a used bike, my father gave a quick and firm no, "If you get hurt on a bike in the street, we wouldn't even know."

We were not allowed to learn to swim or do any sports, nothing that would delay us from returning home after school.

My school in Taiwan, being the island's most selective, offered weekly piano lessons and the privilege of practicing on a beat-up upright for a token fee. My mother said we couldn't afford the fee.

As for the issue of the skirt—the one I had hoped to buy with my prize money—my mother answered, "If I let you have a new skirt, your cousin and your sister will have to get one too. We simply don't have that kind of money."

§

When Small Uncle, Small Aunt, and cousins Paul and Cecilia, first arrived, I had no idea how closely their lives would be associated with ours from that moment on. Our family of five instantly became a family of nine. For better or for worse, we were going to wade through our lives with them.

It was as if my father had adopted Paul and Cecilia as his children. Although we knew they were our cousins, we had to address them as older brother and older sister and defer to them as such. Our two maternal uncles were just residents, but my father's side of family was family.

Cecilia was two years older than I, but we ended up in the same grade at school. In fact, I was a semester ahead of her, in the so-called spring class, where the year's curriculum started in the spring rather than in the fall. Our school had only two spring classes, established to accommodate the influx of refugees in the spring of 1949.

Despite being related and close in age, living in the same house, and sharing the same room and bed, Cecilia and I were not exactly friends until our college years. She was probably a bit wary of me because I was known as a good student at school.

Besides, our temperaments differed. She was also quiet, but guarded, her expression bland like a mask. She seemed unemotional; I could never detect any ups or downs in her moods, whereas people said they could always read me like a book. In addition, Cecilia was pragmatic and ready to look out for her own interests, perhaps a self-protective mechanism she had learned as an "orphan."

Fifth Aunt, Paul and Cecilia's mother, was still alive, of course, but she was in Shanghai and incommunicado on account of the Bamboo Curtain. (She died before the Communists "opened" the mainland thirty years later; Paul and Cecilia never saw her again.) I sensed my father liked Cecilia far better than he did me, and it wasn't entirely due to the fact that she was pretty and the daughter of his most favorite sibling. Years later he told me that he had hoped that she would marry Charley one day. (Chinese mores forbid children of brothers to marry but not those of brother and sister.)

Paul was five years older than Cecilia but somehow kept his childlike innocence and believed that if the sky should ever fall, my father would be there to catch it for him. My father sheltered and dictated to him, and that was exactly what Paul wanted.

Both Paul and Cecilia were much pampered in their early age, each with an individual nursemaid who perpetually attended them. Their life took a steep nosedive when their father died and the Sino-Japanese War drove them to Shanghai, where their mother, Fifth Aunt, married Chang Lao San.

Her second marriage produced two girls, and the family operated and lived above a tiny, shabby stationery store. Their living quarters were so cramped that Paul had to be sent to a Catholic orphanage. When my father went to Shanghai just before the end of the war, Paul was seventeen and too old to remain at the orphanage with no place else to go. Fifth Aunt pleaded with my father to find him an apprentice job and was overjoyed when he offered to take Paul with him to bring up as his own.

Cecilia stayed with her mother and took care of her stepsisters. As she grew into her pubescence, however, there were signs that she was in increasing danger of being molested by Chang Lao San, her stepfather. Her mother was sufficiently alarmed to reach out to her other younger brother, my Small Uncle. Married and having no children of his own, he went to Shanghai and brought Cecilia back to his home in Chongqing.

After living with us for several years in Hangzhou, Paul failed his college entrance examinations and attended an art institute in Chongqing to be near Small Uncle. The Chinese believed in taking care of their kin, and that was how both Paul and Cecilia were brought by Small Uncle and Small Aunt to live with us in Taiwan when they fled Chongqing.

My mother told me about Cecilia's history to underline the importance of my according Cecilia the respect of an older sister. So every night when we packed our lunch boxes from the dinner leftovers, I always had to let her go first, even when it meant that I would have less than enough for lunch the next day.

Small Uncle had been unemployed since his arrival, whereas my father was not only head of the house but also the sole breadwinner, earning a good salary paid in American dollars. My father was happy to assume financial responsibilities for all. In fact, he often bragged that he had five children.

Despite having to provide for so many of us, my parents managed to save and borrow enough money to buy an oil factory in Jiayi, a southwestern city in Taiwan. They put Small Uncle in charge of the factory. I don't remember how long Small Uncle and Small Aunt were away, probably around a year, when they suddenly came back. The factory had folded, all the money had vanished, and Small Uncle got red in the face when my father asked to see the financial records. It was evident that he had embezzled the funds. But my father decided to let it go—after all, Small Uncle was his baby brother.

Small Uncle's timing couldn't have been worse. My father had just changed jobs. He had the same title—director of The Fisheries Bureau—but he now worked for the Department of Agriculture and Forestry in the Taiwan Provincial Government, a government job with notoriously miserable pay. And my father was adamantly scrupulous about not taking bribes.

During the Mid-Autumn Festival, for instance, officials of various fisheries associations would come bearing boxes of moon cakes lined at the bottom with cash, expecting favors returned. My brother Charley was instructed to stand by the front gate to refuse the gifts. Over the years, Charley had no shortage of complaints about our father, yet he never accused him of lacking integrity.

My father's meager salary, our embezzled nest egg, and the debt plunged our family into more than twenty years of poverty. We suffered from it when we were in Taiwan, and Charley and I helped pay for it for years after we came to the United States.

No matter how difficult his financial situation was, my father maintained the same lifestyle. He always ordered the most expensive food at expensive restaurants and insisted upon picking up the bill. He had lived like that since his childhood. No one could detect that we were dirt poor, and relatives living at our house enjoyed free room and board. They gradually moved away and established lives of their own only after many years.

Big Uncle stayed long after we children had left home, until almost the end of his life. Small Uncle and Small Aunt stayed for six years, until I was a sophomore in college. Their baby boy was born while they lived with us and sadly died a year later of leukemia. Except for the brief stint with the oil factory, Small Uncle never held a job in Taiwan, but with his ill-gotten money, he managed to buy immigration to Canada under the so-called "investors quota."

My father liked to lecture us about the advantage of being the "soy sauce dish" in life, allowing everyone "to dip his food in us." He said it was good to let people take advantage of us because it meant that we had something to offer. He had no idea how much some of us had to scrimp and save, how many times I went to school with a half-filled lunch box, how I always had to order the cheapest lunch in college, and how I was always the shabbiest-dressed student.

A related lecture from my father was on how a family should always stick together. The subtext: even if his brother had robbed him, it was forgivable because he was family. I was a mere adolescent when I first heard those lectures, and even then I didn't agree. But I kept my opinion safely to myself.

§

When I think about those years, I realize that my mother never had any friends of her own. She socialized with my father's friends but never showed much enthusiasm for them. She was detached from people in general, even from us, her children. It may be fair to say that she essentially stopped nurturing us when our father came back after the war. Perhaps my father and his activities required so much attention that she was left depleted.

In fact, all of us were like rivers coming from different regions but flowing in the same direction—to the ocean, my father. We were so occupied with catering to his needs and staying within his confines that we never had a chance to get to know one another well.

For much of my life I despised and resented Small Uncle and Small Aunt for what they did to us. As decades pass, however, I'm surprised to find myself taking a different perspective.

We always addressed Small Uncle as such because he was the youngest, but he was also physically small and ugly—short with a balding and pointed head. He was unsure of himself. Severe allergies made him constantly sniffle and clear his nasal passages before he could utter a word. He had lost his father as a baby and was overshadowed by his two much older brothers. There was no hope he could ever catch up to them, let alone outshine them.

He received a pharmacology degree and left Shanghai to make a life of his own, eventually owning a pharmaceutical plant in Chongqing and marrying. If not for the fire and the threat of the Communist takeover, he probably would have led an ordinary life that suited him just fine.

But that was not to be. He was lucky enough to have a caring brother who persuaded him to escape Communist rule at the eleventh hour and provided him and his wife with food and shelter. But he was also unlucky in that he could never strike out on his own.

I thought I was miserable during those years, but I never imagined his daily humiliation, and perhaps even paralyzing, self-lacerating anger at having to live under the wing of a dominating brother who was far superior in every way. Why shouldn't he have helped himself to some of the money? For all he knew, there would always be more from where it came.

As for Small Aunt, I thought I was the lowest person on the totem pole in that house, but in retrospect I realize that she was; we were all related by blood except her. A graceless, uneducated, large-boned woman with a thick Sichuan accent, she had met my uncle while working as a cashier in his plant. In our house, she was ignored and shunned by all of us from the day of their arrival, especially by my father. He didn't like her and never spoke a word to her. She took to her room and rarely opened her mouth; no one ever detected a glimmer of courtesy or friendliness from her.

In the end, their baby didn't survive, and they had to live with their rotten deed. All in all, I believe they had a very sad life.

In all those years, I felt I didn't seem to exist for anyone in that house. Nobody ever asked, "How was school today?" But life is a classroom, and I learned plenty in that house of my adolescence.

Chapter 12

BEHIND THE NARROW GATE

In 1949, when I became a student of *Beiyinu*, the honorific acronym for Taipei First Girls High School, all the Japanese students had departed. They had left four years earlier after Japan lost the war. It was easy for us, the refugees who had come from practically every part of the mainland, to identify the remaining Taiwanese students. They wore old-fashioned skirts with multiple pleats and carried their belongings Japanese-style in a cloth bundle with unmistakable Japanese motif. Most importantly, they spoke Japanese, which had been the official language. To them, we probably appeared a curious and varied bunch. They called us *waishenren*, people from other provinces, or *daluren*, the mainlanders. However, the distinction blurred gradually over the years.

In the beginning, we mainlanders stayed within our individual comfort zones by forming cliques according to the respective dialects we spoke, although we obeyed the rule of using Mandarin, the official Chinese dialect, to communicate with others. My three closest friends and I never had much in common, but the same tongue—the Shanghai dialect—was enough to bond us. We became lifelong friends. Unlike them, however, I spoke two other dialects: my father's Yangzhou dialect and the Hangzhou dialect. I don't remember how I learned to speak Mandarin at school in Taiwan; it just happened.

Although my classmates and I spoke different dialects, we shared the same written language, thanks to Emperor Qin Shi

Huang, the emperor who lived between 259 and 210 B.C. and unified the country. He was notorious for burning books and burying scholars alive (460 to be exact), but he is also recognized for having unified the Chinese written language by abolishing the writings of other warring states. From then on, while words were pronounced differently from dialect to dialect, the written language remained the same.

(Speaking of Qin Shi Huang, Chairman Mao relished comparing himself to the emperor, boasting in a speech in 1958 to party cadres: "He buried 460 scholars alive—we have buried 46,000 scholars alive...We have surpassed Qin Shi Huang a hundredfold.")

§

Originally established to accommodate Japanese students, Taipei First Girls High School was one of the most—if not the most—prestigious high schools in Taiwan. To this day, only the top one percent of aspirants succeeds in passing its entrance exam. The difficulty of getting into this elite institution is often referred to as "squeezing through the narrow gate."

If our school's academic standards were lofty, its discipline was extraordinary—as strict and harsh as those of any nunnery. We wore black uniforms with green shirts (green, for the purpose of camouflage, was a carryover from air-raid days after Pearl Harbor when the Japanese were bombed by the Americans). We wore our hair straight, cut to the length of one centimeter above the ear lobes—no bangs, curls, or waves. What grew underneath in the back was to be kept shaved, presenting a hue called "watermelon skin." If a student's hair started inching toward her ear lobes, our student dean would wield a huge pair of scissors to chop it off. The result was, as we used to say, as if a dog had chewed on your hair.

Furthermore, our principal was the famous, extremely strict, and much feared Jiang Xuezu, who had sworn to remain single to devote herself to her career as an educator. Principal Jiang had a high and mighty attitude that didn't exactly endear her to her students. I, for one, especially resented her haughty tone when she addressed us in assemblies. Whispering behind her back, we referred to her as *The Old Maid*.

Our school stood kitty-corner across Chongqing South Road from the Presidential Office Building, the most imposing structure in Taiwan in those days, occupying a whole city block. Beyond the block was the business district, beckoning us with many enticing bookstores.

My friends kept suggesting that we slip out of school during lunch hour to explore the area, something we were strictly forbidden to do. Even though a doorkeeper was stationed in a small booth at the front gate, we knew other students had managed to sneak out undetected.

I was the only serious student in my clique. In fact, I held an unblemished record during my four years at *Beiyinu*, ranking first in my class for seven semesters out of eight (I slipped to second place during the semester I suffered from diphtheria complications), and I enjoyed a fairly high profile. I was a member of the debate team, participated in speech contests, and a few times even performed in a traditional Chinese duo comic dialogue act called *xiangsheng*.

For reasons I can't explain, I succumbed to the temptation to escape school one day. Perhaps the more highhanded the discipline, the greater the desire to rebel.

Once out of the forbidden gate, however, the adventure instantly lost its allure. We walked past the Presidential Office Building into the business district, all the while keenly aware of our uniform. We looked in the stores, but our hearts were not in it.

On our hasty way back, a rickshaw pulled up from the other direction in front of the school, bearing none other than our principal! At the sight of her stern face we scattered like scared rabbits, with her in her *qipao* and half-inch heels in hot pursuit. While desperately dashing toward the nearby Taipei Botanical Garden, I took the precaution of tucking my glasses in the pocket in the hopes of rendering myself less recognizable. Eventually we succeeded in losing her and slunk back one by one.

Years later, as a writer giving talks to different *Beiyinu* reunions in this country, I mentioned that incident in my opening remark. After repeating the story on several such occasions, I came to realize that our principal had been more benevolent than we had thought. She could have instructed the doorkeeper to wait and catch us. I shudder to think what would have happened if she had decided to do just that and what would have been my father's reaction.

§

Our school had no cafeteria. Every morning we brought our lunch in a metal box, the size and shape of a book with a lid— called *bento* in Japanese—to be steamed on a huge stove in the school kitchen. At lunchtime we would get our bento back and eat at our desks. I often did not have enough food in my bento, and whatever was there, usually the previous night's leftovers, seemed to object to the brutal treatment of being steamed for hours on a hot stove. My lunch simply shriveled and died an ugly second death.

This gave me more reason to cherish the annual Duanwu Festival, also known as the Dragon Boat Festival. To celebrate the festival, every family would make *zongzi* (sticky rice dumplings or "Chinese tamales") to last for several days. The types of *zongzi* varied from region to region and even from one family to the next. What I loved best was our Shanghai version—marinated pork and shitake mushrooms encased by glutinous rice (also called sticky rice or sweet rice and also raw). They were wrapped in bamboo leaves in the shape of an elongated cone, tied with twine, and simmered for hours.

The holiday originated 2,000 years ago when patriotic poet Qu Yuan committed suicide. He had been exiled for speaking out against an ill-advised alliance with the enemy, Qin Shi Huang (the very same emperor who later buried 460 scholars alive and unified the country and written language). On the fifth day of the fifth month of the Chinese lunar calendar when Qin's army did indeed capture the capital of Chu as Quan Yuan predicted, the poet drowned himself in the Miluo River.

This tragic event spawned two customs that have persisted to this day—the eating of *zongzi* and dragon boat races. To mourn

Qu Yuan and pay tribute to his poetry, people dropped *zongzi* into the river to feed the fish—to keep them from eating his body. It was also believed that paddling the boats would scare the fish away and improve the chances of retrieving his body.

Thanks to this tradition, every year I brought two *zongzi* in my bento for several days after the festival and while supplies lasted. Come lunchtime, they were steamy hot and succulent, and they had the added virtue of being substantial enough to sustain me all afternoon.

For the rest of the school year, my gnawing afternoon hunger was often an issue. To make the situation worse, the school store offered a whole host of goodies for anyone with money to spend. I remember watching with envy others licking their popsicles in a variety of tempting flavors—mung bean, red bean, peanut, or milk.

§

Two years before we were due to graduate, we had to declare preferences for our subject of study in college. Going to college was a given, and everyone in our school set her sights on the best. National Taiwan University was an even loftier and narrower gate than *Beiyinu*, and was known throughout the country as *Taida*. Only after failing the entrance examination of *Taida* would any of us consider a lesser college or university.

We had to choose among three subject categories: category *Jia* for those who wished to major in the best and most coveted fields of engineering, medicine, and science; category *Yi* for languages and social sciences; and category *Bing* for agriculture and biosciences.

Because the best students were expected to be in category *Jia*, I was momentarily tempted to state *Jia* as my preference. But I had desired to be a writer since second grade. I didn't know what being a writer entailed, but the idea simply grabbed hold of me and wouldn't let go. I decided that if I studied languages (a synonym for literature in those days) in college, the rest would naturally follow.

Before exams I was always asked by my fellow classmates to explain problems on the blackboard, and I consistently received the highest scores in all my courses. However, math and science were slightly more of a challenge. In geometry, it would take me a while to construct a line for a diagram, and the sulfuric acid in our chemistry lab gave me a nasty headache. On the other hand, I seemed to gravitate to Chinese and English. To the surprise of everyone in my class, I signed up for category *Yi*. Since my parents never asked me about school (or anything else, for that matter), they didn't know.

I was the valedictorian of the school's only two spring classes, a total of around seventy students. It was not a special distinction because it was generally known that the spring classes were academically inferior to the fall classes. Our principal had declared us a lazy and undisciplined bunch, and she repeated her views during our graduation ceremony, delivering her tongue lashing just before my speech. Hers was a tough act to follow. In a humiliated daze, I gave my prepared speech, thankful that because of the Chinese custom in those days, no parents were in the audience—including my own.

Chapter 13

No Regrets

No Exceptions
Letter from my father, 1953

The trouble with you—
head always in the clouds
feet never touching the ground
too young, too impetuous
to know your mind.

Preciously few people
make a living from writing.
What makes you think
you will be the exception?
The world is not holding
its breath for stories from you.
Indulge yourself in writing
you may as well give up eating.

Leave your ivory tower.
Learn something useful.
Study medicine or be a nurse.
No one ever—I repeat—ever
accomplishes
a thing
by being obtuse.

Your mother chose spouse
and children over practice.
Whenever sickness visits us
her medical training
serves its purpose.
If you're lucky
to wed someday
you will use your skills
the very same way.

Putting family over self.
That's what women did
for generations past;
that's what they'll do
for generations to come.
Why should *you*
be an exception?

June 21, 2005

I was eighteen years old. I stood in front of my father in the dining room. We were holding the very first conversation I had ever had with him in my entire life, largely a one-way conversation.

Of course my father didn't write me a letter; he delivered a lecture. I tried to capture the essence of what he said in my poem. To me what he said seemed more like a life sentence. Without parole.

It would have been useless to tell him that my heart had been set on writing since I was seven years old. The Chinese department at *Taida* was more like a department of archeology with courses on ancient works, such as Confucius. There was no study of contemporary literature. My true desire was to be in the Foreign Languages department, where literary heavyweights offered courses on English literature. My father's decision was a sweeping no on all "ivory tower" subjects.

And I wanted to tell him I was *not* my mother. I dreaded the sight of blood, having fainted at each blood test, the first being when I contracted diphtheria and had my veins poked repeatedly by the doctor. Even the odor of disinfectant, ubiquitous in clinical settings, was enough to make me cringe. Having been sick a good deal of my life, I just wanted to stay away from the hospital. I didn't dare say that medicine would be the last field I would choose for my career.

Besides, both my father and I knew my mother hadn't selected her husband and children over practicing medicine. *He* was the one who had made the decision for her. And why should I waste seven years of my life studying something I hated just so I could be useful in case my family got sick? Why couldn't they simply see a doctor like everybody else?

Again, I didn't dare ask these questions. I only stammered again that I was not interested in medicine and that I wanted to study literature.

My father said, "How would a child know what her interest is?"

Ever eager to help, Small Uncle chimed in, "Medicine is like eating rice; literature, eating candy. Only after one's had enough rice should he think of eating candy. The best way is to study medicine for your career and do some writing as a hobby."

Pleased with his own wisdom, Small Uncle smacked his lips and rolled his tongue as if he himself was already eating the candy. But I couldn't connect formaldehyde and the stench of decaying cadavers with eating rice, while I could literally drool over the English literature courses in the Foreign Languages department.

That department happened to be the most popular on campus, boasting the highest number of students. *Didn't parents of those students worry about their children starving?* Still, I remained silent, as I couldn't risk a slap to my face by asking any questions that might be considered impudent.

My father typically rendered his decisions like a judge handing down an absolute verdict. This time was no exception.

That evening after my parents went out for dinner with their friends, I slipped out of the house to a small river several blocks away. In the summer people swam there, and some drowned. I even knew one of the victims; she had been the wife of my father's trusted subordinate and had committed suicide when she couldn't endure the long suffering of tuberculosis.

Standing alone by the water's edge, I thought it would be so easy to slip in—my pain would be over. But frightened by the swift, muddy water, I lacked the courage to take the step.

For three days, I tried to find a way out. I had no one to talk to. It was clear my father was unequivocally against my studying literature, and I was equally opposed to majoring in medicine. I realized I had to find a middle ground; I had to give up literature to avoid studying medicine. I thought of the fact that my father had majored in law in his youth. He must have considered it a practical field, and to me, law was definitely the lesser of two evils.

To my great surprise and relief, my father accepted the compromise, ending our three-day standoff.

In all fairness, my father did take his children's aptitude into consideration when making his decisions on our fields of study. For Paul, I think he chose civil engineering for its practicality and Paul's artistic inclinations; for Charley and Cecilia, business studies, for the fact that they were average students and didn't show much interest in any particular subject. Four years later, for Lining he chose business studies yet again.

None of the other four raised any objections because they didn't have any idea of what they wanted. I was the exception. My father and I were both unpleasantly surprised by the other.

I was also the only one who consistently ranked first in my class. Thus, he probably thought I would be the only one of the five who stood a real chance of getting into medical school. My father's youthful exploits seemed to indicate that he was not ruled by pragmatism; ironically, he was extremely pragmatic when it came to making decisions for his children's futures.

§

The entrance examination to *Taida* was a huge event every July. More than ten thousand students took it in 1953; fewer than one thousand passed.

On the evening that *Taida* posted its exam results, Charley and

Paul went to campus early. A large crowd had already gathered; most had been waiting for hours. When the staff came out holding giant sheets of handwritten names, the ink not yet dry, everyone rushed forward, jostling and craning their necks to search among the coveted names.

As soon as Charley and Paul found both my name and Cecilia's, they rode their bikes home as fast as they could with the news. Afterward, we huddled around the radio to hear our names read aloud and tried to listen for the names of people we knew.

My father was not home that night. At the invitation of the U.S. Department of Agriculture, he was on a three-month tour with a group of Taiwanese agricultural officials. Before he left, he had promised us that if we *both* passed the exam, he would allow us to live in the dormitory.

Despite knowing that I had to give up an important chunk of my life to law, which sounded dry and alien to me, that night was unquestionably the most exhilarating of my life. I don't remember another when I felt so full of hope.

Both Charley and Paul had already finished their junior years in *Taida*. Now we had not two, but four *Taida* students, and all of us had passed the exam on the first try. This made us the envy of a great number of families, for we knew many students who had failed the exam. The majority of those who failed usually attended private tutoring schools all year and took the exam again. Some did year after year. A few even committed suicide after several failed attempts.

Nobody felt like turning in that night; Cecilia and I went to bed when dawn broke, but we were much too excited to sleep. We whispered to each other about staying in the same dorm and speculated what dorm life would be like.

The newspapers in the morning confirmed the bad news that none of my three best friends had passed. Our principal was correct about spring classes being inferior—only seven of us made it, a far smaller proportion than that of the fall classes.

When my father returned from his tour, he immediately broke his promise: Cecilia and I would not be permitted to live in the dormitory after all. Not only that, he set down a new rule—*no boyfriends.* We hadn't even thought about boyfriends, but not being allowed to live in the dormitory was a big blow. It felt as if the outside world had been beckoning to us, and all of a sudden the door had slammed shut.

It turned out that attending *Taida* was quite anticlimactic. The classes were utterly boring. Twice a semester, before midterms

Cecilia and me, circa 1955

and finals week, I would expend minimal effort—two weeks in the library—making summaries of my course notes and memorizing them. The rest of the time, I attended classes but managed to tune out the lectures.

In the spring of my sophomore year, several nursing schools in remote areas of America—such as Montana, Idaho, and Wyoming—offered one-time, all-expenses-paid scholarships to high school graduates in Taiwan. In an effort to solve their problem of nursing shortages, they offered scholarships to entice students who had failed to get into college. Of course, they would have to pass an examination.

I thought this had nothing to do with me. Nevertheless, I was again summoned to stand in front of my father in the dining room. Cecilia and I were to take the exam.

Again, I balked. I was already in college. In fact, I ranked second in a class of 124 law students at Taiwan's most prestigious university. Every semester I received a small cash prize for excellent academic performance. Life was boring but tolerable—why should I give this up? To go to America to empty bedpans, give baths, and stick needles into patients? Just the thought of it was enough to make me sick.

My father was furious. "Why? Is the job beneath you? Nurses are human, too. Do you think you are special, better than they are?"

"No, no, no...that's not what I mean. All I'm saying is that people have different interests. I'm even less interested in being a nurse than being a doctor. It would be miserable for me to spend my life doing something I have no interest in."

My father again said, "How would a child know what her interest is?"

My mother attempted to mediate: "Interests can change. You may not be interested in nursing now, but you could become interested after you study it for a while."

I thought to myself, *what if I never became interested?* I had been studying law for almost two years, and I didn't like it any better than I had before. But I didn't dare argue; to ask either parent a question he or she couldn't answer would be inviting trouble. I could only keep saying "No" until I was dismissed.

One afternoon, however, a man bobbed up outside my classroom window—my father's chauffeur. It was the last day of registration for the nursing exam and he had come to collect me.

Clearly there would be no compromise this time; no amount of imploring would change my father's mind. I was to take the exam and be shipped off to some foreign small town to be a nurse. My fate was sealed.

I was thoroughly frightened, and I was angry. I felt my life was being destroyed and there was nothing I could do about it. I felt lonely and lost. Suddenly an idea flashed in my mind like a meteor shooting across the night sky—the exam! Although my father had absolute power over me, he could not take the exam for me.

I sounded out Cecilia. It turned out she didn't like my father's idea either but didn't dare oppose him. We formed a secret pact. For two days, on test after test, I carefully filled in my name and examination registration number, stared at my paper for half an hour, turned in the blank exam, and left the room. Cecilia did the same.

The morning my father barged into our room, red in the face, waving a newspaper, the pounding of my heart suddenly turned loud and heavy. The names of those who had passed the exam were published in the paper, just as the college ones had been.

"Several of your high school friends passed and *you* didn't?"

I broke out in a cold sweat. "I don't...know why. Maybe...I was...was just unlucky this time."

He stared hard at me. He was more than furious. Obviously he didn't believe me, yet he could believe less that I would have dared defy him. In either case, it was too late. There was nothing he could do now.

Ten years later, when my father saw me for the first time since I had left home to come to this country, he still had to clear his doubts: "Did you fail that exam on purpose?"

It took all my courage to look him in the eye and admit: "Yes."

His face betrayed no emotion, but I had the feeling that he would never forgive me for having challenged his authority and getting away with it. He never suspected Cecilia because she was not a good student. She was so frightened just the same that, to the end of her life, she never alluded to our shared secret, even after he was gone.

For graduate school, I thought journalism was as close to literature as I could get without incurring my father's disapproval. While my friends in English were reading Fitzgerald and Faulkner, I had to familiarize myself with the thirty-seven bullet points on how to manage a small town newspaper.

I wasted seven years of my youth studying subjects of no interest to me. How many seven years does one have? In my case, seven impressionable years, unencumbered by life's later demands were gone because my father had different ideas for my life than I did.

Sometimes I ask myself, what is *interest*? My father dismissed it as something fanciful. He couldn't see it or touch it, and I couldn't prove to him that it existed. For me, interest in writing has always been there, obstinate and inextinguishable. I have never regretted failing that nursing exam. Indeed, I'm grateful I had that choice.

Chapter 14

THE ENGAGEMENT PARTY

During my freshman year, my family moved from Taipei to its northern suburb, the famous hot springs resort of Beitou. For me, it meant a three-hour round-trip commute on two different buses just to attend classes. And I had wall-to-wall classes six days a week. To graduate in four years with my law degree, I was required to complete one year of college and three years of law school and carry an inordinately heavy course load each semester.

College seemed a dreary repetition of high school—with one obvious difference. The university was co-ed. In anticipation of possible complications and in addition to his *no dormitory* decree, my father laid down another of his ironclad rules at the outset: *no boyfriends.*

He needn't have bothered. Taiwan in the mid-1950s was highly conservative, and students were self-segregated by gender. Confucius said, *no physical contact between men and women.* Although he had been dead for more than 2,000 years and we were in the middle of the twentieth century, we behaved as though he were there watching us.

In fact, we carried Confucius' rule a step further. Every day and all day, we sat in the same classroom with the same classmates of the opposite sex, but we didn't converse, exchange greetings, or even show any recognition of one another.

Hoping to break out of these strict confines, some audacious students joined theater, music, dance, bridge, or debate clubs. Military training coaches regularly organized outings in the summer, which were not mandatory but highly popular. Knowing my father would say no, I didn't participate in any—including the debate club to which I was invited in my freshman year.

During the summers after my sophomore and junior years, however, I petitioned my father to go to Taipei for typing lessons. Not surprisingly, he didn't think it was a good idea. But after I graduated in July 1957 and was due to leave for graduate school in America, he relented. Since I would be studying journalism, he decided typing lessons might be useful after all.

He also permitted me to go to Taipei to submit my thesis—a translation of a chapter of a book on the English Borstal system for reforming juveniles—to one of the law magazines for publication.

Then, most unexpected of all, he said yes to my attending a classmate's engagement party.

Most of his largesse came a bit late. The typing class was a three-month program, and my departure date was in less than two months. I only had time to attend classes for a little over a month. (To this day I'm a mediocre typist. Every time I had to take a typing test in my early years in this country, I failed.)

The first law magazine I approached accepted my thesis, scheduling it to be published in several monthly installments starting after my departure from Taiwan.

However, those two pieces of good news paled in comparison to the thrill of being allowed to attend the engagement party.

There were twelve women in our class, and I was in a clique of five. The classmate getting engaged was what we called an "overseas Chinese" from Hong Kong. He invited all five of us. It was the first time in four years that he had crossed the gender divide to speak to us.

When my friends and I showed up that evening, we saw that, in honor of this special occasion, all five of us were in our formal attire, *qipao*. This was the very first time I had worn a *qipao*, one of the nearly ten that had been custom made for me in preparation of my coming years in America.

My friends and I never talked about it, but we had all been looking forward to this unique opportunity to socialize with our male classmates. Having quietly observed them at close range for four years, we knew who were the smartest, the most handsome, or the most outgoing. We also knew who were the best basketball players and who were interested in whom. We even recognized the voices and speech peculiarities of some. In fact, both sides were curious and eager to get to know the other.

In addition, unbeknownst to my friends and family, I harbored a secret wish. When I was twelve, my father had taught Lining and me to dance to fill in as temporary dance partners for his friends. We were taught the foxtrot, waltz, cha-cha, jitterbug, mambo, and even the tango. I loved tango the best. However, as soon as they no longer needed us, our dancing days were over. Thereafter we were strictly forbidden to dance. But I had already become inordinately fond of dancing. Addiction may be too strong a word here, but swaying with the music seemed to transport me to a different realm, free and enchanting. This upcoming party certainly kindled my desire to recapture that old enchanted feeling from ten years ago…

My heart was overwhelmed with gratitude when I learned that my father decided to accompany me on the ride to the party. He was a considerate boss, mainly using his government-issued car during the day and driving himself in the evenings so that the chauffeur could go home. On this evening, however, my father decided the chauffeur would drive us to the party.

When we arrived at the address, a private home, I was surprised to see my father get out of the car with me. At the door, he introduced himself most graciously and inquired, "When will your dinner be over?"

The host was taken aback. He consulted with his fiancée and looked at his watch. "We'll start soon… We should be finished eating by 7 o'clock, 7:30 the latest."

My father thanked him and left.

The house was crowded with familiar and not-so-familiar faces. Music drifted from the record player. Our classmate's fiancée—a vivacious girl with beautiful and expressive eyes—was also an overseas Chinese. The party was still segregated, with girls in the living room and boys crowded in the next room in animated conversation. They were eyeing us, and we pretended not to notice.

Soon we were invited into the dining room with a table laden with food. We served ourselves buffet style and retreated back to the living room to eat with plates on our laps.

Before we were finished, the doorbell rang. My father was there to collect me. It was seven o'clock sharp.

§

I should have known better. I should have remembered the incident a short two years earlier. Charley, having completed his one-year mandatory military training for male college graduates, was the first to go to graduate school in America. He had received a scholarship at Montana State College in Bozeman.

The night before Charley's flight, my father came home late from a dinner engagement in Taipei. Showered and dressed for bed, he asked for Charley. My mother replied, "Oh yes, he called. He's going to stay at the dorm with his friends tonight."

"Which friends? Where's he staying?"

"He didn't say."

"You don't know, and you didn't even ask?"

"What's the problem?" my mother was a little defensive. "He's twenty-three years old; he's leaving for America tomorrow and wanted to spend some time with his friends tonight. Do you plan to check up on him at night after he gets to Montana?"

My father couldn't be dissuaded. He changed from his pajamas, spent more than an hour on the phone calling everyone he could think of, succeeded in finding Charley, drove back to Taipei, and brought him home that night.

Years later, Lining told me about a similar incident.

Twenty-two years old and a *Taida* senior at the time, she was invited by her best friend and classmate Aileen to spend a night at her house. Having reached the end of finals week, Aileen was in great spirits. "We need to celebrate, and I've already talked to my folks."

Lining was not enthusiastic. "I'm afraid my father is not going to let me spend a night at your house. Not even an afternoon."

Aileen didn't believe her. She had often been to our house in

Beitou, and the two fathers were the best of friends. What could be the problem? "If you don't want to ask Uncle Liu, I'll ask him!" she said.

"No, it's not a matter of wanting or not wanting to ask," Lining explained. "I know for sure it's not going to work, so why bother?"

Aileen was surprised. "I can tell that Uncle Liu is the most democratic and the most considerate father in the whole wide world. Besides, even if he doesn't trust me, he should trust my father—they are great friends, for heaven's sakes."

Well, Lining thought, *if you don't believe me and want to get turned down, go ahead.*

Incredibly, my father was all smiles, "Yes, by all means! Have a good time!"

Lining was perplexed. She couldn't figure out what her father had up his sleeve. But she gathered her toothbrush and pajamas and left with Aileen.

On the long distance bus to Taipei, her friend was still gloating—"What did I tell you? Your father's the greatest!"

After dinner, when they had retreated to Aileen's bedroom to listen to her new records, the doorbell rang. My parents were standing there, and my father was all smiles: "We came out for a walk after dinner. Since we're already in your neighborhood, we thought we'd bring Lining home with us."

Aileen tried to protest, but her father stopped her. Lining retrieved her things and got in the car.

§

Living under his inflexible, excessively protective dictatorship, none of us knew my father had an important reason for this totalitarian rule—*his grand plan.*

Chapter 15

The Grand Plan

Perhaps my father started nurturing a secret desire to leave the moment we first set foot in Taiwan. In the beginning, almost all mainlanders, including my father, looked down on the remote, impoverished island. Perhaps the three-month USDA tour he had taken with other Taiwanese agricultural officials (of Hawaii, San Diego, and other *nice* destinations) gave him ideas about where he aspired to live instead. It probably took years for his desire to gradually harden into a concrete plan, a grand plan involving the rest of the family.

As Charley had aptly observed, my father detested the Communists but was a faithful practitioner of their *modus operandi*: "The end justifies the means." He would do whatever it took to achieve his goal of transporting himself to America.

Since he liked to play his cards close to his chest, my father didn't spell out the details of his plan or declare its goal to us, although he used us as the foot soldiers on his battlefield, the pawns on his chessboard. In my case, I had to learn about his plan in bits and pieces on my own. When I did put all the pieces together, it was already pretty late in the game when the hard-earned knowledge was no longer relevant. And I realized that my life, as well as those of my siblings and cousins, had been molded according to this plan.

We lived in a tightly controlled environment until we were sent abroad one by one. Nothing had been left to chance. In my case, given the technological realities of 1957—phone calls across the ocean were impossible, and an airmail letter could take weeks—he was reduced to exercising remote control. He willingly relinquished his daily control over me for one reason and one reason only: to live in America, safe from the Chinese Communists, whom he greatly distrusted and feared.

Although we had fled the mainland in January 1949, a step ahead of its fall to the Communists, we were by no means safe or secure. In August of that same year, the American State Department under President Truman declared that "The ominous result of the civil war in China is beyond the control of the government of the United States," essentially washing their hands of China.

Less than two months later, on the first day of October, the People's Republic of China was established. Mao Zedong proclaimed in Tiananmen Square, "We Chinese have stood up in the world."

Despite their celebratory mood, the Communists did not forget the renegade Taiwan. "Unite our motherland" became their top priority. The slogan "We Will Wash Taiwan With Blood," with its dripping red paint and exclamation marks, appeared overnight on walls, posts, and trees. From Quemoy and Matsu, the outlaying islands still held by Chiang Kai-Shek's Nationalist forces, the same slogan could be heard loud and clear, broadcast from loudspeakers across the water.

The narrowest part of the Taiwan Strait, which separates the island of Taiwan from the Chinese mainland, is only eighty-one miles. On a map it is easy to see how ludicrously puny Taiwan is when compared to the whole of the Chinese mainland. It didn't take a paranoid to hear the drumbeat, to feel the dread of the imminent, palpable peril.

I was fourteen in 1949. What I remember most from that year is my father telling us time and again, "We will all jump into the ocean when the Communists arrive."

One morning at school, all the students were hastily summoned to the auditorium. There we stood, shoulder-to-shoulder, shivering as our principal announced that war had broken out in Korea, our neighboring country. We were shocked. We believed our days were numbered on account of the war.

Instead, the Korean War of 1950-53 actually saved us from Communist invasion, for it showed the Americans the importance of our island's strategic location. Even before a mutual defense treaty between the United States and the Republic of China was signed, the American Seventh Fleet had been dispatched to the area for the Korean War *and*, more than incidentally, Taiwan's security.

Nonetheless, in order to avoid drowning in the ocean, my father decided we had to leave Taiwan as soon as possible—before the Communists reached us—and settle in a secure country.

In retrospect, especially in view of the way historical events unfolded, my father's plan appeared to be an overreaction and was even a bit wacky. Only decades later was I able to connect his plan with his war years when he had endured the most grisly and terrifying experiences of his life, including being arrested twice by the Japanese.

In one instance, he was standing in a line of captives waiting to be executed. Perhaps for sport, to save bullets, or both, the Japanese soldier chose to dispatch each captive by plunging his bayonet into the man's gut and twisting once. (My father demonstrated this to me with a twist of his wrist.) When my father's turn came, his watch happened to catch the soldier's eye. The guy grabbed the watch, shook it, burst out laughing, and let my father go.

Maybe this Japanese soldier was merely intoxicated with his power over the hapless prisoners, but a narrow escape from that bloody bayonet couldn't help but stay with my father and alter him forever.

It wouldn't be far-fetched to surmise that because of the harrowing six years and, in particular, that incident, my father suffered from a subtle form of PTSD—or post-traumatic stress disorder—for the rest of his life. He didn't talk about his war experiences and forbade us to mention the war; only in his old age would he volunteer a select incident or two.

Although my mother and we kids also suffered during the war, our experiences must have seemed trivial compared to his.

It was surprising that he came away from his voluntary military tour with a visceral hatred directed more towards the Communists than the Japanese. The Communists were supposed to be part of the United Front, fighting alongside the Nationalists. In reality, they never engaged the Japanese army. Rather, they waited till the Nationalists were fighting the Japanese and ambushed their brothers from behind.

My father's experiences brought about two important upsides: they prompted him to get us off the mainland while all our friends and relatives hesitated or refused to leave, and they pushed us to leave Taiwan for the United States. Each of us was told just before we left that under no circumstances should we entertain the notion of turning back. For better or for worse, we were to stay in America forever.

To be fair, my father's desire to live in a safe and wealthy country was no different from the prevailing trend in Taiwan at the time. The Taiwanese dream—if you could call it that—was to join the American dream. But I know of no one who took it as seriously, planned it as meticulously, maneuvered it as relentlessly, and executed it as obsessively as my father did. Every step he took, allowed or forced us to take was to advance this goal. He went about it with the same zeal and fortitude that had sustained him throughout his six-year ordeal in the resistance forces.

§

The Chinese who came before us to the United States were known as coolies. They had helped build railroads, while the next wave had opened restaurants or laundries. My generation was the first that arrived in this country as college graduates in pursuit of a higher degree. This drastic change had everything to do with the political situation in China and the rules of the Chinese government.

Shortly after the Communists took over the mainland in 1949, the Bamboo Curtain they erected cut the country off from the rest of the world. No one was permitted to leave.

Taiwan, known as Free China in those days, was comparatively free—but not by much. People, including my father, hardly needed the Communist threat to yearn for escape. The country was poor, its resources having been milked relentlessly by the Japanese for fifty years, especially throughout the war. Job opportunities were scarce, even for college graduates.

And the government stipulated that only college graduates with an admission from a foreign university graduate school were eligible to apply for a passport. In other words, anyone hoping to leave had to start with a college degree. Whether or not he truly wished or was even suited for graduate education was beside the point. In any case, most of those who came to this country did manage to receive a higher degree and become professionals.

The Irish used to say it takes three generations to progress "from steerage to suburbia" in America. Because this new generation of Chinese came with college degrees, this process took approximately ten years.

That was my father's plan. Charley was the first to go abroad and the only one to be apprised of the plan before his departure. He was exhorted to do his best in his studies, earn a doctorate, make money doing odd jobs, and help the rest of the family. As soon as all five of us had established ourselves in the United States, we would apply for my parents to immigrate. Then, and only then, we would be one happy family again—across the ocean, in America.

"You're the locomotive of my train. I'm counting on you," my father told him.

Charley left home fired with enthusiasm to carry out my father's wishes, and he didn't disappoint. He devoted ten years of his life to supporting his one cousin and two siblings financially, plus pursuing his own studies.

To send all five of us to America, my father needed money—and lots of it. To grant a student visa, the American embassy required proof of a

Charley at 23, in charge of executing my father's grand plan

deposit of an astronomical $500 in an American bank, plus money to cover one-year's tuition and living expenses. We also needed, of course, to buy a one-way ticket to the States. Like the majority of other Taiwan families of the time, my father had to borrow money for all of these.

In 1955, both Charley and Paul had received their bachelor's degree a year earlier from *Taida* and had undergone one year of military training required for male college graduates. The next hurdle was the examination given by the Ministry of Education for students going abroad. Charley passed, and Paul failed.

In a way, it was a lucky break for my father, since it cut all the expenses to half for the year and postponed the other half to next year. Besides, the $500 deposit could be recycled—sent back, paid off, and borrowed again. But he made sure that Paul spent the year preparing for the Ministry of Education exam. Come summer, Paul did pass.

But there was yet another significant roadblock for Paul, whose weak spot seemed to be English. To be granted a visa at the American Embassy, students had to prove their English competence by translating a few paragraphs of an article from *Time* magazine and writing an essay. Paul acquired several essay topics from people who had taken the test, so my father ordered me to write essays on those topics for Paul to commit to memory. Again, Paul passed.

Despite his USDA tour of America, my father learned very little about the country, so he didn't have specific destinations in mind for us. We were like a handful of seeds he scattered in the wind, landing willy-nilly, trying to take root.

He found out about Montana State through a college friend, and Charley, a business studies major, was lucky to be granted a one-time scholarship of $500 in agricultural economics.

The money only lasted Charley less than two quarters, but before his money ran out, he was granted a research assistantship on account of his good grades. In addition, he shoveled snow, mowed lawns, and took all manner of odd jobs. He even worked all summer shearing sheep to send money for Paul's journey.

Paul left Taiwan in September 1956 to join Charley at Montana

State on the strength of the axiom "two can live as cheaply as one." In reality, it was "two can live cheaply on one assistantship." However, the same courses Paul took in college, now rendered in English, were like Greek to him. For a whole year, he studied nonstop but failed every one.

Aptly recognizing that Paul's talents might lie outside of school, Charley borrowed $150 from his college friend and sent him to New York City where, with his civil engineering degree from Taiwan, he found a job as a draftsman, earning $145 a week. Paul was finally independent.

That same summer in 1957, both Cecilia and I graduated from *Taida*, but Cecilia, like her brother before her, failed the Ministry of Education exam. It became my turn to leave; I was twenty-two.

I chose the University of Oregon in Eugene for one reason: cheap tuition. Because Big Uncle worked for the Taiwan Provincial Shipping Bureau, I received a discount for my freighter fare, though my father also had to borrow that amount. The first thing I did after arriving in Eugene was to send back the $500 deposit and the rest of the money, keeping a total of $100.

Charley by then had graduated from Montana State with a master's degree and was a PhD student at Iowa State with a research assistantship. For three years he sent me half of his $175 stipend every month—except summer when I worked as a typist—until I finished all requirements for my master's degree and found a job in New York.

While I was at school, in addition to his support, I babysat, shelved library books, and stapled pamphlets. My grades also exempted me from paying tuition.

Cecilia left a year after me, in 1958. She went to New York City to join Paul, whose salary as a draftsman supported them both.

When Lining came along in 1961, I was self-supporting, but Charley had a new worry: Lining was going to Peabody College in Nashville, where tuition per semester was a whopping $500. Charley was in the middle of working on his PhD dissertation. He took a job as assistant professor at Colorado State in Fort Collins until Lining finished her degree in Library Science in a year and a half, and went back to finish his degree.

In a span of seven years, my father had succeeded in launching all five of us abroad. He became the envy of his friends and colleagues, many of whom tried to send their children to stay at our house for a while in the hopes of "catching" a bit of our luck.

§

In addition to money and passing exams, in view of our ages, another possible complication in my father's plan was romantic relationship. Therefore the strict *no boyfriends* rule for Cecilia and me.

Charley became a Catholic in *Taida* and met a girl in church. My father took the budding romance most seriously. He discovered the girl was the daughter of a concubine (a second wife living in the same house but with the status below that of the first wife), and commented that a person having grown up in complicated family dynamics would not fit well in ours.

I thought he meant our family was special; we had high standards. Later I understood that any emotional entanglement could jeopardize my father's plan—he himself had given up the idea of going to the University of Michigan largely because he had met my mother.

When Charley and the girl both graduated in 1954, Charley had to go off for his one-year military training, and his girlfriend left for America. Their relationship cooled considerably on account of my father's objection, the one-year separation, and the fact that Charley wasn't an enthusiastic or particularly impressive correspondent. While Charley was in Montana and his girlfriend was studying back east, their connection withered.

§

On a dark and drizzly afternoon in early September, my parents took me to the port of Jilong to board a freighter named *Chungking Victory*.

For days before departure, I had wept when I was alone, forlorn and apprehensive, knowing there was no turning back, and my life would never be the same again. Both of my parents were dry-eyed that afternoon, but our family friend Auntie Zhou started crying in the car and couldn't stop.

All my parents' friends were mahjongg friends, and Auntie Zhou and her husband were no exception. Second- or third-generation Chinese Americans, called overseas Chinese, they appeared at my parents' mahjongg tables some time during my sophomore year in college.

My passage on the freighter Chungking Victory; September, 1957 (front left)"

They were refreshingly different, and I was impressed by Uncle Zhou's American sense of humor. He was self-deprecating. (My father was known for his sense of humor, but like other Chinese, he never laughed at himself—it was considered undignified.)

More outrageously, Uncle Zhou made fun of his wife in front of everybody. At dinner, he described their first date: "Oh, how hard I worked, shoveling snow in winter, cutting grass in summer, to save enough money to take Emily out for dinner. You know what? She hardly touched her food! My heart was bleeding when the waiter cleared the table, but I consoled myself—*Good, a dainty eater. She'll save me lots of money in the long run.* Now, wouldn't you know it? She can eat a whole chicken in one sitting!" We didn't laugh. We all looked toward Auntie Zhou in trepidation, but she didn't protest or appear to mind. She merely looked at her husband with loving indulgence. I thought, "what an eccentric couple!"

Now, of course, I understand they were just being them: Americans born and bred. I can appreciate the courage it took them to uproot and transplant themselves to an entirely different culture. I also understand why Uncle Zhou—"call me Ben"—didn't get very far in the Department of Defense. Being too American, he didn't fit in.

It was probably toward the end of my junior year when Auntie Zhou volunteered to tutor both Cecilia and me in English.

Cecilia, like her brother Paul, had an artistic bent but was not academically or linguistically inclined. She became so distraught before each lesson that she would literally become sick and run to the bathroom. It was so painful for her during one recitation that Auntie Zhou suggested her to get married and forget about higher education abroad—a comment not taken well by the recipient.

In contrast, I had no problems with recitation. As a result, Auntie Zhou probably thought I showed great promise. When she learned I was leaving for her home country, she asked to come along to see me off.

Years later, at the ripe old age of seventy, I wrote a poem in memory of her, for she was the only adult connected with my family who believed in me. In it I remember my mother's once-in-a-lifetime humor but make no mention of my father, who did not shed a single tear the day I left home for the United States. Later I learned he cried profusely at Cecilia's departure.

The Farewell Gift

What crossed the Pacific with me
forty-eight years ago
are mostly gone—
mother's camel hair coat
the silver chopsticks
I had used since childhood
carved with symbols
of happiness and longevity
various beaded and embroidered
satin *qipao* I never wore
books
my youth
youthful hopes

an acute case
of homesickness…
Some lost to time
others through carelessness
or disuse.

But that Chinese Dictionary
Cloth-bound
four inches thick
is still on my desk
its pages yellowed
edges frayed
inscription faded but still readable—
a farewell gift

I hadn't known
her given name
in Chinese
till I read the inscription
in my lonely cabin
on the Pacific.

Atrocious accent
worn luster of being *overseas Chinese*
faded *qipao*
that seemed to date
back to the war years
she cut an unusual figure
among my parents' friends.

She never stopped sobbing
that gray drizzly afternoon
Not even after mother quipped
at the pier: *better stop
else people'll think
you're her mother.*

Only now, too late
I realize with a start:
perhaps she did think of me
as the daughter she never had—
heading for a bright future
in *her* native land

the land she abandoned
in her youth, to join her
Chinese American husband
in the Chinese war effort.

What was it like
to be out of sync
with one's adopted society
unable to go home?
In my callow youth
I never paused to ponder.

Not even when, in the guise
of English lessons
she had me recite
the Declaration of Independence
the Gettysburg Address
Gen. McArthur's farewell
speech to the Congress.

After that day at the pier
she went to teach in Thailand
two years later
died there
alone.

Revised, June 28, 2005

Part Two:
The New World

Chapter 16

ONLY SCIENCE MAJORS NEED APPLY

As I climbed aboard the freighter, my ears were still ringing with my father's farewell instructions: "Under *no* circumstances should you marry anyone who is *not* a science or engineering major."

Unaware of his plan, I found this order perplexing. I knew that science and engineering were all the rage because students in those fields were awarded assistantships in America, while those who studied languages and the social sciences waited tables.

But my father had already made me forsake literature in favor of a more practical field—why this sudden added requirement? I didn't realize that he was thinking a step ahead in his plan. Someone in the sciences or engineering would have a better chance of acquiring a green card or citizenship, to sponsor my parents' immigration to the United States.

Of course, I didn't question my father. I knew better.

My surprise was made more distressing because that same afternoon, after my last typing class in Taipei, I had been handed a thick, well-sealed letter from my boyfriend—to be smuggled on board and read during the voyage.

My father's sweeping new decree had just relegated the letter writer to the previously empty dustbin of "possible applicants."

Except for deliberately flunking the nursing exam, I had never disobeyed my father. My offense against his *no boyfriend* rule was far from premeditated; I had "misbehaved" without intending to.

Like many other students, I had taken free English lessons at the local Catholic Church when I was in high school. In fact, the American nuns who taught English at the church were on the faculty of the prestigious Foreign Language Department at *Taida*.

The classes conducted by Sister Margaret—a young and willowy woman with a great sense of humor—were often filled with laughter. The nuns also offered Bible Study in English. Most students took both; so did I.

Sister Rene taught Bible Study, where we studied handouts with questions and answers. Having been brought up with no religion, I found my doubts addressed neither by those questions nor their answers, but there was no forum for discussion, so I kept my mouth shut.

At the end of the semester, a sheet was circulated for us to sign up to be baptized. Already uncomfortable with the stock questions and answers, I felt railroaded by their tactic. I took the Bible Study class twice; twice I passed the sheet on without signing. It was time to quit.

I did, however, acquire my English name from my lessons there.

Because our Chinese names proved too difficult for the American nuns to pronounce, we each had to adopt an English name. We usually tried to find something similar to our Chinese names. Since mine is An-nuo—I spelled it An-no then—and the names of Anna and Anne were already taken, I went to the back of the Merriam-Webster Dictionary and found "Annabel," not knowing American high school textbooks contained a famous poem by Edgar Allan Poe titled "Annabel Lee."

My father, who gave me a special dispensation to attend the lessons, was none too pleased about my choosing an English name without getting his permission. "Annabel, Annabel, it sounds like 'animal,'" he said, but he let it go.

Charley had attended the nuns' lessons a few years earlier. Unlike me, however, he had converted and become quite evangelical about his newfound faith.

He succeeded in convincing our father to attend a discussion group headed by Father Gong, a priest known for his intelligence and eloquence. Because I had been in Sister Rene's Bible Study classes, Charley thought I should also join the group to give Father

Gong a chance to finish the job that had eluded Sister Rene.

The discussion group was held at 5 p.m. on Thursdays on Yang Ming Mountain, not easily accessible by bus. I had to wait at my law school campus for my father to get off work early and give me a ride.

It was fall, the beginning of my junior year. Thursday happened to be a short day—no classes after 3 p.m. Instead of rushing to catch the bus for home as I usually did, I now had some time to kill.

I was on my way to the law library when I ran into a classmate. "K" was a prodigy of sorts, having achieved the unusual distinction of passing the higher of the two national Civil Service Examinations during our freshman year, an exam people typically wouldn't attempt until at least after college graduation. An avid basketball player, he was also known for his calligraphy.

He seemed surprised to see me and asked why I hadn't gone home. He spoke casually as if he had known my schedule and we had always conversed together. We both knew we were not supposed to talk, but it seemed so natural we didn't resist it. It felt like we knew each other well.

Once we started to talk, the feeling of familiarity mixed with something new and exciting, and it propelled us along. We walked back and stood outside the empty classroom, talking all the while until I had to go out to meet my father.

We continued our conversation the following Thursdays. I can't recall what we talked about, but he was well-read and interesting to talk to. On the other hand, the discussion group didn't go well. Father Gong grew visibly nervous every time my father asked a question, and we quit the group after less than two months. But K began to show up at my city bus stop, and we rode to the Taipei Train Station together. Sometimes he even took the Beitou-bound long-distance bus with me.

However, we continued to be discreet at school; we would tacitly revert to our "regular" mode, never exchanging a word or showing recognition of the other.

One day, while riding the Beitou bus together, he surprised me with two thick, beautiful volumes of *Anna Karenina*, translated from Russian into English—a gift after my own heart. He had gone to the Registrar's Office at the main campus to find out my birthday.

I had always been a glutton for books. My appetite was insatiable. I had read the Chinese version of this classic, and I couldn't wait to devour the English translation once I got my hands on them. But those two luxurious, precious volumes, signed to me in his own hand—many of our classmates were in the habit of requesting his calligraphy—struck terror in my heart. Where could I keep them? What would I say when they were discovered, as I knew they surely would be?

I told him I couldn't possibly accept his gift.

I had never talked about my family; this time, of all times, if I gave any reason for my refusal, I would have to tell him about my father, and I couldn't expect him or anyone else to understand. (Perversely, when the chips were down, I was as tight-lipped as my father.) Difficult as it was to hurt his feelings and to part with the two beautiful books, my fear was so overwhelming that everything else was secondary. I never knew what he did with them.

K was hurt and dejected, but he was forgiving; we continued to meet as if the incident had never happened. Sitting side by side on the Beitou bus constituted our most intimate moments together. I don't think we ever held hands, but we did manage to have a lunch date.

By that time, we had graduated and our classmate's engagement party was over. Although I was taking typing lessons in Taipei every day, I was expected to go home immediately afterward. To buy some extra time for our date, I told my father that I would bring food (which I did) to my friends in the dormitory. Two of them had stayed behind in the dorm studying for the exam to qualify as lower court judges.

K and I met at an eatery of his choosing near the Taipei train station—a formal, traditional restaurant named Zhuangyuan Lou. He kept piling food in my bowl, as if he had infused his feelings into the elaborate meal. But I was so petrified on account of my flagrant lie to my father that I had no appetite.

The last time we saw each other was outside my typing class when he handed me the letter. Neither of us had any inkling that we were parting forever. We were young and full of hope, and we believed we would be together in a year or two.

I read K's letter on the deck of the freighter. In it, he declared his love for me and laid out his plans. He would seek a doctoral degree in America, an essential for his future, but he loathed wasting a year in the requisite military training. Since anyone with a domestic advanced degree would be exempt from the military training, he would enroll in a master's degree program in Taiwan so that by the time I received my master's, he

Eugene, Oregon; October, 1957

would be getting his and on his way to America. He asked me to wait for him for two years.

I was torn—too ashamed to tell him that he had already been disqualified by my father and too selfish to give him up. He wrote several times a week; sometimes the letters would arrive in a bunch, and, as a joke at the co-op I lived in, the girls threw me into the shower once for getting the highest number of letters in one day.

The biggest problem I had in my first year in this country was, of course, a lack of money. Between tuition and other initial expenses, the $100 I retained was gone in a jiffy. From then on I had to live on half of my brother's assistantship and whatever I could earn on my own.

I met two female students from Taiwan. They came a year before me and both were working as waitresses in a local Chinese restaurant. From what they told me I learned that I didn't even have enough stamina to work as a waitress. I chose the lesser of two evils: to work longer hours and earn less (even if it was far less). My new friends found me a job babysitting for the Chinese restaurant owner for fifty cents per hour. Eventually I also shelved books at the university library for seventy cents per hour.

The two part-time jobs and the work I had to do as a member of the co-op—taking turns cleaning the bathrooms and kitchen and waiting on tables—took up a huge chunk of my time, time I badly needed for my studies.

Two of my courses, American History and International Relations, required outside reading in addition to the textbooks, and I could only read one page an hour, looking up each new word in my English-Chinese dictionary, a tedious task I soon gave up.

Everyone around me spoke in such a fast-flowing stream that I failed to catch anything from it. In class, whenever the professor cracked a joke, everyone would laugh, leaving me red faced and baffled.

I had never felt so stupid in my entire life.

The evenings when dusk began to fall were the worst of all, bringing on loneliness, anxiety, and unchecked melancholy. I yearned for my life back home where I was sheltered, and I missed K.

For obvious reasons, the Chinese students in Eugene thought I was foolhardy to study journalism. The conventional wisdom was that library science would be a far better choice, as it was much easier and job opportunities were plentiful. But library science seemed safe and dreary. After some thought, I decided, to everyone's surprise and disapproval, to transfer to the mecca of journalism (at least in Chinese eyes), the University of Missouri-Columbia.

§

Throughout those extraordinarily painful nine months in Eugene, K's ardent and articulate letters brought me much-needed solace and hope. They followed me from Oregon to Iowa—to spend my first summer with Charley—and then to Missouri in the fall.

When I was in Missouri, K sent me his picture and asked for

mine. I obliged and once even sent him a newspaper clipping of a book review of mine that I was particularly proud of. He had perfect vision, but chose to wear glasses because I did. He selected an English name similar to mine.

Our two years dragged to three. I was finishing my coursework, plunging ahead with my thesis, while he was doing the same in Taiwan (a domestic higher degree was notoriously difficult to earn).

Deciding it was time to declare his intentions to my parents, he took the liberty of paying them an unannounced visit. However, he didn't inform me ahead of time and encountered an unpleasant surprise. My father wasn't home that day, and my mother was distant and cool. K was probably surprised that they knew nothing about him and were not interested in getting to know him. I understood my parents were triply angry because I had broken the *no-boyfriend* rule in Taiwan, withheld that fact from their knowledge, and chosen someone who was *not* a science or engineering major.

Neither of my parents mentioned the visit in their letters, treating the suitor as a nonentity. Only my sister declared him *disgusting*, as if he had been some kind of a depraved character. I don't think she ever even laid eyes on him. I understood the seriousness of the word, and I knew where it came from.

More than 7,000 miles away, I could feel my father's wrath like the *Tai Mountain on top of my head*, to borrow a Chinese expression. But he knew distance was on his side. Since he didn't order an immediate break-up, I figured time was on our side.

Alas, I was wrong, so wrong. Time was running out, and we didn't know it.

With my graduation in sight, my father told me to start applying for doctoral studies: international law or criminal law. But I had no intentions of returning to law or continuing in journalism; my heart was still set on English. But I knew no English PhD programs would take someone with a zigzagging background of law and journalism.

More importantly, how would I pay for it? My father hadn't sent me a penny since I left home. Did he know Charley had already supported Paul for a year and me for three years? Folding flyers at my school's Freedom of Information Center for a dollar an hour didn't go far in keeping my body and soul together. It was time for me to get a "real" job.

The bulletin board at school was replete with ads for reporter jobs at small town papers in Missouri. I decided, however, that instead of spending the rest of my life slowly suffocating in a small Midwest town, I might as well take a chance and go to New York.

It was summer of 1960. I had finished my research. I was on my way to write my thesis in Iowa, where Charley had rented the attic of his rooming house for me. I received a letter from K with the devastating news that the mandatory military training had just been extended to two years, *and* those with an advanced degree were no longer exempt. He was trapped by fickle government rules, and he asked me to wait for another two years.

I brought K's letter with me on the bus to Iowa to mull over. I had always lived my life simply propelled by outside forces; now, for once, I had to take serious inventory and weigh the pros and cons for myself.

Two additional years meant a total of five, very likely even six; I had already waited for three. It would mean at least five years of our living in two different worlds: he staying in his familiar surroundings while I struggled in an alien environment and culture, fighting daily battles he couldn't even imagine.

Like a weary soldier in the trenches, I was told to wait two more years. Two more years! I felt I had already changed a great deal and was no longer the same girl he had said goodbye to outside the typing class in Taipei. Surviving in New York could only be harder. I had heard so many stories of couples breaking up because they had grown apart, and I was afraid to imagine the possible scenario between K and me.

I wished I had known him better so that I could better predict our future. How would he feel when he had to start his life in America? I couldn't envision him waiting tables.

All of a sudden *time* had turned into our worst enemy. All around me, everyone was getting married and settling down. What if he chanced to meet someone, or I did, in the next two years? I was dreadfully afraid of suffering the eventual heartbreak.

Even if we could conquer all the odds—and those were formidable odds—there was my father. I still remember his expression when he specified that I could *only* marry a science or engineering major. Even though my father was an ocean away, I shuddered.

I had a feeling that whatever I decided would be irreversible and that it would be the gamble of my life. Was I willing to put my future on the block when all I had to gamble with were a promising man whom I still had deep feelings for, memories from three years ago, and a pile of love letters?

Life was cruel, and it made me cruel. On the bus, with my churning, chaotic, and tangled thoughts, I learned something about myself, something unpleasant and unflattering: I was more pragmatic than romantic, and I was mortally afraid of confrontations—especially with my father, when I felt I was destined to lose.

All things being equal, I tended to gravitate to the sensible solution, the lesser of two evils, the path of least resistance. I was too ready and willing to sacrifice my feelings in the bargain. Emotionally, I was a coward.

Though I was a coward, I was an obstinate one. My mind knew what I should do, but my heart refused to do it. I did *not* want to write that letter to K. *I can't, not now, it's too difficult, and I'm too busy.* Everything had to wait until I finished writing my thesis.

Everything except, of course, an afternoon off to serve as a bridesmaid at Clara's wedding.

Chapter 17

CLARA'S WEDDING

When Clara wrote to ask me to be her bridesmaid, I assumed it was because she had heard that I owned a cocktail dress, acquired the previous summer when I was a bridesmaid at Paul's wedding in New York. Paul had paid for the dress. Unlike Paul who was working, Clara and I were foreign graduate students, dirt poor, penny-pinching a dire necessity.

Still, I was a little taken back—I hardly knew Clara. I had only met her once or twice. As if she had read my mind, a second letter soon arrived saying that she would really appreciate my doing her this favor because she was new at Iowa State and didn't know anyone well. She had heard from Charley that I would be in Ames in August.

On the day of the wedding, waiting for the bride in the church's front foyer with the rest of the wedding party, I knew most of the guests who came in—including Grace and Sam. I had met them in 1958, during my first summer in Iowa, and I certainly didn't expect that Grace would give me a hate-filled stare and walk past me without saying hello. I was stung by her hostility.

Little did I know that Clara was using me to deliver a double whammy to Grace. By inviting me as her bridesmaid, Clara was snubbing Grace, her roommate—usually the natural choice for that honor. More importantly, Clara knew Grace's boyfriend Sam had been interested in me for some time.

I was not exactly in a celebratory mood myself. I had been cooped up for days in an unbearably hot, tiny attic, pounding out my thesis on a dilapidated manual typewriter, all the while struggling to keep the dilemma with K out of my mind. I assumed Grace was being territorial because Sam was at her side, so as a sort of retaliation, I did something naughty. I gave Sam a sweet smile.

That was all the encouragement he needed. He didn't follow her in but lingered to talk to me instead.

Admittedly, Sam and I had a bit of a history.

Sam was the first person I met in Ames. Two years prior, he had been with Charley at the depot when my Greyhound bus arrived from Oregon, where I had spent my first nine months in the United States. Charley needed a car to transport my luggage, and Sam was the only one among the Chinese students who had a car—a beat-up Chevrolet.

Years later, Sam told me that I had been pale and unsmiling (not surprising as the journey took three days and two nights, with the bus only stopping briefly for quick meals and trips to the restroom) and had been wearing a dress with a collar that was too low (a dress my mother had made).

Charley had found me a summer typing job in the agricultural economics department where he was a doctoral student. I started work the morning after my arrival. The rest of the typists in the department were high school graduates, whereas I had had a year of graduate studies in journalism. I was given the glorified title of research assistant and assistant editor in the hopes it would look better on my resume.

It was summer 1958. Most of the roughly fifteen Chinese students at Iowa State were from Taiwan, most from *Taida* and nearly all male. The arrival of a new girl, even only for the summer, was a big deal. Before I had had a chance to wash up and unpack, Charley's friends dropped by with various excuses to look me over. In a couple of days, despite the less-than-impressive impression I had made at the bus depot, Sam showed up with several others, including Grace.

The Chinese students on campus were a tight-knit group; they got together every weekend for a movie, a meal at a drive-in hamburger joint, or a picnic. When they heard Charley call me *xiaomei*—little sister—everyone took to calling me little sister, too.

One weekend Sam was absent from the Chinese group gathering. I was told he had gone to Nebraska to visit his girlfriend, the choice of Sam's father, Homer, and daughter of Homer's best friend. Next I heard, his girlfriend had broken up with him. He was "disqualified" because he hardly wrote and rarely visited her, whereas another suitor was local and more attentive. In the following month, Sam looked rather glum.

At the end of the summer, Charley and I got a ride from Sam to the Midwestern Chinese Students' Rally held in Madison, Wisconsin, where Sam's older sister Rose lived. We were the only three from Ames.

Afterward, Charley sent several pictures home—he was proud of his new sunglasses. But the photos generated some unexpected attention from our parents; Charley and I had to vouch that the third person in the photos was *not* my boyfriend.

I left for Missouri that fall. Before my departure, Sam invited Charley and me for dinner at his apartment. What promised to be a sumptuous meal of roast duck was botched—he forgot to turn on the oven before our arrival.

The University of Missouri's School of Journalism was well known in China; most of the Chinese students on campus were in the so-called "J School." Several were middle-aged and had come to reinvigorate their careers. The only female, I joined the Chinese "crowd" of five or six.

One day, some fellow students told me, snickering, that a letter for me with an Iowa return address was on the school bulletin board. It was from Sam, telling me he had just come back from presenting his first physics paper at a conference. The content was rather matter-of-fact; he was probably just trying to share his proud achievement with someone, but I found it somewhat offensive. Did he expect me to write and congratulate him? I threw it in the wastebasket.

The next summer I was back in Ames, doing the same job with the same title. Charley and I stayed at a unit he had rented in Pammel Court, Iowa State's married student housing complex. At the beginning of that summer, Sam's father Homer died in Taiwan, and Sam appeared depressed for quite a while.

Then came the news that Paul was getting married in New York. Cecilia had made it to New York the year after me. Because of our unusual family situation, Paul decided he would go to the extra expense of having two bridesmaids at his wedding—Cecilia and me. But Charley could not afford two airplane tickets, so he decided that I should go by myself. The cheapest airfare was from Chicago. When Sam heard that I needed transportation to Chicago and back, he said he was thinking of visiting his sister Rose in Madison and would be glad to give me a ride.

We left early in the morning, reached the airport around 4 p.m. for the 5 p.m. flight, but the flight was delayed a few hours due to foul weather. Since it was already near dinnertime, Sam suggested that we go to Chinatown for dinner.

The food wasn't memorable. What struck me that evening was the debris that littered the streets of Chinatown and an old man, a fellow countryman, squatting outside the restaurant.

The familiar term *lao huaqiao*, "old overseas Chinese," was suddenly no longer an abstraction; instead, it was made vividly real to me—skin and bones, empty eyes, wooden expression. Had the hardship of living as an alien turned this old man into someone reminiscent of a character from the Qing Dynasty, or an opium addict? Was that the price of being a foreigner? It was chilling.

Sam stayed with me until I boarded my flight around midnight. He then drove to Madison and picked me up on Sunday for the ride home.

Only years later did he admit that he had used his sister as an excuse for driving me to the airport. At the time, he was probably disappointed that I dozed through most of our return trip to Ames. I hadn't slept on the flight to New York; the plane had been delayed due to a severe storm that failed to abate. The lightning was fierce and unrelenting, and the decrepit plane shook and shuddered alarmingly. Once I arrived in New York, I found that the floor of Paul's tiny apartment was crammed full of sleeping guests. His bride Francene slept with us on the living room floor before the wedding and moved into the bedroom after the ceremony.

Other than the church where the wedding was held, I didn't see much of fabled New York City. I left Ames Friday; by Monday morning I was back in the typing pool. Losing my Friday's wage was already enough of a "luxury."

Shortly after the wedding weekend, Sam asked me to a movie. I felt I owed him a favor for the ride to Chicago and understood that it took him some courage to invite me. I liked to see Cary Grant in *North by Northwest* but was put off by his choice of words: "Let me *take* you to the movie…"

I tried to be diplomatic. "Why don't I check with Charley? I think he would like to see it, too."

That was when Charley sat me down and delivered his *elder-brother-as-father* speech: I shouldn't encourage Sam by going to a movie with him. He was an introvert as much as I am an extrovert and the relationship would never work.

It was true that I was not interested in Sam. Consciously or not, I was in the habit of comparing those who were interested in me with K, and they always came up short in more ways than one. Besides, K's vulnerability—being thousands of miles away—made me more protective towards him. But I thought Charley's analysis about introverts versus extroverts was too much of a generalization. Besides, what was the big deal about going to a movie? Since the issue wasn't worth arguing, I didn't bother. I turned down the invitation.

That winter, I was back in Iowa working in the same typing pool as before. One day, just as we were sitting down for our break in the adjacent coffee room, the phone rang. It was for me, and it was Sam. He came right out and asked, "What do you think if we get engaged?"

What? I couldn't believe my ears. *A marriage proposal over the phone? How preposterous!*

I quickly looked around me; everyone was still in the coffee room, talking and laughing. I was alone in the typing pool. The secretary in charge of the typists was the only one with a desk and a phone, and I was standing by her desk and holding her receiver. "But why? I hardly know you."

He was obviously prepared for this argument and responded readily. "We can get to know each other after the engagement."

"Don't you think that's putting the cart before the horse,

though? What if we don't get along?"

"I'm sure we will."

"But I'm not sure. Why should *I* take that chance?"

The conversation was getting more ludicrous. As I searched desperately for a way to end the call, he played his trump card:

"I can teach you to ride a bike, and I can support you to finish school."

That did it—he thought I was desperate enough to sell myself for a graduate education! I checked my anger and said coldly, "No, I don't think it's a good idea. It wouldn't work. But thank you just the same." I hung up.

If courtship came with a three-strike rule, he had already exceeded his quota. But this phone call was the most thoughtless, most pathetic proposal I had ever heard of. I walked slowly back to the coffee room feeling rather depressed, and I never breathed a word about it to anyone—not Charley, not K.

Between that winter phone call and Clara's August wedding, Sam and I had not been in contact. I did hear from Charley that Sam had been tutoring Grace in physics and that she had become his girlfriend. I thought, *that figures; the guy's desperate*. Not so long ago, he had offered to teach *me* to ride a bike.

Now that he walked into Clara's wedding with Grace, who deliberately antagonized me, I smiled at Sam and immediately regretted it. *Why did I do it? What am I going to do with him now?*

To my surprise, he didn't seem to mind offending Grace by staying on to talk to me, and he didn't hold a grudge about our last phone call. In the few minutes before all the guests had to go inside, he wanted to know what I planned to do in the fall. When he learned I was going to New York City after finishing my thesis, he brightened and said he had just taken a job at the new IBM Research Center north of the city.

Charley must have noted our conversation in the church lobby, for that evening he took pains to tell me that Sam and Grace had left just after the ceremony and were on their way to New York. Grace would be teaching at a small nearby college. I knew what he meant—"Stay away from this guy; he's taken." I was a little baffled by this bit of information, however. It didn't sound right. The way

Sam operated, he and Grace should have been engaged by now, or even married. But I didn't ask Charley any questions.

I went back to Missouri to start the grueling process of typing my thesis, a task far more frustrating and painful than the combined efforts of researching and writing it. The summers and winters in the typing pool had done little, if anything, to improve my skills. I remained a miserable typist.

As soon as I passed my oral exam, I left by Greyhound bus on a Friday morning in early October and arrived in New York City after lunch on Saturday. My cousin Paul met me at the bus depot. Within minutes of our arrival at Paul's apartment, the phone rang. It was Sam. He was on his first trip to the city since he had started his new job and was wandering the streets by himself that afternoon when it occurred to him to look up Paul in the phone book. He had been a roommate with Paul and Charley during their freshman year at *Taida*.

Departing Missouri for New York City; October, 1960

I never did convince Paul that Sam's call that day had not been preplanned.

Was it mental telepathy or was it fate? While "Mr. Right" languished 9,000 miles away, "Mr. Wrong" hit perfect timing, showing up at just the right time.

In retrospect, coincidences seem to have had a pivotal impact in shaping or changing Sam's life and mine. Indeed, it would be difficult to believe that fate didn't have a hand in this whole matter.

When Sam graduated from high school, he wanted to study physics. However, his father Homer—who had longed to be an engineer all his life—had pushed his son into electrical engineering instead. "Do you want to spend your life teaching high school physics?" he argued.

As a result, Sam majored in "Double E," the hottest field in *Taida* at the time, and went on to receive a master's at Iowa State. Whenever he was bored by electrical engineering, he would read physics books for fun. He took two courses in physics the year before graduation and did so well that he blew everyone else away and attracted the attention of Roland Good, the young and upcoming professor who had taught Sam in both courses.

Professor Good happened to be at Sam's graduation ceremony in 1958 because he had a student receiving his PhD that same day. He was surprised to see Sam get his master's—Good had assumed he was a doctoral student. After the ceremony, he cornered Sam and asked him, "Have you ever thought of switching to physics?" The result of this encounter was that Sam was offered a fellowship in physics that same afternoon.

It proved to be a timely intervention. Sam had received a fellowship in electrical engineering from Stanford University and would have left Ames for the West Coast before I arrived. We would never have met.

And in New York, suddenly, miraculously, the clueless and blundering "Mr. Wrong" did everything right.

We all went on a walk in Central Park the afternoon I arrived in the city. While Paul and his wife Francene tactfully kept their distance, Sam caught a grasshopper and told me a little bit about insects. He confided that as a child in Chongqing he had wanted to be an entomologist.

Perhaps he was inspired by the surroundings, for Central Park in early fall was beautiful. Perhaps I was more receptive toward having a friend in that intimidating new city. But most importantly, talking about insects, he sounded like the scholar that he later proved to be. He seemed more interesting and appealing than before.

Sam came to the city every weekend, spending his nights on a cot at a nearby YMCA. A fervent opera aficionado, he invited me to *Aida*, a breathtakingly beautiful performance at the old Metropolitan Opera House, with Leontyne Price in the title role.

I have been an opera fan ever since.

Before the opera, Sam lent me his record set of *Aida*. The following week he was shocked to find his treasured records on top of the radiator, warped from the heat (*mea culpa*). He kept his mouth shut and bought another set on his way home.

Chapter 18

NEW YORK, NEW YORK

That first Saturday afternoon in Paul's apartment, the first words out of Sam's mouth were, "So are you all done with your thesis?"

I also had a question but didn't ask it: "Where's Grace?"

I didn't have to wonder for long. Grace, a Chinese Indonesian, had been the only girl in the group of Chinese students I met in the summer of 1958. She had arrived at Iowa State a few years earlier for doctoral studies in physics but hadn't done well. After repeatedly failing her qualifying exam, she had been notified by the department that she should get a master's degree and leave.

Sam probably started helping her after he switched to physics in the summer of 1958, and they went out together after I had turned him down. Sam told me he broke up with her on account of cultural differences, but that Grace asked him not to reveal the breakup until after they had left Ames. It was important for her to save face.

Frankly, Grace was not foremost on my mind in those days. I needed to find a job. The Monday morning after I arrived in New York, I began pounding the pavement. My first stop was *The New York Times*. I knew they wouldn't hire me as a reporter, but I was willing to sweep floors and work my way up to something a little more interesting—such was the naïve, romantic notion I had. My hope was dashed in two minutes.

Similarly, *Time Magazine* was not interested in me as a fact checker for their research department.

The Chinese have a proverb—*If you don't go into the tiger's den, how can you get a tiger cub?* But all I got from venturing into various "tiger's dens" were outright rejections. In desperation, I applied for typist jobs at the United Nations, book publishing companies, and women's magazines, but I failed my typing test every time.

Finally, an ad in the paper led me to a company I had never heard of: Scholastic Magazines and Book Services. I became their one-person copyright department on the strength of my combined law and journalism background.

My work involved requesting publishers to grant permission to reprint their materials and granting permission to various entities to reprint works owned by Scholastic. It was boring work, though I did enjoy sitting in on negotiations for book contracts and the occasional visits to the venerable New York Public Library to find copyright owners.

I often cast a longing gaze at the offices of *Literary Cavalcade*, a literary magazine for high school students published by Scholastic. I didn't have the proper background to be on their staff.

Once I started my job, the next important item on my agenda was writing the long-delayed letter to K, a task made more urgent by the fact that he had sent me a pair of pearl earrings for my graduation present.

We had always communicated via aerogram, a cross between an airmail letter and a postcard. Sky blue in color, the aerogram was a single sheet of very thin paper that could be folded into the shape of an envelope and sealed.

Half crazed with emotion, I scribbled the letter on two aerograms during my lunch hour; I never paused while writing and sealed them immediately without reading them over. I don't remember most of what I said except that, in two more years, both of us would have changed so much that it would be impossible for us to pick up where we had left off.

That *was* my main concern, but it shouldn't have taken two aerograms to convey. I must have repeated the message over and over again, trying to convince myself as much as him.

It had been five years. How do you sweep away five years with two aerograms? There were so many layers of emotions at play, but most remained unexpressed: how many times I wished he had been here and how I valued the meeting of our minds and regretted that we would never have the opportunity to find out whether we were compatible.

I was too ashamed to mention my father. During all those years I had been unable to tell K my father's *no-boyfriend* rule and his marrying-a-science-or-engineering-major requirement—and I wasn't about to tell him now. I realized I hadn't been entirely honest by keeping that crucial information from him. And I didn't mention Sam.

Sam was only too happy to drive me to mail back the earrings. As I descended the main post office's wide, open steps, I gazed back at the building's imposing Grecian columns—so strong and sturdy, a mute reproach to the fragility of human connections.

With those two aerograms and the return of the earrings, the tenuous thread that had connected K and me for the past five years was severed forever.

Time was against us; it was not meant to be.

But there was the guilt. I thought I had made a rational decision and hadn't expected to be assaulted by so much guilt. Had I strung K along all that time? I must have. I didn't mean to be callous. Young and thoughtless, I didn't know how to be otherwise.

Poet Marianne Moore wrote, "The deepest feeling always shows itself in silence." Maybe. But how I wished that I could have reached across the divide somehow to make my true and deepest feeling known so that both of us could have been comforted in the process.

I have had a bad conscience ever since—not for the decision I made but for the crude way I handled the breakup. I have always wished I had known how to tell K in a gentler way.

I still dream about him once in a while. In my dreams, he never grows old, always gives me the cold shoulder, and never speaks a word to me. I take it as my deserved punishment.

§

Meanwhile, life went on. Cecilia and I rented an apartment in upper Manhattan on West 104th Street. Charley was finally able to stop sending me half of his stipend, and I was mailing part of my salary home every month.

One thing I noticed in those days was that my cousins and I had grown apart. Paul was married, of course, and he had a baby boy, but even Cecilia and I had drifted apart, though we had been close in college. (I never told her or anyone else about K, however.)

Only three years later, she appeared to be interested just in day-to-day things. Was she always like that, or had I changed? The difference kept us feeling a little alienated from each other. In a way, the new distance in my relationship with Cecilia told me I was right in my decision about K: over time, people tend to adapt and grow with their respective environments. This realization should have comforted me, but it made me sad.

In contrast, Sam and I discovered we had more in common. We were interested in similar things and spoke the same "language." He came every weekend, and the city never failed to fascinate us. What an indescribable experience to be young in New York! I was spellbound by its diversity and vitality. Even crossing the street with crowds of people was thrilling.

We went to the museums and galleries. After exploring the sights and sounds the city had to offer, we used to frequent a nearby restaurant on Broadway named "East Garden."

The Cantonese still dominated the Chinese restaurant business in those days. Americans had never heard of Kung Pao Chicken, or Mu Shu Pork, let alone jicai stir-fried with winter bamboo shoots. "East Garden" didn't have those dishes either, but this being New York, the restaurant did offer some Shanghai-style cuisine: braised fish, stir-fried shrimp, and pork, dried tofu, and *zhacai* (spicy preserved turnip), all shredded and stir-fried in one dish.

When the steam rose languidly from the table, the dishes emanating their familiar, long-lost aroma, the pain of my past three years in America seemed to dissipate...

Ah...the soothing, healing powers of a meal like home!

§

Before Charley came to New York City to visit us for the Christmas holidays, I was more than a little worried about his reaction to the suitability between Sam and me. Sam gave me a couple of his own graduation photos and suggested that I display them in the living room of the apartment I shared with Cecilia. The open declaration worked wonders—not a word about introvert versus extrovert.

After the holidays it was time for Sam to write a letter to my father in Taiwan to ask for my hand, so to speak. We were concerned that my father might object to the fact that Sam and I had the same last name.

We were only too familiar with the Chinese belief *Tong xing bu hun*, no marriage

One of two photos Sam enclosed in his letter to my parents, 1961

between couples with the same last name. This unwritten law probably stemmed from the fear that the two might be closely related.

But wars and constant political upheavals in the twentieth century had uprooted and scattered a great number of the country's population. Many traditions had fallen by the wayside. Though not nearly as taboo as same-sex unions, some Chinese still frowned upon same-name marriages. As I told Sam, "With my father, you just never know."

It turned out we had no need to worry; my father's considerations were very different. In the matter of his daughter's future, he was surprisingly pragmatic.

When Sam's letter from New York—he had shrewdly enclosed a couple of his photos, one of him in his PhD cap and gown—reached my parents in Taiwan, my mother took a look and declared, "This guy's got a temper." She was right.

For all they knew, their prospective son-in-law could have been a potential wife beater or a budding alcoholic. But it didn't matter to my father, for he was a science *and* engineering major *and* a PhD to boot!

I should have been happy that my father bestowed his instant approval, but somehow I couldn't shake the uneasy feeling that I was like a commodity sold to a qualified bidder.

Chapter 19

MY CUP RUNNETH OVER

Sam and I became engaged on Chinese New Year's Eve in 1961, which fell on Valentine's Day that year, and married four months later. It was a double engagement, for Cecilia was engaged to her boyfriend Ed that same day.

Ed was one of the two groomsmen at Paul's wedding. In that dorm room during their freshmen year at *Taida*, Charley and Sam

were assigned to one side of the room, and Paul and Ed to the other side. Furthermore, like Paul, Ed was a civil engineering major (thus perfectly adhering to my father's rule, although I don't know whether or not my father had given the same order to Cecilia). He had received a master's degree from the University of Michigan before coming to New York.

Cecilia's wedding was held a week before mine. Charley came to New York to attend her wedding and to give me away at mine.

Our wedding day; New York City, 1961

Sam's professor, Roland Good, and his wife also flew from Iowa to attend our wedding.

Before the ceremony, Paul delivered his *elder-cousin-as-father* talk to me. Sam was great in every way, Paul said, except that his health was poor.

That was no news to me. Before we had even met, Sam had gone through six operations, five of which had been major procedures. He was not eligible for the requisite military training because he had failed his physical exam—on account of a tumor on his right upper leg the size of a large grapefruit.

Doctors puzzled over this tumor, as it grew ever larger throughout his college years. No one had dared to do anything until a young doctor, fresh from medical training in Japan, diagnosed it as a rare type of benign tumor of the lymphatic system called lymphangioma and was willing to take on the risk of performing surgery.

Because of the tumor's sheer size, it took three operations over the course of a whole year to remove, leaving huge, horrific scars and damaging local nerves in the process. While his classmates were away for military training, Sam spent the year in the hospital.

Compared to his health problems, mine were minor. Ever since my childhood encounter with diphtheria, my energy has been in short supply. Morning is not my shining hour, and neither is evening.

Because of our health, we needed to avoid lengthy daily commutes. The IBM research lab in Yorktown Heights where Sam worked and the offices of Scholastic Magazines in Times Square were forty-two miles apart. My boss Betty kindly suggested that we live somewhere in the middle, like Yonkers or White Plains, so I could take the train to work. People did that all the time, she said.

But not us. Commuting more than twenty miles to work every day was not possible. Not realizing that scarce job opportunities in the suburbs and my newly married status would likely render me unemployable, we chose an alternative that had Betty shaking her head in disbelief. I resigned from Scholastic, and we took a tiny apartment in Mount Kisco, six miles from Yorktown.

Our timing was poor in the extreme. It was summer 1961. My

father had taken on the responsibility of supporting our three cousins in Hong Kong a year before, and my younger sister Lining had just graduated from *Taida* and was on her way to Peabody College in Nashville.

Although Charley and I tried to send home whatever we managed to save, my father had always lived beyond his means; hence, his accumulated debt plus interest had come to $2,500.

Charley, who had been bearing the brunt of our family's financial burden and was in the middle of writing his PhD dissertation, decided to put that on hold and apply for a teaching job. He became an assistant professor at Colorado State University in Fort Collins to support Lining through school.

Paul and Francene were expecting another baby, their second in less than three years; Cecilia and Ed had just started their new life. Neither cousin was any help financially. It was imperative that I find a job.

After several fruitless searches, and after failing my typing test at IBM, I took the only job I could find—typing addresses in a huge warehouse for *Reader's Digest* in nearby Pleasantville. I never told anyone at work that I had a graduate degree in journalism; mercifully, nobody asked. Since I didn't have to support myself, I was able to send all my earnings home.

At the same time, Paul's warnings about Sam's health became a reality.

Sam was one of ten young theoretical physicists in a group nicknamed "Fruitcake"—full of nuts. They had been handpicked and headed by M, a brilliant physicist. Apparently, M was also prolific at home, having produced an eyebrow-raising number of children, somewhere in the vicinity of eight or ten.

Everywhere M and his family went, he would be driving his red Porsche, with his wife and their brood in a Volkswagen bus close behind. One day, out of the blue, M left IBM (he in his Porsche and his family in the VW) for a fabulous new job in Washington, D.C. He was gone, and his ten young physicists became instant orphans.

"Fruitcake" was a highly competitive group, and IBM a highly competitive— and sensitive—company. When IBM's stock went down a fraction, say a quarter of a dollar, the company's headquarters

At a party, 1962

in Armonk, New York *and* the research lab at Yorktown felt the gloom and doom. It was difficult to even go to the stock room to ask for a pack of pencils, something the theoretical physicists used plenty of in those days.

Some of the Fruitcake members began to look for jobs elsewhere. Sam's anxiety came out in the form of a severe case of stomach ulcers.

In those days, doctors believed that a milk diet should be used to treat ulcers to neutralize the acid; I was issued several mimeographed sheets of recipes and a schedule of what and when to feed him, while he was kept sedated with tranquilizers. When that failed to work, he was put on baby food. For months afterward, whenever we were invited to dinner parties, he had to bring his two jars of Gerber.

After almost a year of typing addresses, I found a job as a receptionist/secretary at an orthopedic surgeon's office. I worked there until a day before my first child, Andrea, was born in October 1962.

As a new mother, I was seized by maternal feelings I didn't know I had. I suddenly felt all sorts of fear. For example, I was so afraid that she might suddenly stop breathing that I would repeatedly go to her crib to listen for her breath.

When February rolled around, I was horrified when Sam suggested getting a babysitter so we could go out for dinner to celebrate the second anniversary of our engagement.

"We can't do that!" I said. "What if Pam dropped the baby by accident? She's just a teenager."

"She won't. She has experience," Sam replied. "Besides, do you realize you haven't been out since the baby was born?"

With the various baby paraphernalia, we quickly outgrew our one-bedroom apartment in Mount Kisco. When Andrea was five months old, we moved into a two-bedroom apartment in Peekskill—with a playground next to the complex—nine miles from Yorktown. We bought more furniture, and Sam delighted in holding Andrea by her feet, while she stood upright, giggling, reaching for the ceiling. She thought she was on top of the world.

§

One late spring morning, as I was busy fixing breakfast, the phone rang. It was K. He had obtained my number from a friend who knew my high school classmate's roommate.

We had never talked on the phone in Taiwan, and he sounded like a stranger. More than three and a half years had gone by since we broke up. It had been almost seven years when we last looked into each other's eyes, innocent of what tomorrow would bring, but it seemed like a lifetime. Words came rushing up to my throat; I felt I owed him more explanation than he had received. But I couldn't talk, not with Sam a few feet away, eyeing me with suspicion.

Sounding stilted, K congratulated me on the birth of my daughter and said he had wished for a girl but had gotten a boy instead.

It was strange, our talking about kids, his boy and my girl. Not a word about when he had gotten married, how long he had been in the States, where he was going to school, or how long he would be in town. He didn't say, and I couldn't ask.

Desperate to break the impasse, I invited him over for dinner; to my surprise, he accepted.

I realized after hanging up the phone that I had been characteristically thoughtless. He was new in this country—how could he get to the suburbs? How would we feel when we saw each other? How would Sam react?

He called the same time next morning to say he wasn't coming after all. Again his timing was wretched—Sam was a few feet away from the phone, looking more annoyed and accusatory. K said he was glad to learn I was happily married and decided it was best not to disturb us. All I could do was say goodbye and wish him luck.

§

In the summer of 1963 Lining moved to New York. Having graduated from Peabody, she had found a job as a library cataloguer in Queens. Jobs in library science were indeed abundant and New York a natural choice—an easy subway ride to visit our cousins during the week and a train ride to spend her weekends in Peekskill with me.

Every Friday evening she would arrive by train and leave bright and early Monday morning for work. On Thursdays, I would stock our refrigerator with her favorite foods in happy anticipation of her arrival.

Lining and I had not been close when we were home, but our family ties were so surprisingly strong that from her first weekend visit, she became my best friend and an integral part of our life.

Growing up as the pampered child in the family, she had no use for reading or studying. Everyone readily succumbed to her charms. Once I tutored her for an exam. On the question of the capital of Argentina, she replied "Hot Dance" with a triumphant smile (a movie titled *Hot Dance in Argentina* was in theaters at the time).

It was a rude awakening for Lining to discover that her charms and wiles didn't go far in entrance examinations to *Beiyinu* or other public high schools. The shame of spending three years in a private junior high for the academically lowest of the low was what probably straightened her out.

Now that she had grown up and was capable of holding her own with the rest of us, I was delighted to discover that we had so much in common. We had the same sense of humor and subscribed to the same family narrative—that we were special because we belonged to a special family. We were considerate of each other, respected our elders, and protected by our virtuous ancestors.

Meanwhile, Sam was doing well. Because his work dovetailed with that of IBM's research lab in Zurich, he was informed he might be sent to Switzerland for a year or two. In the end, however, it didn't happen—they sent someone else instead. Though disappointed, he seemed to take it in stride.

In fact, we began looking to buy a house. I admired the stone houses in the area and was holding out for an affordable one, when Sam received a letter from the chairman of the Iowa State Physics Department offering him a position of associate professor with tenure. He decided to take it.

I was horrified. I hated leaving the area and what the city had to offer. Most of all, I didn't want to abandon my sister. Leaving her was tantamount to pulling the rug from under her; it would be against my father's wishes—my father, who had explicitly entrusted me with taking care of her. Yet how could I object to Sam's career choice for my own personal reasons?

Andrea had just turned two when we made our journey of more than 1,200 miles to Iowa. We left New York the day after Thanksgiving in 1964.

Chapter 20

OUR YEAR OF MOTHERS

If anyone should ask me to describe Iowa in one word, I would say, "cold." Two words? "Brutally cold." Three words? "Soul-crushingly cold."

I don't mean to exaggerate, but Iowa winters tend to remind me of the story of the Chinese patriot, Su Wu.

More than 2,000 years ago, Su Wu, an ambassador of the Western Han Dynasty to a neighboring state and long-time adversary, Xiongnu, was detained by Xiongnu and exiled to herd sheep. For nineteen years, he endured extreme hardship but refused to surrender. Finally, he was allowed to return home; there, he found his mother dead, his wife remarried, and he himself a legend in Chinese history.

In my junior high school music class, we used to sing a famous song called "Su Wu the Shepherd." While the lyrics tell the poignant story—*Su Wu never betrayed his country. Snow on the ground, ice from the sky, for nineteen years, drinking snow for thirst, swallowing wool for hunger, he herded sheep by the side of the North Sea...*—the melody is so horrendously monotonous that every time I tried to sing it, I dissolved into hopeless giggles.

I had no idea that many years later I would be like Su Wu, with snow on the ground, ice from the sky, persevering for nineteen—no, seventeen—years.

I grew up hearing stories about frigid Manchuria where, if one uncovered one's nose and ears, they would fall off from the cold. Now, for seventeen long years we made our home in a small town in the American Midwest, at the same latitude as Manchuria. In the winter, cold fronts from the North Pole, unhindered by mountain ranges, would relentlessly assault the home of this modern Su Wu...

In September our lawn was covered with thick frost in the morning. Beginning in early October, the outdoor thermometer frequently registered zero degrees. Come November, snowstorms started making courtesy calls. By December, no matter how much I wrapped myself up from top to toe and layer upon layer, the wind cut right through me and rendered all those layers useless.

In January, Mother Nature turned even more punishing. For several weeks, temperatures would hover between ten and twenty degrees below zero—any exposed skin would turn blackish purple in minutes. By the time February arrived, I was hysterical, dreaming of sunny, balmy Hawaii. Snow and ice didn't melt in March. In fact, they had hardened into a grayish black rock.

"April is the cruelest month," T. S. Eliot wrote. He seemed to have written that line just for me because in April, there would come a morning when the "rock" turned into dirty, worn, and loose "cotton," exposing the long-invisible lawn and driveway. The message was clear: *Spring is here; can winter be far off?*

Throughout the years, my desire to relocate to a warmer climate was paramount, but it was a desire that met with equally strong resistance. I was married to someone whose priority—whose only priority—was physics. Was there anything in life, in this world, more important than physics?

§

After spending two summers and two winter breaks typing in Ames, I was no stranger to the town or its harsh climate. However, in addition to the cold, there was the guilt of abandoning my sister and the pain of leaving the most cosmopolitan city in the nation, the epitome of urban sophistication and diversity, in exchange for small-town smugness and homogeneity.

As it turned out, we had worse problems. We had no sooner arrived in Ames and moved into a tiny, dilapidated rental house—

the best available—than my mother-in-law descended on us to commence an indefinite stay. She lived with us for six months and during that time, came close to destroying our young marriage.

To this day, I'm reluctant to write about my mother-in-law Irene, for I'm aware that no matter how honestly and fairly I try to portray her, my account would seem overblown. As the cliché goes, life is stranger than

My mother-in-law, Irene

fiction. Irene was certainly stranger than fiction. Like a diva in an opera, everything about Irene was bigger than life; rules for ordinary human beings simply didn't seem to apply.

If I had met her before my marriage, I would have run a mile and then kept on running. But she was far from my mind when I walked down the aisle. She was thousands of miles away in Taiwan. Chances were I wouldn't see much of her. I didn't learn much about her either, except that she was a college professor in Taiwan with a master's degree in nutrition from Oregon State College.

Suffice it to say that she turned out to be the very antithesis of anyone's image of a professor. More alarmingly, she emanated an air of provocative belligerence, of fighting swagger. It suddenly occurred to me that I had never seen any of Sam's family photos.

Every morning, after I dropped Andrea off at nursery school, Irene would follow me from room to room, as I made beds and tidied up, delivering her monologue in her booming, lecturing voice. The content of her lecture was always the same: *me, me, me; me and my four extremely brilliant children.*

Curiously, she never said a word about her husband Homer and didn't once utter his name in those six long months. It was as if he had never existed, as if she had had her four brilliant children by "immaculate conception." I thought, *Good heavens, she is truly exclusive.* Nobody was worth a darn except her and her four brilliant children.

The subtext was also clear: I was so undeserving, so lucky to have landed the most brilliant of her four extremely brilliant children.

She made sure she always went grocery shopping with me. She must have thought I was extravagant because any meat that cost more than thirty-nine cents a pound she would take right out of our shopping cart. We had pork butt, beef tongue, and chicken wings for six months—they were all thirty-nine cents a pound. She liked Red Delicious apples, but she liked them soft. Any apple failing her finger test was rejected.

My cooking made her wheeze, she claimed, so she took over and boiled everything. I had to be at her beck and call and was not allowed to stand by idly. Every time she cooked, she made a huge mess. For example, she would carry a piece of pork butt from one end of the kitchen to another, dripping bloody water all over the floor.

I gagged from her beef tongue boiled with spinach. More alarmingly, Andrea was losing weight.

I asked Sam, "How long do I have to put up with this? I think someone has to tell her she cannot behave like this. She can't come in and take over."

That someone obviously was not going to be him. In fact, he warned me against reasoning with her. "You don't know what she's capable of. She never reasons. She'll scream at the top of her lungs and roll on the floor. She'll grab a knife and threaten to kill you or herself. She doesn't care who hears her. You're no match."

He added ominously, "She used to blow up every few days even *without* provocation."

"Now you tell me," I said.

But I saw terror, pain, and shame in his eyes.

Chinese culture has its own version of original sin. Because your parents gave birth to you and raised you, you are forever in their debt, and you can never repay such debt. To strengthen that line of reasoning, there is the ubiquitous, unequivocal saying: *Tianxia wu bushi de fumu*, parents can do no wrong under the sun. Even if your mother beats you brutally for no reason—which I later found out Sam's mother had indeed done.

I realized that although Sam was no longer a child, he was still terrified of his mother, to the extent that he would be willing to give her his right arm or anything else she demanded, just to keep the peace and avoid a scene.

Would he sacrifice his daughter and wife? The answer seemed to be yes. I contemplated packing up and leaving with Andrea but felt trapped because I was pregnant, and we were in the process of buying a house.

Meanwhile, Sam was sinking into a deep depression. His mother promptly went to bed every night at 7 p.m., and he would sit alone in the living room with the television off, brooding and drinking. I was in no position to help him. In those last months we were no longer on speaking terms, and I suffered from insomnia. The house was quiet; even the air seemed taut. It was as if we were bracing ourselves for the impending detonation of a time bomb.

In the end, the anticipated catastrophe didn't happen. Irene grew bored and decided to go to Chicago to stay with Sam's older sister, Rose, ending our six-month siege.

What a reprieve!

Like survivors of a devastating natural disaster, we couldn't stop talking about what we had just experienced, and Sam came forth with some details of his hellish childhood. I was finally able to serve Andrea her favorite foods. Watching her eat ravenously, we smiled.

To this day, I have not bought beef tongue or chicken wings again. It has been fifty years.

§

Soon after Irene departed, we moved into our new house, and *my* parents came for *their* indefinite first visit. A change of dynasties. We had a scant two months between Irene's stay and my parents' visit.

I hadn't seen my parents since I had left Taiwan eight years before. My father had left his government job a few years back and had just concluded a two-year stint as a fisheries consultant in Saigon.

It had been only ten years since he had set his grand plan in motion, and he had succeeded splendidly. Since my siblings and two cousins were all on the East Coast, my parents visited all of them before visiting us. To save them the trouble of changing planes, we drove to Chicago, with Andrea in tow, to pick them up at the airport.

When our car came to a stop in the driveway of our spanking new, four-bedroom colonial house with a two-car garage, I could see my parents were impressed. None of my siblings and cousins appeared to have done as well. Unlike my siblings who were still single, I was married with one child and another on the way. My parents surveyed "their kingdom" with more than a little satisfaction.

By that time, I had figured out my father's plan and realized that his order to marry a science or engineering major was totally unnecessary. They didn't need me after all. Charley, having finished his PhD from Iowa State, was now on the faculty of North Carolina State and was perfectly qualified to apply for green cards for our parents.

After we accompanied them for their obligatory visit to Minneapolis, our nearest big city, and a few other tourist sights, we returned to Ames. My parents were ready for mahjongg—their favorite form of recreation—and Ames was ready for them.

Shortly after Sam and I had moved to Ames, I had received a call from a Mrs. Bing, wife of the Chinese physician who headed the Iowa State Student Clinic. Both Bings were second- or third-generation Chinese Americans. After the usual pleasantries, she asked me, "Do you play mahjongg?"

I said, "No."

"What a pity!" she said.

"But would you like to learn?" she asked.

"No."

"What a pity! Do you play bridge?"

"No."

"What a pity!"

Of course I didn't tell her mahjongg tended to bring up unpleasant memories for me. I had not been fond of the men and women who came to our house in Taiwan and immediately sat down at the mahjongg tables, playing and engaging in idle talk for hours, breaking only grudgingly for meals. *What a waste of life*, I thought.

To make the matter worse, I had always been assigned the duty of filling their teacups, serving them snacks, and waiting until they had finished playing late at night so that Cecilia and I could walk to the bus station and hail taxis to send them home.

My mother often chided me—not in front of our guests, of course—for failing to be sufficiently cheerful while performing those tasks. "Why do you insist on pulling a long face, as if someone owed you ten sacks of rice, and sticking your lips out far enough to hang several bottles of oil?"

I still remember a particularly humiliating incident connected with mahjongg.

In my freshman year of college, we had physical education classes three times a week and were required to wear black regulation culottes. I didn't have any and had no chance to ask my mother for money for them. Finally, I brought it up at her mahjongg table.

Aunt Liu, a close family friend whose long-deceased father had been the governor of Guizhou, my father's superior, was generous to offer, "We'll lend you a pair." Her daughter was two years ahead of me in *Taida* and was well known in the Foreign Languages Department for her beauty.

"What's your waist size?" she asked.

"Forty-eight centimeters," I said. (About nineteen inches.)

"Too bad, hers is thirty-eight centimeters." She smiled.

Years later, my daughter Andrea observed that I was always nervous when my parents were around. Was I? I didn't realize that. But their presence did stir up certain memories, not all of them pleasant.

I have no idea how the small Ames Chinese community got wind of the fact that my parents played mahjongg; soon they were inundated with invitations. People I hadn't even met or heard of wanted to play with them.

We even developed a routine. I would drive my parents to a particular address, and they would be brought home late at night.

This went on for a good while, and I was beginning to worry that we would be expected to set up mahjongg tables at home to reciprocate for all that hospitality when letters and telegrams started to arrive from Taiwan, pressuring my father to go back to start a new job.

We were saved by Taiwan's budding prosperity. So close to the triumphant completion of his grand plan, my father was reluctant to leave but powerless to resist. He went back to head several fisheries and shipping companies in the Veterans Administration. He was to work for another twenty-four years before retiring to America at the age of eighty-two.

Since it was only a couple of months before the baby was due, my mother stayed behind to help. Clifton was born at the end of November, and my mother proved to be a doting grandmother, bent on satisfying Andrea's every whim and holding a diaper by Clifton's crib, eager for him to wake up. I had never seen that side of her.

Toward the end of December, she decided that if she didn't leave then, she would never be able to tear herself away. She left on New Year's Day, flying from Des Moines to Raleigh on her way to Taiwan. She told me later that for days afterward she kept hearing Clifton's cries in her sleep.

With the birth of our son, we were now a family of four. Our first year in Iowa began with the residence of Sam's mother and ended with the departure of mine—*Our Year of Mothers.*

Chapter 21

THE THREE HUNDRED POEMS OF TANG DYNASTY

My mother-in-law Irene was so extraordinary and had such a devastating impact on Sam's life and behavior that I would be remiss not to include her story in a narrative of mine. In fact, since the day I met her, I made many efforts to learn more about her because the more I abhorred her, the stronger and more irresistible grew my urge to understand her.

To me, she seemed a vainglorious personality run amok. I wanted to know how she got away with her type of behavior, whether she knew how profoundly she had wounded her children, and how a personality like hers could have developed in the first place. Most of all, why hadn't anyone, especially her husband Homer, ever taken her aside and talked some sense into her?

I had to learn about her in bits and pieces in my forty-four years of married life, mostly from Sam after he retired, when he became more relaxed and open. But there were things he could never bring himself to reveal and that I only learned later from his sister Rose after his death.

§

Irene was the very proud descendant of the famous Ho Tungjiao, the last general in the Ming dynasty to resist the Manchurians. The victorious Manchurians became the new rulers and established the Qing Dynasty. General Ho was killed in battle, but his loyalty to the Ming regime was punishable by the beheading of the so-called "nine relations"—members of his immediate and extended family on his father's side, as well as the families of his mother, wife, teachers, students, colleagues, friends, and anyone else remotely connected to him.

Luckily, the fledgling Qing rulers were an ethnic minority; they needed to show mercy in order to quell unrest among the Han— the ethnic majority. So instead of beheading the "nine relations," they made General Ho's ten sons *xiang ba qi*, rendering them *de facto* Han nobility, and exiled them to Manchuria—the Chinese equivalent of Siberia. In other words, the new emperor showed them mercy on one hand and punished them on the other. Each son was allowed to ride a horse from sunup to sundown and claim the area he covered as his own.

For the general's ten sons—reared in comfort and luxury in the southernmost province of Guangdong—the primitive and harsh life of the north was the most severe punishment imaginable. Some did survive, but they didn't flourish. Infant mortality was so high in that brutal climate that Irene's forebears were barely able to carry down the bloodline, rarely producing more than one surviving son in each generation.

More than two hundred years (the duration of the Qing dynasty) later, Irene's father faced the same problem that had beset many of his forebears. His wife had bore him a total of eleven children, but only one was tough enough to survive: Irene.

If Irene's father was poor in his number of surviving offspring, he was staggeringly rich in land. He owned 5,000 *qing*, or about 83,000 acres. No man, not even a general's son, could have covered this much area riding from sunup to sundown on any horse. It seems that given the sparseness of the human stock and the expansiveness of his property, Irene's father and his forebears must have inherited from heirless uncles or cousins for generations.

Even in Manchuria, the backwater lands of China, 83,000 acres of land was considerable—especially when it was producing mostly opium.

Irene's father saw his sons and daughters die one by one as stillborn babies, infants, or young children. When he was certain he would not have an heir (a daughter didn't count because she would eventually marry and belong to another family), his cultivation of opium began to gnaw at him. He feared that the reason his *Ho* bloodline had become extinct was because the heavens were punishing him for growing opium, a product that brought destruction and ruin to so many.

He sought solace from the missionaries, was converted to Christianity, became a minister himself, and stopped growing opium.

When Irene's mother died years later, he quickly married a very young wife, most likely with the hope of producing an heir. In fact, she was Irene's high school classmate. Irene was livid, but by that time, she was living far away with children of her own and was powerless to intervene. To his great disappointment, however, the second wife bore him a daughter and no sons.

Irene's father had no way of knowing that he had no need to worry about the inheritance of his land. The Chinese Communists soon took over Manchuria and solved his problem by taking all 83,000 acres off his hands.

To further punish the landowner for his sins, the Communists forced him to watch as they beat his young wife. They first wrapped her in a heavy quilt so that not a single bruise could be found on her body when they were done, but every bone would be broken.

After the family was dispossessed of land, house, servants, and other earthly belongings, the three were begging in the streets when a distant cousin happened to spot them and alerted Irene. The wife died shortly afterward from her injuries.

§

During her childhood, as the lone survivor of eleven offspring in a family with so much land at stake, Irene's importance could not be overemphasized. (As a last resort, her father could make a son-in-law heir by having him take the *Ho* name.)

She grew up feeling entitled to behave any way she pleased, with no consideration for others, including her own parents. By nature extraordinarily forceful and tyrannical, she believed in her own omnipotence and expected the world to conform to her whims.

She relished bragging that as a child when anyone tried to deny her wishes, she would bang her head hard against the wall, hollering, "I'll kill myself. In eighteen years I shall be another strong young man!"

Buddhism was the dominant religion in China for many years, and Buddhists believe in reincarnation. This oft-repeated expression came from convicts facing execution. The minute before their heads were to be chopped off, they would yell, as a show of bravura, "In eighteen years I shall be another strong young man!"

It was bizarre and astonishing for a little girl to make that threat, but of course it worked like magic.

Manchuria being sparsely populated, its *tufei*—pirates who terrorized on land instead of at sea—preyed upon landowners with impunity. There were no police or government forces, for the simple reason that one's nearest neighbor was a several-days horse ride away.

Irene—no doubt proud of her ancestor General Ho's exploits—was the natural defender of house and property. I was told that in her youth she used to ride on a galloping horse while firing guns with both hands.

Though this story was hard to believe when I heard it, I couldn't help thinking, *what rotten luck to have unknowingly acquired a mother-in-law capable of dispatching me with twin guns blazing!*

It was astonishing to me that someone with that background had received any education at all, let alone possessed the mental wherewithal to reach the level of education she did.

Irene attended Shenyang High School in the province of Liaoning, passed the entrance exam for Yenjing University (the best in the nation at the time and still one of the two best) in Beijing, graduated with a degree in nutrition, and earned a scholarship to Oregon State College in Corvallis to continue her studies in nutrition.

You could probably count the number of Chinese women with that level of education in the mid-1920s on the fingers of two hands.

Up until then she had been on top of the world, but something seems to have happened that stopped her in her tracks—and it seems to have happened in Oregon.

I once mentioned to Irene that I had attended the University of Oregon when I first came to this country and had gone to Corvallis for a party one Saturday. I told her this shortly after she came to stay with us in Ames, in an effort to establish some common ground for conversation, but I was greeted with a loud expelling of air through her flared nostrils. She said nothing.

There was yet another aspect of Irene that I later discovered. In the 1980s, two of Sam's sister Rose's friends, like many other Chinese Americans, made their trek to China, the homeland that had been closed to them for decades due to Communist policies.

In a Nanjing museum they happened to see one of Homer's books on exhibit. (Homer was a scholar and wrote books on soil chemistry.) They were so excited that they called Rose when they came home. Rose, of course, was proud and happy and told her mother, who retorted, indignant, "But I'm not any less capable than he!"

Under the same circumstances, any Chinese woman of that time—including my mother—would have taken pride in the recognition of her husband, but not Irene. She always had to come first. She probably resented him all those years for being academically superior.

It's interesting that my mother bitterly resented my father's strenuous efforts to thwart her desire to put her hard-earned education to use, but if anyone criticized my father in his absence (as Charley did on several occasions) she would be indignant and instantly rise to defend him. Maybe it was love, maybe just loyalty. But it was likely Irene never loved anyone except herself.

Homer had received a PhD in agronomy from the University of Maryland and did his doctoral research in soil chemistry. Unlike Irene, he was of a more scholarly bent and had managed to write and publish papers and books despite the war and the attendant relocations and job changes.

Why was Irene so resentful of her husband on that score? Did she think his accomplishments reflected badly on her?

More importantly, what exactly happened in Oregon?

I know her English and knowledge of nutrition were dismal to the point of non-existence. She never even showed the slightest interest in nutrition. The fact that she did not pursue a doctoral degree and was completely mum about her experience in Oregon led me to suspect that for the first time in her life, she had discovered that the world would not bend to her wishes. It was as if a door had suddenly slammed in her face.

In fact, I suspect that because of the general racial atmosphere of the time and her language ineptitude, she suffered profound humiliation in Oregon, and the fury she carried with her manifested in telltale ways throughout her life and formed a toxic legacy to her children.

Irene and Homer happened to have returned to China around the same time and met while they were teaching at Yenjing University. Academic standards were not exemplary at the time, and a foreign degree was highly prized. In the rarefied arena of singles with higher degrees from abroad, it seemed perfectly natural and inevitable for them to wed. I suspect they only had a brief acquaintance before marriage, as a long engagement would have been deemed unnecessary and unseemly at the time.

For Homer, it appeared to be a logical, impeccable choice to marry a modern woman, educated in the United States as he was, so they would have more in common. Unfortunately, they couldn't have had less in common. In addition to their disparate American experiences, Homer came from the opposite kind of dysfunctional family.

His father had been married at fifteen—the nuptials having been arranged by the families involved—and had a son by the time he was sixteen. His wife, Homer's mother, had a pair of properly bound tiny feet and was properly illiterate and self-effacing; she carried out household duties efficiently and obeyed her husband absolutely. She produced five boys.

Homer was eleven when the Americans came calling at his home in Taiyuan, the capital of Shanxi province and where his father had achieved local renown by successfully passing the last imperial civil service exam. Although he had passed the exam at the lowest rank, he was considered *the* scholar in the city.

The Americans were recruiting promising Chinese youths for a new preparatory school in Bejing, named Qinghua. When

Homer's father learned of the visitors' purpose, he tilted his head back and let out a stream of loud laughter:

"I have three sons, but they are all pretty dumb—except *lao er*, number two. You may take him."

Homer's fate was changed in that instant. He became one of two students from the province of Shanxi to receive the all-expenses-paid scholarship.

Like their father, Homer's older brother, the eldest son of the family, was also married at age fifteen and had a son at sixteen. He was nineteen when Homer left home, and he wished to attend college in Beijing.

He was finally allowed to do so. However, each semester when he needed money for tuition and expenses, he was made to kneel, to wait till his father deigned fit to throw money on his head. And each time he had to suffer the added humiliation of picking up the scattered money on all fours.

The poor fellow later became the founder and principal of the renowned school in the province but died at fifty, a grandfather of many, from a stroke while kneeling in front of his father.

Born and raised in that environment, the eleven-year-old Homer was turned over to the Americans when his father gave his consent. He was immersed in American culture, attending Qinghua, a boarding school 250 miles away, for eight long years. The school then sent him to America to attend Iowa State College (later Iowa State University), the foremost institution in the country in the field of agriculture.

He received his undergraduate and master's degrees and went on to the University of Maryland. When he received his PhD, his professor wanted him to stay to continue their project, the same kind of research in soil chemistry that led to the discovery of streptomycin that later landed a Rutgers University soil microbiologist a Nobel Prize.

But Homer was more than thirty years old. He had lived among Americans for more than twenty years and was yearning to go home.

He lost no time in starting a family of his own. He and Irene wed in 1927 and had four children: Lily (she later changed her name to Monica), 1928; Rose, 1929; Sam, 1933; and David, 1938.

The war started in 1937. By the time David was four months old and the war one year old, the family had relocated to Chongqing, the war capital, where Homer had taken a government job, as there were no universities in Chongqing at the time. They bought land outside the city, built a large house, hired more servants, and settled down for eight horrifying years.

Chongqing during the war was, of course, not a pleasant or safe place to be. The Japanese bombed the city day after day. A conservative estimate was that more than 11,500 bombs were dropped by the Japanese, mainly incendiary bombs targeted at the civilian population.

But the bombing raids, though terrifying and deadly, were not nearly as devastating to the children as their mother's behavior.

Irene had always had an unpredictable, explosive temper. She could blow up at any time, any place, for any reason or none at all. It was more than a mere temper tantrum. She would roll on the floor, feet wildly kicking, arms wildly waving, while emitting ear-splitting screams and ear-scorching curses. Servants knew enough to stay away, and she couldn't care less who could hear her. She would grab, without pretext or warning, anything at hand—a chair, a broom, a dustpan—and beat the children savagely, shouting, "Go ahead and die!" "Why aren't you dead?" "I'm going to beat you to death!"

Even in his adult years, Sam couldn't bring himself to describe these scenes, which happened every few days or so. Afterward, her outburst would blow over, and the family would live in peace for a while, as if nothing had happened—until the next episode started the cycle all over again.

These tantrums didn't just happen in Chongqing, of course. As far as Rose can remember, they started before the war. But it was in Chongqing, when Irene was not teaching and Homer only came home on the weekends (on account of the distance to his job), that her "temper flares"—as they were euphemistically called by family members and servants—occurred with such frequency, and to such an extent, that all four children bore deep scars for the rest of their lives.

Incredibly, Homer was present at many of these episodes but did absolutely nothing, as if he wasn't there and didn't see or hear anything. He never uttered a single word or took any action to protect his defenseless children. Perhaps that was the only way he knew how to cope. Perhaps cowed by his early upbringing by his father, he was not emotionally capable of confronting Irene, so he resorted to being emotionally, if not physically, absent.

While I cannot begin to imagine the pain and suffering Homer had to endure on those occasions and during his marriage, I find it unconscionable that he never lifted a finger to intervene for the sake of his children.

After all, everybody only has one childhood; nobody can start over and obtain a second one. And the childhood shapes the person.

Sam told me he seriously contemplated suicide at age eight. All his life, depression and death wishes never left him. He also suffered from various physical ailments, including prostate cancer. Multiple surgeries took him in and out of hospital throughout his life. Even after his mother's death, she forever lived in him. Haunted by her insidious shadow, Sam continued to spend his life running from fear and pain. He died at seventy-two from a massive stroke.

§

Though Irene beat her children mercilessly, she also paid relentless attention to their education, an undertaking none of her children ever gave her credit for. She had a deep-seated, visceral yearning for glory—and was frustrated and furious when the world denied her that glory.

Thus, the children were drilled from childhood that they must all get a PhD *and* become famous (she herself had accomplished neither). They existed to vindicate her, to prove *her* greatness. To that end, she spared no effort or expense.

She supervised their homework, paying special attention to math and science. When the girls were in junior high, she learned that the school had an excellent math teacher, so she hired him to come to their home to tutor.

The high school math teacher/tutor also happened to be an accomplished amateur Chinese opera singer, so he was pressed into double duty to teach all four children Chinese opera.

A young bachelor with no home of his own, he proved to be so indispensable that he was soon invited to move in with them. In time, he introduced the family to a nearby prominent professional Chinese opera troupe, and all four children performed onstage in one role or another.

When Sam was young, his mother made him memorize *The Three Hundred Poems of the Tang Dynasty*, the holy bible of Chinese poetry. In his retirement years, he could still recite many of the verses.

One day, after lunch with two friends, in a rare unguarded moment, Sam mentioned that he had learned those poems as a child from his mother but that she had always beaten him *before* each session.

That was the first time I had ever heard him mention his mother's way of teaching. Noting the shocked expressions on all our faces, he tried to make light of it, "You know, all Chinese parents did that."

The husband of the couple shook his head. "No, mine never did." His wife also disagreed, "Mine didn't either." I said nothing. I didn't get any beatings, *and* my parents didn't try to teach me anything.

I never asked Sam how often those poetry sessions occurred and over how many years. I didn't want to know.

§

Even after her children had grown up and were living too far away to be thrashed into submission, Irene still proved to be a formidable adversary.

Being from Manchuria and of the lineage of General Ho, Irene had always taken great pride in being a northerner and categorically rejected anything and anybody southern. In fact, Irene went so far as to include the word *north* in the Chinese

Sam's family after the war: Rose, Monica, Sam, David, Homer, and Irene; Shanghai, circa 1947

names of all her children. Therefore, Monica is River North; Rose, East North; Sam, West North, and David, Sea North. All the *Norths* were brought up with the explicit order that they were to marry only northerners.

In 1957, when Rose wrote home for permission to marry, Irene flew into a rage. Rose's boyfriend James was tall and attractive, with a nice disposition. Furthermore, he came from a good family and was a doctoral candidate at the University of Wisconsin. Rose and James had known each other since they were in Taiwan, but he had *the most unforgiveable flaw*. He is a southerner.

Instead of her mother's approval, Rose received daily raging, blustering letters. One question stings her to this day: "You're getting your PhD; why do you need a husband?"

Sam had joined Rose two years earlier at Iowa State. Each day Rose would come home and be greeted with the sight of a newly arrived blue aerogram from Irene. She would burst into tears, close the door to her room, and cry her heart out.

Luckily for her, there was a third member of the family in their apartment—their father, who was on his sabbatical, also at Iowa

State. Homer, who had never in his life opposed or contradicted his wife, gave Rose his blessings for the wedding.

In the following year, Monica, who had left home in 1954 for Rome to study art, presented her mother with a *fait accompli*. Apparently taking a lesson from Rose, she informed her mother by mail that she had joined a convent and had changed her name from Lily. In her fury, Irene disowned her, destroyed her paintings and belongings, and wrote her, "I shall cry till my eyes go blind."

After the fiasco with her two daughters, Irene's letters to Sam, "the most brilliant of her four extremely brilliant children," took on a more urgent tone. And the bar was set higher. His future spouse had to have two additional attributes: height and strength. She promised, in every letter, to send him some of her students who possessed those necessary qualifications. "And they are beautiful," she never forgot to add.

But before Irene could carry out her promise, news came that her older son also wished to marry a southerner. After swallowing her bitter tears, Irene met my parents and my sister, a college senior living at home. As soon as she saw Lining she asked, "Is your sister as tall and strong as you?"

That I managed to fail all three of her prerequisites was unforgivable, and Irene was not one to hide her feelings.

§

To me, Irene's brutal beatings of her children and her other exploits were shocking and unbelievable enough, but there was more.

The few times Sam and I visited my parents in Taiwan, Irene would come to call, invariably bearing stinky preserved duck eggs.

She knew my kids wouldn't eat them, and I absolutely detested them, but she claimed they were Sam's favorite. In all the years I knew Sam, he never expressed any desire for stinky duck eggs, preserved or not. But Irene was there to provide her much-deprived and beloved son this very delicacy, its odor—aggressive and obnoxious—permeating my parents' apartment.

I can't remember whether he ate them in her presence (or at

all), but I do remember every time she would also urge him, "Go visit Mr. Jia. He'd love to see you," and she would hand him the address on a slip of paper. Like the dutiful son he was, he did as he was told.

At the time, I had no way of knowing this Mr. Jia was *the* Mr Jia, the children's math and Chinese opera tutor, *and* the cause of Sam's very last beating by his mother.

Sam only divulged the story after he retired. One day, Mr. Jia had some kind of spat with his mother; he threatened to leave and move out of the house for good. Irene told David to go and apologize to him. David did so, to no avail. So Irene ordered Sam to do the same.

It was a weekend. Sam had just returned home from boarding school. Hot and weary from the journey, he protested, "But *I* didn't offend him. Why should *I* apologize?" Those words came out before he realized that he was, in essence, "pulling whiskers from the tiger's mouth." Infuriated, Irene grabbed his belt hanging by the bed and started whipping him with all her might.

He grabbed the belt back. For a moment, he stood trembling, staring into his mother's eyes. At twelve years old, he was already taller than Irene, who turned, speechless, and stomped out of the room. She never attempted to beat him again.

The upshot was Mr. Jia stayed. In all, he lived with them for more than ten years, until one day Rose told him to get out of the house.

And even that was not the whole story. It wasn't until later, when Sam was undergoing some deep bodywork, that some long-buried ugly facts started to dribble out.

It was the sudden and unexpected surge of his long-suppressed anger and shame about Mr. Jia and his mother's "special relationship" that gave Sam his courage and precipitated his impulse to grab back the belt.

When I first learned this, it was almost impossible for me to wrap my head around that piece of information.

Moral issues aside, how could this happen with Irene's husband, all the children, and servants afoot? I don't wish to comment on her looks, but why would a young bachelor even be interested in a middle-aged woman with four children? Living for ten years right under the same roof. Did Homer suspect anything at all?

I later found out it was open knowledge among the children, though I still don't know how aware Homer was about the situation. Chinese culture certainly didn't condone a married woman having an affair. It's derogatorily called *tou han*, stealing a fellow.

It's easy to understand why Sam buried it deep under his consciousness, but why did he feel obliged to pay those courtesy visits to his mother's former adulterer in Taipei? He himself was already a father of two and a physics professor. Who knows? Sometimes, human nature can be quite unfathomable.

§

After Homer died of strokes in 1959 at age sixty-two, Irene was comparatively happy and content. Other than visiting to assert her will over us once every few years, she continued to teach at Taizhong Agricultural College. Later she switched to the College of Chinese Culture on the Yang Ming Mountain.

On the evening of May 1, 1979, Irene was found collapsed outside her apartment on campus. It was allergy season, and her asthma had probably brought on the heart attack that killed her. In her kitchen, the braised pork was still warm in the pot. She had survived Homer by twenty years. None of the children knew her actual age.

Hundreds attended her funeral, most of them her distraught students, bereft that their beloved teacher was gone. For her children, it was puzzling that so much affection was shown at her funeral. From what they heard, she had been a miserable and embarrassing teacher, using the same tired material year after year and spending a lot of her lecture bragging about her children. Sam looked around the hall, touched but incredulous. All his life he had lived with the shame and knowledge that his mother's notoriety was unequaled. Had time alone wrought a miracle that nothing else could?

After the funeral, before Sam was to return to the United States the next morning, my father took the four siblings out to dinner and was shocked—and chilled—to see them having a great time, laughing and joking without a shred of grief. They had just buried their last parent.

As a woman at war with the world for the glory she thought it owed her, Irene didn't achieve much glory in the end. And none of her four children achieved the kind of fame she so desperately craved. However, if life proved to be a disappointment for her, death was exceedingly kind. She died the way many aspire to but precious few achieve: fully alive and functional till the last minute.

Not given to introspection, she likely died remorseless about what she had done, without an inkling of the fact that petrified children tiptoeing through a minefield of a home are not likely to achieve future greatness.

§

Since Irene's death, I have had many occasions to reflect on her legacy to Sam. In addition to the obvious pain and fear she inflicted on him during his childhood, the effects of which he suffered throughout his life, the emotional damage that I sustained can neither be calculated nor discounted.

Though Sam was regarded a brilliant physicist and—according to some of his friends—a "Renaissance man," he was as emotionally stunted as a five-year-old. His intellectual IQ might have been high, but his emotional IQ was pathetically low.

He had a craving for love and affection because he had received none during his childhood. Because I also suffered from the same problem, only to a lesser degree, I can empathize.

His Achilles heel—an inordinate need for love and affection and his appalling lack of emotional acuity—contributed immeasurably to the greatest unhappiness of his life and mine.

Chapter 22

OF LEMONS AND COUNTRY BUMPKINS

After *Our Year of Mothers*, we settled down to our daily life. Each morning Sam closed the door behind him and went to work, and I was left with two small children and their respective needs, demands, and wills.

Nobody had warned me that parenting was one of the toughest jobs in the world. You need a license to drive a car, but you don't have to meet any requirements or receive any training to be a parent. Most people I knew fell back on how their own parents had raised them, but in our case that wouldn't work. Sam and I never discussed it, but coming from the childhoods we had, both of us wanted to try our best *not* to repeat the same pattern. In addition, our environment presented unusual challenges.

The number of Chinese in mid-1960s Ames was about a quarter of one percent in a town of around 39,000 residents—less than a drop in the bucket. Naturally, Sam and I wanted our children to be bilingual, capable of navigating both cultures with equal ease, but we were fighting a losing battle.

My pride in having sent Andrea, fluent in Chinese, to nursery school at age two, turned into her anger at me for being the only child who did not understand what her teacher was saying. Even before entering nursery school, Clifton told me, "If you spank me, I can spank you. We are equal." My jaw dropped. Where had he learned that?

I was filled with envy and frustration during those years. I envied Sam's opportunity to grow academically and gain professional stature, leaving childcare and housework to me with a clear conscience. I envied other parents who didn't have a different culture to contend with, whereas I only succeeded in getting my children to eat Chinese food after an epic struggle.

Despite my valiant and persistent efforts to the contrary, our children grew up one-hundred-percent American.

In those years, I also had to learn how to be a young faculty wife, attending parties and baking cookies—not exactly the expertise I had been groomed for growing up.

The 1960s seemed to be the burgeoning years of the Iowa State physics department. Chairman Daniel Zaffarano assembled a large number of cocky, ambitious, competitive, and fun-loving young faculty members. And true to his Italian heritage, he ran the growing department like a benevolent Godfather.

There were parties galore: the department dinner dance in the spring, the summer fish fry in the park, costume parties, Christmas parties, and so on. We were invited to dinners or parties every Friday, Saturday, and Sunday night; each lasted way past midnight.

I was often so groggy in the morning that when Clifton woke up, all I could do was to stumble into his room and find him a pacifier in the hopes of going back to bed for a few more winks.

We were caught up in this whirlwind of parties when a letter came from my father. My mother had sunk into a depression. She suffered from several chronic illnesses and had undergone through long periods of severe dietary restrictions after their 1965 visit. He told us to come home for a visit—a *long* visit.

The timing was baffling. In 1949, after we had escaped to Taiwan ahead of the Communists takeover, the island had been critically short of all kinds of professionals, including doctors. My mother was offered the chance to join the practice of one of her schoolmates. But my father threatened divorce. We weren't even told about this at the time. She gave up her once-in-a-lifetime opportunity willingly. Why was she depressed now, twenty years later?

Instead of letting her work in some capacity in medicine where her heart was, my father, in addition to mahjongg, wanted her to take up stamp collecting to fill her hours. We were all told to save interesting stamps for her. Over the years, Sam had been getting requests from physicists in different countries for reprints of his papers, so I laboriously removed these stamps and sent them in batches to my mother. My father was genuinely hurt, even outraged by my mother's lack of interest, complaining in his letter, "She just stuffed them in a drawer and never even bothered to look at them!"

But where had he gotten the idea for her to collect stamps when he himself had never had the time or interest for such patient pursuits? In the process of whittling her into a subservient wife, he was burying her alive, just as he had tried to wrangle Cecilia and me to be nursing students. He was always so determined to get what he wanted that he never considered what others might want and the human costs to others if they acceded to his wishes.

Obeying my father's wishes, Sam and I flew to San Francisco in the summer of 1968 to catch a charter flight—our first trip home to Taiwan—with a five-year-old and a two-year-old.

My father was doing well in his new career at the Veterans Administration; for the first time in over twenty years, they had no money worries.

The overall changes in Taiwan were striking. The economy had quickly developed to the point that the tables were turned. Those of us who had made it to America used to be envied; now we were pitied. People in Taiwan characterized us with the three *qis* or "ishes." Our speech tended to be *yangqi* (foreign-ish); when we spent money, we were *xiaoqi* (stingy-ish); and what we wore was *tuqi* (country-ish).

My mother felt the same way, and she was sorry for us, four country bumpkins from rural America. She had seen Iowa with her own eyes—miles and miles of corn or soybeans but not a single Chinese restaurant! She was determined to compensate for our deprivation by getting us to sample the culinary delights Taipei had to offer during our five-week stay. This gave her such an important purpose that she snapped out of her depression.

My parents' friends were only too glad to help. We were booked for almost every breakfast, lunch, and dinner. Unfortunately, being used to simple fare, we were easily saturated at banquets of twelve courses or more. At such occasions, I only wished I could have had all those dishes frozen, wrapped, and shipped home to savor.

Three years later, my father expressed his disapproval when he heard that Sam was to be a visiting professor at the University of Copenhagen, which meant that we were to spend a year in Denmark. "Denmark is practically next door to the Soviet Union. What if...?" But Sam couldn't be dissuaded. My father did talk us into buying around-the-world tickets, so we could stop in Taiwan on our long way to Europe. And we had to drop Bangkok from our itinerary because my father deemed it unsafe to visit.

Taiwan was even more prosperous by then. One day we were taken to a resplendent hall for lunch. A huge band was playing; the excellent variety show onstage drew continuous applause. The eyes of our two little country bumpkins were glued to the stage, so dumbstruck that they paid no mind to the elaborate courses being brought to our table in quick succession. With all my senses overloaded, I, too, lost my appetite and didn't know what I was eating.

Our host shouted over the loud music: "Is it true that you don't have shows like this in America? And you don't have dishes like these in America?"

"You are absolutely right," I admitted, shouting back. My answer brought a satisfied smile to his face.

§

Though Sam did well professionally over the years, he truly excelled in illnesses and surgeries. Depression and ulcers were the twin scourges of his existence. Starting in his forties, he acquired a third problem: hypertension.

Sam suffered nearly forty surgeries over the course of his seventy-two years of life. One time we were asked to list all his operations; it took more than three pages, single-spaced. He parted with everything he could do without, namely the "non-essential organs," such as tonsils, appendix, gall bladder, and later, prostate gland. His body was also adept at producing "superfluous parts" like a blood clot, benign tumors, hemorrhoids, and even a hernia.

The most exotic, of course, was the lymphangioma that required three operations over the course of a year to exorcise when he was twenty-one years old. But that was not the end of the story; it later made two rather dramatic comebacks.

Before leaving for a dinner party one night, Sam showed me his left arm. What looked like an irritation, a minor bump, or swelling more than quadrupled in size by the end of the evening. The next day, it had grown to the size of a small lemon. His doctor, despite having never seen or heard of a case like this, decided to operate instead of waiting for confirmation of the test results.

When we arrived at the hospital and an attendant grabbed a wheelchair for me, I had to decline, pointing to Sam: "No...*he's* the patient." At the time, Clifton was overdue by more than a week. Luckily, he was considerate enough to wait two more days before making his appearance.

A few years later, after having returned home from attending a European conference, another lymphangioma suddenly materialized on Sam's right arm. This one had to be removed just as expeditiously. (I love the surgeons' use of the word "remove"; it sounds so bloodless and pain-free.)

A more urgent and life-threatening case was a blood clot that developed in the vein of his left leg, the "good" leg. He was hospitalized on orders of strict bed rest and medicated to dissolve the clot. They failed to work, and the whole vein, which traversed the entire length of the leg, had to be stripped—a brutal procedure involving lengthy and excruciating recovery.

Since small children were not allowed in the hospital to visit, I bundled up Andrea and Clifton—Clifton was a few months old—and waited outside so Sam could wave to them from his window.

Over the years, Sam's surgeries spanned several hospitals and three geographic areas where we consecutively made our home. Because of the complications he suffered, we had to seek out university hospitals further away from home.

As the years went by, I began to compete with Sam on the frequency and severity of health problems and surgeries. Not to be outshone, he came home one Friday with the news that his doctor suspected a heart aneurysm and prostate cancer. A subsequent test exonerated the aneurysm, but the prostate biopsy was so badly botched that he suffered its aftermath for weeks. At sixty-one years of age, he decided to retire, and we moved to California.

No sooner had he bid adieu to his prostate gland in San Diego (it was cancer) than an echocardiogram found he had defective heart valves and a congenital heart disease. The muscle wall between his two heart chambers was much thicker than normal, rendering him particularly susceptible to bronchitis and other ailments.

Indeed, his cardiologist's words brought back my memories of the numerous times Sam had been laid up in bed from respiratory ailments—or recovering from surgeries—doleful and wretched. When he was well enough to sit up, he would pass the time teaching the kids a physics or mathematics idea or two.

Ah, the kids. They were fortunate to learn some science at their father's knees, so to speak, but unfortunate in that they inherited our allergies and sickly constitutions.

Andrea had her first severe bout of bronchitis when she was five months old, and she got sick practically every month no matter how careful I was. Before she was a year old, Sam was playing with her one day after she had just recovered from yet another illness. He suddenly stopped and declared, "I know what you are; you're a little lemon. If you were a car, you would've been recalled already!"

Too young to understand the meaning of "lemon" but gathering it was no compliment, she started to cry.

She was soon in good company—her brother was also a lemon. Many times, when the children were ill, Sam and I would debate whether or when to bring them to the clinic. One day too early, the doctor might refuse to prescribe antibiotics; too late, it might be full-blown strep, ear infection, bronchitis, or pneumonia. Sam learned to put his ear to the sick child's chest to detect whether a case of bronchitis was brewing. Viruses and bacteria were kept so busy in our home that they saw no need to move elsewhere. We were nicknamed *The Ailing Lius*.

Sam could be accused of lacking in self-knowledge when he called his children lemons, but I knew I had been a lemon since my diphtheria episode.

During the days he was young and felt healthy, he would be raring to go to work in the morning, like a racehorse restrained at the starting line. *I* was the lackadaisical one, who could hardly get going in the morning and needed rest during the day.

But by and by, his energy level dropped—especially after his congenital heart disease caused atrial fibrillation (irregular heartbeat). After a heart operation called ablation, he felt fifteen years younger—for three days. In other words, the surgery was a dismal failure.

Sam was compelled to stare mortality straight in the face whenever surgeries were required. However, despite having had a death wish since childhood, he was frightened. His favorite words, "We'll muddle through," were as much to reassure me as to allay his own fears. He did manage to muddle through every time—until one autumn night when he didn't.

§

Intellectually, Sam was a smart man, smarter than I could ever hope to be. His intellectual prowess was the silver lining in the cloud of his emotional problems and physical ailments. The two were

Before spending summer in Bochum, Germany, 1970; Sam, Andrea, Clifton, and me

highly connected, of course. His illnesses and surgeries were mostly psychosomatic, his body's way of manifesting his turbulent emotional state.

It has been said that when a person suffers from profound, unbearable emotional pain, he sometimes resorts to cutting himself, inflicting physical pain. Sam's surgeries were perhaps his body's way to alleviate or divert his emotional pain.

Unlike Irene, who blew up every few days, Sam would have only occasional emotional outbursts. His rage was directed more to himself, but no less devastating. And it continued throughout his life.

He was so fearful of the possibility that I might be as disapproving and critical of him as his mother that he searched for her in my words and deeds. Sometimes when he thought I blamed him for something he had done, he would turn morose and hit his head and chest with both hands in such despair that the incident left me emotionally shaken for days.

And the unpredictability was hard to bear. Once, looking at photos he had taken during our summer in Bochum, Germany where he had served as a visiting professor at Ruhr University, I made a casual remark that those ordinary house rooftops in the photos didn't appear to be particularly photogenic. He flew into a rage and threw the camera across the room with such force that his new Leica was totally destroyed.

Freud's statement about the marriage bed is, of course, only a metaphor. We are all flawed human beings, and our flaws are more than genetic. Intentionally or not, our parents shaped us when we were small and vulnerable.

As forces of nature in our lives, my father and my mother-in-law both registered extraordinarily high on the "Richter scale," although their methods were poles apart. While Sam's mother employed in-your-face brutality, my father was capable of cutting you down with words or a smile. When those two forces intersected, the effect became devastating.

Chapter 23

I, TOO, WAS THAT RABBIT

Once in the late 1960s when my father stopped by Ames on a business trip to the United States, I made the mistake of mentioning to him that I was getting restive at home. That casual remark provoked a lecture I hadn't heard since I was eighteen—"a woman must put her family before self," as my mother before me had done for him.

As it turned out, I was destined to disappoint my father—he who had rescued me from the knife when I was still in my mother's womb, the one person in the world to whom I twice owed my existence.

My writing certainly was not my father's idea of "putting my family before myself." But it just so happened that in February 1971, I had the opportunity to serve on the jury in a driving-under-the-influence case. The disparities between American and Chinese law unleashed emotions that compelled me to write a long essay in Chinese and send it to the literary page of *Central Daily News*, the leading newspaper in Taiwan at the time.

I chose *Central Daily News* because I was a subscriber to its four-page "airmail edition," which included the literary page. Within a short time, my essay was serialized as a leading piece, taking up most of the page for three days.

The reaction from Taiwan was immediate and gratifying: both my father and my mother-in-law were pleased. In those days almost everyone in Taiwan read that paper.

Their pride of my so-called accomplishment was short-lived,

however. Soon after, we spent a year in Denmark, where my struggles with learning Danish resulted in a humor essay. Again, *Central Daily News* serialized it as a lead piece.

The reaction this time was also immediate. It really tickled the funny bones of many people I knew, but to say my father and mother-in-law were displeased would be an understatement. Rather, they were furious. (It was amazing how the two agreed on so many issues.)

How could I have forgotten what happened at sixteen, when my father humiliated me after I won the essay contest? At the time, I thought it was because I had failed to ask for his permission, but now I knew it went deeper than that. By describing some awkward situations caused by my language problems and my clumsy efforts in dealing with them, I had disgraced our respective families and tarnished our name.

Just as in my "Nose" essay, if I was making fun of myself, I was, by extension, making fun of everyone in my family and my in-law's family—a most serious offense.

I did submit a third essay, a non-humorous one, which was again serialized as a leading article, but I learned my lesson. I didn't attempt another essay in Chinese, humorous or otherwise, for another fourteen years.

§

After returning from Denmark, I cast about for something else to do and found a volunteer opportunity to write publicity stories for our new local art center, the Octagon. I assisted Bess, also a volunteer but a retired faculty member from the Iowa State journalism department.

Using the information Bess gave me, I would write about the coming exhibits of The Octagon for the *Ames Daily Tribune*, our local afternoon paper. When its offices were closed at night, I would simply slip my story under the door. I never got a byline, of course, but there was some satisfaction in seeing my words published.

Perhaps it was Mark Twain who once said that writing editorials (and in my case, publicity stories) was like peeing in a blue serge suit—nobody knows about it, but you feel warm all over.

Feeling warm all over, one afternoon I was across from the refreshments table at an Octagon reception when I overheard the wife of one of Sam's older colleagues questioning my professional qualifications for the work. Bess defended me by emphasizing my academic credentials, but the lady—a Swiss with an admirable accent—remained unconvinced that they were sufficient proof of my competence. (Later, however, she became one of my most enthusiastic supporters, steering several story leads my way.)

Bess had four children. They lived in different corners of the country, and none seemed to ever find time to visit. Instead, she traveled to see them every summer, leaving her duties at the Octagon to me—including hosting a weekly, thirty-minute radio program. The Octagon would schedule one or two local artists to be interviewed each week. I was to arrive at the station a half hour before the show to meet with the guest and talk over what we were to cover. Then we would be on air.

Bess did it every week, and she didn't think it was a big deal: "Just chat with them and ask a few questions to get them to talk, and before you know it, the half hour is over." But to me that half hour was pure agony—under duress I sounded like an idiot. If I were religious, I would have prayed to God to let no living soul hear my halting, stammering, inarticulate performance. Luckily, as far as I knew, nobody ever heard the shows.

One afternoon, my guest was David Williamson, a young sculptor-poet who had just won a commission to produce a piece of sculpture for the terrace of the public library in Jefferson, a rural community west of Ames. As he described his twelve-foot abstract steel sculpture, I envisioned him pounding and welding that huge piece of metal, to render the face of the goddess rippling like a flag in the wind. Suddenly I heard words come tumbling out of my mouth: "Why don't you let me write a feature story about you and this piece of work?"

I was shocked by the way the words appeared to have come of their own volition. Even more shockingly, he responded, "Sure!"

We did the show, walked a couple of blocks to the Octagon,

and sat in the empty auditorium where I interviewed him for two hours and filled several pages of my notebook. I found I liked asking questions; I liked learning what motivated him to do his work and how he did it. And his views about art were refreshing.

It was only that evening, as I rolled a blank sheet of paper into my typewriter that it occurred to me that I was in trouble: I had no idea how to write the story. It had been twelve years since I was in school. What possessed me to think I could write a feature article? Who would publish it? Why hadn't I thought of these problems before?

I thought it was Williamson's fault. If he had asked, "Is your English good enough?" "Can you write feature stories?" or "Where can you publish?" I would have told him "I don't know" and backed out in time.

But after having interviewed him for two hours, I couldn't call him and say, "Sorry, I don't know how to write the story." I had no choice but to go ahead and write it.

I don't know how I wrote it, but I did. Everything after that seemed a blur: The *Ames Tribune* used the article with my byline and a photo I took of Williamson. Bess encouraged me to do a different version for *The Des Moines Register*, which was published three months later as a cover article in the *Sunday Register*'s *Picture Magazine*, with a circulation of half a million. More surprisingly, the story received first prize in that year's Iowa Press Women Awards.

§

Shortly after I mailed the story to *The Des Moines Register*, Williamson had his second one-man show at the Octagon.

It was a scorching weekday afternoon, when most people were either at work or in the swimming pool. The gallery was deserted. The sculptor accompanied me as I looked at his exhibited works: steel sculptures of varying sizes and shapes, bas-reliefs, etchings, oil paintings, watercolors, and charcoal sketches.

The oak floor creaked as we walked from one end of the gallery to the other, and I noticed that although his show had opened two weeks ago, not a single piece had been sold.

I bought a charcoal sketch with a large rabbit, a small tree, and a moon, in a simple wood frame.

I didn't understand the piece, and I didn't ask him what it meant. He never offered either, for he had said in the interview, "To appreciate art, one needs to look, and look again and again. I hope there's more to my work so that each time the viewer takes a look, he will find it more meaningful and can share to a larger degree what I have to offer."

Rabbit sketch by David Williamson, 1973. Photo by Sylvia Durian

I hung this sketch in our dining room, where it provoked an opinion from everyone who saw it for the first time. Our Chinese friends would bluntly say, "It's too weird," while our American guests were more tactful: "Unusual, isn't it?" Some would simply shake their heads and say, "I don't understand it." After making their comments, our guests would turn away. The sketch was no doubt too enigmatic, a failure even as a conversational piece.

After we moved to Oak Ridge, the rabbit sketch became my study's solitary artwork. I had switched to writing literary essays and short fiction in Chinese.

One day, out of the blue, I decided to take a good look at it. The drawing is done on cream-colored paper. To the right, a small black moon hangs starkly in the sky, too uniformly black and perfectly round, as if it had been produced by a draftsman rather than an artist. A solitary tree stands in the lower middle of the sketch, with a large white rabbit flying over the tree towards the moon.

The rabbit's eyes look meek and melancholic, slightly surprised and perplexed, as if he can't believe he's really flying. His forelegs are struggling to go up and forward, but where his hind legs should be is a flapping fish tail.

Rabbit legs are for jumping and running in the woods; a fish tail implies an ability to swim. One thing this fish-rabbit is singularly unequipped to do is to fly, but he does. No wonder everyone thought the sketch weird and nonsensical.

I'm no art connoisseur, and I certainly didn't understand this sketch. Why had I chosen it among so many of his works? It was neither aesthetically pleasing nor spiritually uplifting, just a simple, strange drawing.

Perhaps I was attracted by the rabbit's passion for doing something deemed impossible. Totally unaware of his limitations, he tries. For one instant he finds himself soaring over the tree, embracing his dream of reaching the faraway moon. The next instant he may fall or continue to rise, possibilities he is apparently not capable of considering.

Was it that passion—that single-mindedness personified by the rabbit—which drove me to choose this sketch that scorching afternoon years ago? I don't know. But more than two decades later, contemplating it in my study in Oak Ridge, I suddenly understood. The young sculptor was that rabbit.

Life as an artist is never easy. In an agricultural town, especially in Ogden (a village of a mere 1,000 souls) where Williamson lived, how many could have shared his vision of art? How many would buy his works? He admitted he didn't know but explained that "Iowa is my home and I've made a total commitment to art; it's not a matter of choice anymore."

To write that story for *The Des Moines Register*, I had made a trip to Ogden to interview Williamson for a second time and to see his work-in-progress. His wife was a potter, and their daughter was not yet a year old. He was working twelve-hour days in a converted chicken coop, pursuing his vision of art in a town largely devoid of culture. How would they survive?

But when I came to think of it, he was not alone. Because I, too, was that rabbit.

I had no idea whether I could write the story. Because I passionately, desperately wanted to and put myself in a position of no retreat, I did turn the impossible into reality. I was just as insane as that rabbit.

Perhaps anyone who has ever tried to pursue his life's passion is that rabbit. In the process of trying, we may meet with different degrees of success or failure, while the object we pursue, that eternal, perfect black moon, is still hanging in the sky—bewitching, unreachable, and indifferent.

As for Williamson, he did just fine. He is still doing what he set out to do in 1972, though he now has an emphasis on environmentally-friendly projects. He is quite well known in Iowa.

I went on to write nearly ninety lead stories, mostly about people in or around Ames who were undertaking unusual, difficult tasks. In the process I met many amazing people and learned about fascinating subjects.

I wrote about a Harvard-trained Iowa State University archaeologist excavating late stone-age sites in Kenya; a visiting physicist from Berkeley discussing the "Big Bang"; an animal ecologist keeping a lonely vigil in the Peruvian Andes, studying vicuna, a small, graceful member of the South American camel family; and the local community theater's ambitious production of "Marat/Sade," a play within a play.

One night I attended a sedate Renaissance music concert, with its exotic medieval instruments, and rushed right afterward to the eardrum-shattering gig of a rock band at a bar. The young musicians were on their way to Los Angeles in their quest to replace The Beatles and The Rolling Stones. I wrote about both events, and for both I had my family in tow.

It was hectic, but the process was nothing short of thrilling. Each story presented its unique problems; when I finished, I was too excited to sleep. In those years, I also wrote an occasional guest column.

I remember walking to the podium to receive the first prize for the Williamson story in Des Moines and hearing some in the audience gasp: "She's an *Oriental!*" Perhaps this was beginner's luck; thereafter I only received second or third prizes.

After six years of having my byline in the papers, I received a call from the Iowa State journalism department offering me a teaching job. Teaching presented a different set of challenges, especially for a foreigner in this field. I did poorly at first but gradually learned to introduce humor in my material and conquer my inexperience and stage fright.

Meanwhile, Sam's job reached a point where he lacked both the emotional strength and cultural savvy to handle the politics. Consequently, he committed what our daughter Andrea later termed his "second professional suicide" (the first being leaving IBM). He quit his position and accepted one at the Oak Ridge National Laboratory in Tennessee. I had been teaching three years when we left.

I had mixed feelings as we pointed our car southward in the summer of 1981, with Andrea and Clif, who were now college and high school students, respectively. I was happy because I was finally leaving frigid Iowa for good. On the other hand, I knew that while Sam would always have his professional stature wherever he went, I would probably have to start my career from scratch again.

Chapter 24

FATHER KNOWS BEST

Before we made the move, I knew very little about Oak Ridge. I knew that it has a national laboratory and it is in the South, meaning it is much warmer than Iowa. Through Sam, I knew something about national laboratories. After all, for seventeen years, in addition to being a professor at Iowa State, he held a joint appointment at Ames Laboratory, a national lab that had been involved in the Manhattan Project during World War II. The indispensable role of both Oak Ridge National Laboratory and Ames Laboratory in making of the atomic bombs that brought Japan to its knees was not lost on me.

Before we moved, I also learned that Oak Ridge was almost identical to Ames in its population size, and was touted as having the highest number of PhDs per capita in America. The former was disappointing, for work opportunities would be limited. The latter turned out to be disappointing as well, for the PhDs turned out to be narrowly focused in the applied sciences and technology.

Unlike Ames, Oak Ridge lacks a university. While Iowa State is ridiculed as "Cow College" or "Udder University," the importance of a higher educational institution in a town cannot be overly emphasized. Granted, cultural life in Ames cannot be compared with that of the nearest big city, Minneapolis/St. Paul, but it is infinitely richer than that of Oak Ridge.

In terms of climate, we moved nearly 900 miles southeast, out of the "frigid zone" into the "temperate zone." Culturally, we found ourselves in Jim Crow country—directly above Mississippi and Alabama.

We made our home in that conservative small Southern town for thirteen years.

Our living environment was irrelevant to Sam. In fact, he found a haven in Oak Ridge. He had rejected a joint appointment in the physics department at University of Tennessee in nearby Knoxville. For the first time in seventeen years, he could devote all his working hours to research, free of teaching duties, numerous and interminable faculty and committee meetings, and backstabbing departmental politics.

He was ecstatic, like a kid in a candy store. To maximize his time in this candy store, he asked me to take over our household financial matters. If I had letters for him to mail on his way to work, he couldn't wait for me to go upstairs to fetch them; he was simply too eager to get to the office. I would have to wait till the next day.

The orthopedic surgeon I worked for before Andrea was born loved to tell the story of his father, who was a carpenter and did a lot of work for IBM. The fledgling company wished to pay him with stocks, but his father preferred cash. Dr. Pisnali always ended his story with a rueful smile: "Just think, if my dad had taken the stocks instead, I'd be a playboy on the Riviera today."

I always had the feeling that if Sam ever had a chance to be a playboy, he would still be doing physics. The psychologist who taught him biofeedback for his hypertension seemed to agree. She said people with childhoods like his tended to become alcoholics, but Sam was using physics to get his highs and block out his pain.

Sam was happy in his work as a fish in water; Andrea went back to college at UC Berkeley in the fall; Clifton had to adjust to a new high school, where he was not exactly embraced by his fellow students; and I, with a bulging scrapbook filled with clippings of eighty-six lead stories, hit a dead end at the town's only paper. Although I did get an occasional guest column published, my hopes of freelancing were soon dashed.

Instead, I got a part-time teaching job at UT Knoxville. Correcting student papers one day, frustrated and desperate, I had an idea. Since freelancing in English was no longer possible, why not do it in Chinese instead?

After publishing a few *serious* pieces, I happened to read an essay entitled, "The Cocktail Party" by Wu Luqin, a revered Chinese humorist. Suddenly, my years of attending cocktail parties in Iowa came rushing back with stories that demanded to be told.

I was fifty years old and hadn't forgotten the lesson I had learned at sixteen (and again at thirty-seven) from my father—he didn't like my writing humor essays.

But I just couldn't let those inner voices die, so I wrote the piece and sent it to the literary section of *World Journal*, the leading Chinese language paper in the U.S. that published daily on both coasts and had subscribers across the country.

Thus I embarked on a twenty-year freelance career, writing literary essays and short fiction in Chinese.

Beginning with "The Cocktail Party" (mine shared the same title as Wu Luqin's), the majority of my essays contained a touch of humor. For this I have to thank my progenitor; humor came naturally—I didn't force it, and I couldn't stop it. Whenever I was powerless to change what pained me or irritated me, I would simply find an amusing angle, write about it, and feel better. It became an important part of my coping mechanism in life.

Regrettably, my father still didn't like it. He was angry, and his anger found its expression in various unmistakable ways.

§

I was not the first one to run afoul of my father; Charley was. Back in the sixties, after Charley had devoted ten years to his education and to supporting all of us through school, he probably thought he had accomplished his mission and was free to live his own life. But he was wrong.

I suspect Charley's next phase of obligations was never spelled out for him. My father certainly dropped so many hints that even I was not unaware of them, but Charley seemed peculiarly obtuse. He consistently rejected "perfect" marriageable candidates my father sent him from Taiwan. Communications between them became so unpleasant that Charley stopped writing home every week, claiming he was too busy. In the meantime, he found he didn't like academic life, so he left North Carolina to join the U.S. Department of Agriculture in Washington, D.C. He bought a townhouse in Arlington, Virginia.

In the spring of 1970, he surprised us all by getting married, and my parents traveled from Taiwan to attend the wedding. Perhaps Charley hoped his marriage would relieve some tension between him and our father, but he chose the wrong bride—a Caucasian from New England.

Instead of "Father" and "Mother," the titles my parents considered unquestionably theirs as the groom's parents, she addressed them as Mr. and Mrs. Liu, striking chills in their hearts. To their relief, the marriage lasted only two years, and the couple had no children.

While Charley's behavior didn't exactly please our father, Lining's life was also problematic. Shortly after Sam and I left New York, she relocated to Albany, New York and discovered she absolutely detested small-town living. After two miserable years, she went back to school at the University of Maryland. Fortunately, she fell in love with the D.C. area and worked as a librarian at the Library of Congress while going to school. She rented an apartment near Charley in Arlington.

My father was very much heartened by the fact that Charley and Lining were now living in close proximity. He had always wanted his children to stay together. Taking care of my baby sister was a priority he exhorted tirelessly in his letters to me in New York.

On the ashes of Charley's failed marriage, a joyous family reunion was held in Charley's home in the spring of 1974.

We were all there. Paul, Francene, and their three children drove down from New Jersey; Cecilia and Ed came from Akron, Ohio with their two children; Sam and I flew from Ames with Andrea and Clifton; even Small Uncle and Small Aunt made the journey from Toronto. Our mother had been on a long visit with Charley, so she simply stayed put, and our father flew in from Taiwan. He was in top form, king of his domain and the star of the show.

Rushes of warm and cozy feelings engendered by the occasion were destined to subside. On the eve of our departures, as Cecilia was busy in the kitchen preparing blue crabs to take back to Ohio, Lining announced to us that she was contemplating moving to China.

In 1974, Chairman Mao was still alive, and the Cultural Revolution showed no signs of abating. Moving there from America was tantamount to suicide. The rest of us fell into a hushed silence when my father started to cry, declaring, "Go if you must, but remember, the moment you leave these shores, I will commit suicide."

Perhaps Lining made the dramatic statement just to get attention (an ill-considered gesture), but for the first time, our father was reduced to a toothless tiger and exposed by his beloved "breast-hugging baby." It was embarrassing, even pathetic.

Of course nothing came of it. Everyone just pretended the incident hadn't happened, and it was never mentioned again.

Although what Lining had said was merely an empty threat, she had hit our father's sore spot. He was so paranoid about the Communists that it bordered on the irrational. In fact, a few years later, he sent a letter telling us all to move to Brazil because he had heard it would be safer than the United States.

Since I was geographically isolated from my siblings and cousins, I had no idea how they responded. But Sam did write a letter explaining the impossibility of his finding a job in Brazil; he didn't even know a word of Portuguese. My father never replied, and the matter was dropped.

§

Over the years, I had tried my best to stay in my father's good graces. When Sam served as a visiting professor at UC Berkeley and we were living in California, my father was in his late middle age and had become interested in health and nutrition. For his personal perusal, I spent the year there translating Adelle Davis' book *Let's Eat Right to Keep Fit*. My translation was serialized in the "Home and Family" page of *Dahua (Big China) Evening News*—ironically the same paper that sponsored the essay contest when I was sixteen—and later published as a book. I never received a word of thanks from my father, but he understood I did this for him and he approved.

A few summers later, when my father suffered a heart attack, I went home to help and slept on the couch in his Taipei Veterans General Hospital room for two weeks until he was released. I could tell that he was glad I was there.

In the summer of 1980 we were in Berlin, where Sam was a visiting professor at Free University. My mother suffered a severe heart attack while she and my father were visiting Charley and Lining in Virginia. I flew back to help, leaving Sam and the children to fend for themselves for the remaining two months of the summer.

Twice at my father's urgings, I helped Lining with her thesis. During the seventeen years we lived in Iowa, she only came to visit us once—to get help with her master's thesis. By then she had already spent six years at the University of Maryland, and her adviser had criticized her writing mercilessly.

Reading and writing had never been Lining's strong suit. There was a dearth of books in her apartment. Instead, it was filled with appalling piles of yellowed, dusty, and unopened issues of *The New York Times* and *The Washington Post*. At times she could be caught asleep on her living room couch, a newspaper covering her face.

I took nearly three weeks off of my own writing to work with her. The thesis passed the scrutiny of her professor, and she finally received her master's degree.

She made her second trip to visit us shortly after we moved to Tennessee. This time she came for help with her PhD dissertation— her advisor had scribbled on her draft, "Your English is barbaric!"

My daughter Andrea, having grown up adept at catching my mistakes in English, had edited my stories when she was in high school. Now a graduate student in theoretical physics at Cornell University writing her own PhD dissertation, she was recruited to help. We mailed drafts back and forth, sometimes at a furious pace. We rewrote Lining's introduction, reorganized and edited the rest of her dissertation—learning some Russian words and pre-Soviet history in the bargain.

Lining would sometimes excitedly exclaim to me on the phone, "That was *exactly* what I wished to say. How did you know it?"

We polished every page of her dissertation, including the acknowledgments section, in which she thanked Charley (for paying for the typing of her dissertation) and everyone else under the sun, but not Andrea or me. She received her PhD and never uttered a word of thanks to us for our work. Neither of us confronted her, figuring it was of no use.

And everything I did for her and for my parents over the years—at much personal and family sacrifice—didn't earn me any brownie points with my father, either.

He never had a good word to say about my writing. None of my book titles pleased him (he lived to see four published), and he consistently made disparaging remarks such as: "Different papers continue to publish you because they *happened* to use one of your earlier essays." (I never did understand this logic.)

My father, however, loved to mention Joyce, Sam's sister-in-law, a famous poet, essayist, and painter. "Look at her! Her world is immense, her experiences rich, while you're just cooped up in your house. What can *you* write?"

He also took pains to praise the foremost essay writer at the time, "I really admire Qijun. Her essays are perfect; not a word can be changed."

As my father's words washed over me again and again, it gradually dawned on me that he didn't wish me well and that parental love—like other kinds of love—couldn't be bought, not with any amount of hard work, filial devotion, or wishful thinking.

When my friends wrote home, they usually emphasized the good news so as not to worry their parents. By and by, I discovered that maximizing my bad news seemed to please my father more. It became my default approach.

Once I made the mistake of mentioning that both my children were in the gifted students program. My mother was delighted. I happened to turn my head; my father's face was frosted over. Several times when others praised my writing in front of my father, his face would instantly fall and he would change the subject.

Perhaps as a result, self-doubt has been my lifelong companion.

I often feel I'm fighting a losing battle against a deep sense of unworthiness. Sometimes I have also detected a self-hatred in myself, a self-destructive urge. I seem to be anxious to validate my father's judgment and belief that I won't amount to anything no matter how hard I try. I seem to have developed paradoxical tendencies: I work hard and strive to do well, yet I can't help sabotaging what little success I achieve.

Every time someone compliments my work, I feel embarrassed, uncomfortable, and undeserving. It is as if I am not standing on firm ground, as if something has been pulled out from under me, or nothing was there to begin with.

Baffled and pained by my father's attitude throughout the years, I have never ceased to ponder why my success was so repugnant to him.

Sam's sister Monica, who spends six months of the year in Taiwan, had been friendly with my father. During one of her visits, he confided that Lining was by far the best, the smartest of his three children. "She knows what she's doing," he emphasized.

Could it be that time and again I failed his expectations by doing well? Had I violated his sense of justice and challenged his vision of the rightful family order, the order that he tried to uphold above all—that I was meant to fail and my sister to succeed?

In his mind, the battle lines seemed to have been drawn. I wondered whether each time I achieved something, it was perceived as a blow to my sister, who he believed rightfully deserved the prize over me.

Fathers are supposed to know best, and mine was one who could never be wrong.

Chapter 25

COLLATERAL DAMAGE

To My Mother

And so we revolt against silence with a bit of speaking
— Carolyn Forché

The darkness
in the cave near Chattanooga
overwhelming
suffocating
obliterating all senses—

I could hardly breathe

yet the fish
in the cave's underground lake
live and breed for millennia
just like their brethren outside
with one difference—

they have no eyes

the first girl in your village
to rebel against foot binding
to fight for schooling

to graduate at top of class
with a medical degree

you struggled dauntlessly
out of one dark cave
only to fall in another—
the black hole—

your marriage

the young bride
radiant with hopes for a bright future
in the wedding photo
the strong valiant capable
single parent
who protected and nurtured us
in the war was transformed
by our father

to his ideal helpmate

too busy attending to his wishes
you stopped being a mother to us
submitting your will to
his stronger will you
who had excelled in everything you tried
became an appendage
a gracious hostess
whiling away
your energy and intelligence

playing mahjongg

for years you let him
correct and *approve* your letters
before you stopped writing
to us

COLLATERAL DAMAGE

seeing you
knuckles and knees ravaged
by rheumatoid arthritis
squatting struggling
to tie shoes
for my able-bodied father
I clenched my teeth

to keep from crying

never talkative
you grew quieter still
spending more and more time
in your darkened room

staring at nothing

when the early tendrils of Alzheimer's
pried loose the floodgate
of your psyche
away from Father's presence
the pain the quiet fury that encompassed
the arid desert of your life
for six decades
like dammed acid rain
came bursting forth

for weeks I listened and listened to you
letting tears

quietly roll down my cheeks

that was all I *could* do
all I ever did for you.

Revised July 21, 2005

T he battle of wills between my parents must have been intense throughout the years, but it was never waged in our presence. The hierarchical thinking of Chinese parents simply didn't allow them to bring these matters to their children's attention.

Therefore, when my father complained to me one evening during my visit in Taiwan, I was taken aback. "I've always done what *your mother* wanted," he said. "I went along with her on everything, and she's *still* not satisfied."

So this was how he saw it? I started trembling before my words came out—I had never contradicted him verbally in my life, but I had to do it now. "No, it's just the opposite, and it has taken a tremendous toll on her...." I began to cry but struggled to get the words out. "...And Charley and Lining think so, too."

He was stunned. I could see that he was angry, but he could tell that I hadn't pulled my siblings' opinions out of thin air. I didn't tell him that we had talked about our parents many times and had agreed that our mother was the more intelligent and sensible one. We all would have been better off if she had taken him up on his threat of divorce back in the early fifties. Oh yes, even Lining, who was always on our father's side, agreed with Charley and me.

"He's just like a candle; he'll only buckle when some heat is applied," Charley had said with undisguised contempt and bitterness.

My mother stayed with Charley for months at a time when he lived alone for several years between his two marriages. One time, over a dish of ice cream, a favorite midnight snack for both of them, he asked her, "If you knew what you know now, would you have married him?"

A quick and resounding "NO!" was her answer.

"If you knew what you know now, would you have had kids?"

She waffled, "You guys turned out okay, didn't you?"

The years 1965-66, during which my mother went back to join my father after their two years in Saigon and their first visit to the United States, were the watershed that marked my father's steady career rise and my mother's corresponding rapid deterioration in health.

After several years of misdiagnoses, she was found to be suffering from an autoimmune disease—rheumatoid arthritis. Nothing, not even the exotic silver injections in her knees, eased her symptoms except cortisone.

Despite the excruciatingly painful and debilitating disease, she worked for a while as a cashier at the International House, a youth hostel in Taipei. I still have a hard time imagining that: my mother...a cashier.

My mother had always been a quiet woman. In her old age, she was practically mute. In my weekly phone calls, my father would hold forth on different subjects, while she was completely silent. I would become anxious, "*Muma, Muma,* are you there?"

"Yes," she would answer. "I'm here."

"But you didn't say anything!"

"I was listening."

During my last two visits home in the late 1980s, I was heartbroken to overhear her mumble an old ditty to herself like a mantra: "Marry a man, marry a man; clothes to wear, rice to eat..."

She bore his frequent, contemptuous putdowns—"What do *you* know?"—as her just deserts. When we walked to a restaurant, my father and his close friend Auntie Ren would stride a block and a half ahead, chatting and laughing, leaving my mother dragging painfully behind. She didn't seem to mind.

It was not surprising that my mother's physical and mental decline went hand in hand. When what little fighting spirit was left in her was gone, she began to show distinct symptoms of Alzheimer's disease.

§

My parents were entering their eighth decade. They had enjoyed forty years of peace and prosperity in Taiwan—contrary to my father's dire expectations. Since autumn 1965 when he was called back to work for the Veterans Administration, he had served as president and chairman of the board of several fishing and shipping companies.

In addition to a car and chauffeur, he had an office suite

complete with private bed and shower, enabling him to work for ten more years, if he so chose. He was a man comfortably situated in every way.

After four decades, Taiwan had become home, and it was undoubtedly where my father preferred to live out his remaining years. However, as friends around him began to pass away, my father began to realize that having a child or two nearby would be a help and comfort.

Unfortunately, the grand plan my father had devised and set in motion so many years ago was working too well; all five of us had put down long roots into foreign soil. My parents had no one in Taiwan.

My father wrote a seven-page letter detailing what had happened to his friends in recent months—eleven cases in all. One had suddenly collapsed and died in broad daylight, while trying to hail a taxi after a pleasant visit with friends; another, in a hospital bed with tubes in and out of every orifice, showed his recognition of the visitor with tears. He died alone shortly afterward. My siblings, cousins, and I each received a copy of that letter. What could we do except urge them to move here and promise we would take good care of them?

Did my father think of K then? He had been adamant about K's unsuitability, but life has a way of mocking those whose judgment tolerates no argument.

Over the years, K had become a renowned scholar and sociologist. The most significant among the numerous honors showered on him was being elected a fellow of Academia Sinica, the highest academic institution in Taiwan.

I read about his successes in the Chinese newspapers. For a few years, after those two brief phone calls in New York, he seemed to know where I was. I received an occasional Christmas card, signed with no message, probably during the time he was in the U.S. studying for his doctorate.

When he first went back to Taiwan and became the editor of a prestigious magazine, he wrote me to solicit article contributions. It was a scholarly magazine, and I had nothing to contribute. I think I last heard from him when he sent me a copy of his seminal book.

I knew I came off as cold and unfeeling because I never responded, but I didn't know how to respond. I felt dishonest from the beginning for having hidden my father's edicts from him. That he had gotten the brush-off from my family and I had kept him in the dark about the reason throughout made me feel all the more guilty and unworthy.

The worst was when he asked me to return his letters, probably sometime in the late sixties. I was too ashamed to tell him I no longer had them.

Charley, who for years had handed me those blue aerograms with no question or comment, had at last felt compelled to speak. The fact that I kept them after I married Sam seemed to challenge his sense of fair play. He eventually succeeded in shaming me into burning them on the gas kitchen stove in my Mount Kisco apartment.

I should have had the decency to tell K the truth. I owed him that, but I didn't tell him. I did the cowardly and hurtful thing—I didn't reply.

Once, when I was on a visit home, K happened to be in the newspapers. My father saw it and asked me, "Are you sorry?" I wanted to ask him, "Are *you*?" but I didn't need to. I knew he was sorry. He probably thought that had it not been for him, events might have turned out differently. But he was ascribing too much power to himself. The primary reason I broke up with K was the new two-year military-training rule. In my letters home I never told my parents about the breakup. In fact, I had never once mentioned K or even alluded to his existence.

Except for knowing he did well for himself, K's life has been a question mark to me. Our worlds are so far apart that, for the rest of my life, I won't know anything about him. That decision was made long ago.

No, I was not sorry. But I was angry at my father just the same, for casting a pall over the relationship, for dismissing K so summarily, and for forgetting that he himself had once been a young man—a law student, very much in love, as yet untried and unproven by the vicissitudes of life...

I was also angry with myself for lacking the fortitude to point out to my father that *he*, being neither a science nor an engineering major, would also have been rejected outright had my maternal grandfather had the same rule. Ironically, my mother's field did fall under the desirable category, but how had that helped her?

Like my mother, I was just collateral damage. Unfortunately, some decisions in life are irreversible. Life is not a scientific experiment; you can't simply change one of the variables and run the test all over again to observe the results.

§

My parents were both eighty-two years old in September 1989, when they finally moved to the United States. It was a well-planned and well-executed operation. Charley took two months off work and brought our mother here first. I went to keep her company in a furnished apartment in Virginia, while Charley turned around and flew back to Taiwan to pack and helped our father wrap up their affairs.

The Taiwan apartment sold and the furniture and belongings in a freighter container, our father and Charley landed at Dulles Airport. No one could deny that the whole operation had been a splendid success.

Charley, Paul, Cecilia, and I all attended the reunion dinner with our respective spouses. Lining, who was single, was also there. Of the next generation, only my newly married daughter Andrea was present with her husband Doug.

The patriarch presided over dinner at Peking Gourmet Inn, the Peking duck restaurant in Falls Church, Virginia and favorite eatery of former President George H. W. Bush. My father was head of the house again but in name only, because he was new in this country, a fact that was not lost on him.

Since Charley had been away for two months, leaving his consulting work and his home affairs unattended, he and his wife Sandy left right after dinner. The rest of our party reconvened in our parents' temporary apartment.

As soon as we were seated, Paul's wife Francene launched into a proposal that my parents should transfer their money and apply for welfare. Her parents—former schoolteachers—had done just that. Ironically, Lining, a research analyst in the Social Security Administration, chimed in to agree.

It was apparent that Francene and Lining had discussed the matter ahead of time and decided it was the best way to "protect" my parents' financial resources. They hadn't bothered to inform the rest of us.

They didn't seem to realize they were proposing fraud and that all involved, including our aged parents, could go to jail.

Thanks to Taiwan's prosperity, our parents had more money than they needed. I was not apprised of their actual worth, but we were told that they had sold their apartment on Ren-ai Road in the best district in Taipei at a most opportune time and had converted all of their money to dollars at the most opportune exchange rate.

They probably had more money than all of us put together. Why would they need to stoop to this egregious—not to say illegal—scheme?

Perhaps Lining was too young to remember the times our father had refused bribes when our family desperately needed money. Integrity aside, he had always been protective of his dignity. Why would he want to lose that now? Why would he want to lose control of his money? I knew he wouldn't agree to the plan.

Perhaps Lining's advocacy for the scheme hinged upon the way she had been brought up. She seemed to have a lawless streak since she was a child. With our father as her sword, the world was her oyster. She could get away with anything.

The youngest in the family, she appeared to crave power and relished the chance to play the big sister. Indeed, Charley had told me a rather shocking story that highlighted her reckless behavior.

Our cousin, Peter—one of Third Uncle Yong-Choen's children who had escaped to Hong Kong and was supported by our father in the sixties—came under Lining's wing in Washington, D.C. Lining adored Peter so much that she was willing to go to any and all lengths to help him. Somehow Peter was acquainted with people in China who wished to sell copies of ancient Chinese volumes on palace sexual techniques—the Chinese equivalent of the Indian *Kama Sutra*, if you will. It happened that Lining had a close friend—nicknamed "Little Canton"—who worked in the rare books division of the Library of Congress, and that section had those very volumes in their archives. The scheme was for Lining to act as the intermediary for Little Canton to "lend" the volumes to Peter, who could get a copy made and airmailed to China.

Charley didn't know whether or not Little Canton had been informed about her role, but he was sufficiently horrified and told Lining, in no uncertain terms, not to attempt any such thing, as all participants would surely be caught and land in jail. He succeeded in forestalling the operation.

Her ideas could be hare-brained. Another time she wanted to hire herself out as an au pair in the Soviet Union to learn Russian. Over the years, Charley shot down so many of Lining's ideas—not all of them lawless, of course—that he was convinced she lacked judgment.

Proposing that our parents go on welfare certainly fell into the extralegal category. What would Charley say about this if he had not gone home early?

Meanwhile our father became enraged and burst into tears, but surprisingly he didn't address the crucial issues: the law or the ethics. Instead, overcome by self-pity, he spoke through sobs, "I worked and suffered all my life to come to this new land. Now that I'm finally here, entrusting our two sets of old bones to your care, you want to leave me to the charity of the Americans? I can see that nobody's going to come and collect my dead body after I die!"

Lining was quick to protest, "*Baba*, how can you say that?"

"I shouldn't say it? I shouldn't bring up the matter of collecting bodies? Would you rather leave mine on the streets for the dogs to gnaw on?"

Incredulous, I sat motionless and speechless. It crossed my mind that our only other family reunion had ended with another one of Lining's preposterous ideas, and our father in tears.

It had been fifteen years since that disastrous night—so long ago that it almost seemed like a dream. However, this night was no dream. Our parents were here, in the United States, to live out the rest of their lives.

Chapter 26

THEIR GOLDEN YEARS

Surprisingly, as flagrant as Francene's and Lining's scheme was, my father didn't hold any grudges against them. In fact, the next morning he and Lining seemed to have formed a team and were thick as thieves. Lining seemed to have undergone a physical transformation overnight—she looked more relaxed and secure, even younger. For the first time in many years, she appeared to be in her element.

Though we were a party of four in the following few days, as Lining and I accompanied our parents to several different banks to deposit their money, it was a party of two as far as my father and sister were concerned. I was relieved, however, there was no more talk about my parents applying for welfare.

We had to go to different banks because the maximum guaranteed each customer by the government in the event of a bank closure is $100,000. I don't know how many banks we went to each day, but on the morning of the third or fourth day, my father carried a briefcase containing what he alluded to as his "little goldfishes" (gold bars) and my mother's important jewels.

Unlike me, my mother loved jewelry. She was fond of saying that she could easily spend a million dollars in a matter of hours by visiting the best jewelry stores.

After my father received the key for a big safe deposit box, he said casually, "It would be too crowded in there." He didn't look at me when he made the comment, and he didn't need to. I took the hint and stayed with my mother in the lobby while my father went

My parents at their 60ᵗʰ wedding anniversary; Maryland, 1991

in the vault with Lining.

Sam and I stayed for a week after the reunion dinner. We were all expected to help our parents get settled. The most important aspect was, of course, the management of their estate. To this end, Lining had already made an appointment with a hotshot attorney at an exorbitant fee of $500 an hour. All three children were expected to accompany our parents to the meeting.

The day before, Lining gave Sam a ride to the airport to pick up our rental car. When he got back, he was ashen and shaking with anger.

He told us that as soon as he had gotten in the car, Lining began complaining about Charley and me, demanding, "Who are they to behave as if I did something wrong? What did I do wrong?"

Sam said he tried to diffuse her anger by staying neutral: "When people don't get along, it's usually because both sides have problems..."

Before he'd had a chance to finish, Lining exploded at the top of her high octave voice: "Who are *you* to tell *me* I was wrong? Get out of my car! Get the hell out RIGHT NOW!"

She was driving seventy miles an hour on the Beltway. Sam lost his temper too: "Pull over and I'll get out!"

Sam seemed shattered by the incident. I was upset too. But I was not surprised that Lining had complained about me. For some reason, whether I opened my mouth or not, I seemed to trigger her hostility. However, her blowing up at Sam was new. She had always liked him and had been appreciative just the day before when he had helped her fix her car.

My father's reaction to the incident bordered on the bizarre. He said to Sam, "What's wrong with your wife's younger sister taking a bit of liberty with you? After all, you're her brother-in-law. If not you, whom can she tease and be playful with?" He completely dismissed the fact that what she did could hardly be characterized as playful.

But I was troubled for an additional, more serious reason. While Sam was out in the morning, my father was talking to me about Charley.

He told me that when he and my mother visited us for the first time in 1965, they had deposited the bulk of their savings under Charley's name. They felt safer to have their money in an American bank. After Charley married his second wife Sandy in 1977 (twelve years later), they informed Charley that they needed to take the money back.

His reason for doing so, my father said, was because Sandy came from a problematic first marriage, and her two boys were constantly in and out of trouble. What if something should happen and Charley got caught in a difficult situation because of his stepsons? What if Charley needed extra cash and used that money?

This incident happened so long ago, and nobody had told me—not that I had needed or wanted to know. Now, in 1989, another twelve years later, why did my father suddenly see fit to fill me in on this?

I wasn't baffled for long, for immediately he hit me with the clincher: "Charley has been mad at me ever since, but it was probably *you* who suggested to me to take my money back from him, wasn't it?"

What? The hell I was going to take that rap! But as I opened my mouth to defend myself, it occurred to me that there was no use. Why would he tell me about this history if I had been the one who had made the suggestion? Why did my own father, accuse me when he knew I was innocent? It seemed as if a hand reached deep inside me and snapped the primordial tie that connected me with my father. Suddenly my heart felt heavy.

He was going to make me take the blame in front of Charley to protect my sister.

§

Even before my father arrived, our family dynamics had undergone subtle changes. As the favored child, Lining had never been expected to pull her own weight. This time was no different: I took care of our mother in Virginia while Charley helped our father in Taiwan. Among other chores, Charley had to pack up our mother's room (with strict instructions from her not to leave anything behind). Lining didn't do anything at all.

Without a car, I had walked around the unfamiliar neighborhood to scout for the nearest grocery store or a restaurant I could walk my mother to. Not once in the three weeks did my sister come to visit her or ask if we needed any help.

I knew our relationship had been steadily deteriorating over the years. At first I thought she was suffering from general unhappiness. She was approaching middle age after all and had to struggle with life's demands all by herself. I felt guilty because I had a family and she didn't.

By and by, her unhappiness appeared to focus on me. She didn't bother to hide her disappointment when things went well for me or to cover up her glee when she heard about my misfortunes.

I didn't understand why she seemed to hate me even more after I had helped her with her thesis and dissertation—why, in addition to hatred in her eyes, I saw disgust and contempt.

In time, her hostility expanded like an iceberg under the surface of the frigid sea. It was huge and unyielding, poking out at the slightest opportunity. I grew wary of its sharp tip but was powerless to prevent its jabs.

I often asked myself, "What have I done to make her hate me so? Have I neglected her because I'm too involved with my family? Even little kids have the instinct to know who truly cares about them; why doesn't she?"

Sometimes I would think, "We are sisters, born of the same flesh and blood; how can we be enemies?" Every life has its trials and tribulations. For someone who had been used to everything going her way, setbacks were harder to take. When she found herself downhearted and alone, whom could she take it out on, except me, her own family? As long as I continued to love her, she was bound to turn around one of these days.

I also thought, life was difficult enough. Family members should come together to help one another.

That was what I kept telling myself over the years, but her fierce explosion at Sam seemed to be a declaration of war, a point of no return. It seemed now that our father was here, she no longer needed us.

Sam was not in the mood to analyze the situation. He was so miserable that he became adamant about leaving right away, skipping the attorney's meeting. Rattled by my father's false accusation, I agreed, but I thought I should talk with Charley before going home.

Poor Charley! My father's demand to take his money back must have been a slap in his face.

As a teenager, Charley had been immensely proud, standing guard behind our front gate and refusing boxes lined with cash. Later, he willingly, ungrudgingly shouldered the burdens of supporting us for years. He must have taken great care of our parents' money. Both he and Sandy had well-paid jobs; they were not hard up for money.

Why had my father accused him of possibly embezzling his savings?

The trouble was that our father never cared for Charley. Charley had been given more responsibility simply because he was male and the firstborn. No matter how hard Charley worked, it was not enough. Having left the USDA several years earlier to work as an independent consultant, Charley had taken two months from his lucrative consulting work to devote himself to the move. He had done the lion's share of the work, at great personal financial sacrifice.

But ever since the reunion dinner, my father's anger had been focused on Charley, who had shown a lack of respect for the patriarch by leaving early. He had been busy trying to catch up with work that had accumulated in his two-month absence. He hadn't even bothered to call. In fact, they didn't see eye-to-eye on many issues and had never gotten along well. Two months of enforced togetherness only made the situation worse.

There was a deeper reason for my father's unhappiness with Charley over the years. To please our father, you didn't necessarily have to *do* the right thing, but you did have to *say* the right thing. Charley worked so hard to do the right things, but he consistently said the wrong things, things that greatly offended our father.

Years ago, our father once complained to Charley, "Your mother is so darn stubborn. If I say the sun is round, she insists it is square. Of course she never contradicts me out loud, but I know in her heart she doesn't agree with me."

Charley smiled. "All of us, including *Muma*, don't have the freedom to speak our minds, and we don't have the freedom *not* to speak our minds. Your thought control is as tough and thorough as that of the Communists!"

My father's persistent attempts at dictating to Charley about his marriage caused their worst conflicts. When his wish for Cecilia to be his daughter-in-law failed—"It would be like incest!" a horrified Charley exclaimed when he found out—my father started collecting "dry daughters."

The dry daughter (or dry son) is a peculiar Chinese relationship in which a middle-aged or elderly man or woman expresses fondness for a youngster by "adopting" the latter as a dry daughter or dry son. For a girl, a gift of jewelry is usually offered, and in both cases, special favor and status are bestowed. The closest Western counterpart would be a goddaughter or godson, although there is no religious connotation attached to dry daughters and sons. The word "dry" denotes the lack of a blood connection.

The dry daughters my father chose were daughters of his good friends. Beautiful and talented, they shared an additional virtue—they adored their dry father.

But Charley refused to cooperate. He wouldn't even buy a plane ticket to go and visit a girl. Time and again he told our father not to bother, that it was *his* business to find a wife, only to be told, "You're my son; your business is *my* business. Why do you differentiate yourself from me? Have you been poisoned by thoughts of freedom because you have spent too many years in America?"

Sometimes my father would try a different tack: "Let's say you are going to Florida, and I prepare a map of Florida for you. What's wrong with that?"

Charley replied, "I'm not going to Florida. Why would I need your map?"

He insisted he was looking for *his wife*, not for his father's daughter-in-law. But my father countered that Charley's wife *would* be his daughter-in-law. What was the difference? Why couldn't Charley understand that?

Charley did find his own wives. His second wife Sandy was a colleague of his at the USDA, but she is also a Caucasian. Since it was a second marriage for both, a simple wedding was held at Charley's house.

Again, both my parents made a special trip from Taiwan, and the rest of our family attended. We met Sandy's two sons from her previous marriage.

Again my parents found the bride didn't pass muster, and on this subject, my mother happened to agree with my father. Ironically, while the two parties in the marriage were able to ignore the boundaries of race, my parents' racism was showing—not atypical of most Chinese parents' attitudes.

Disappointed as they were about Charley's marrying a Caucasian, it didn't stop my father from immediately lobbying his new daughter-in-law for a grandson. Sandy said she was willing, but it was up to Charley. To which my father responded, "What does Charley have to do with it?" Not surprisingly, Charley felt *he* was the one to decide whether he wanted a baby, *not* his father. This time, however, he kept his opinion to himself and took steps to ensure my father would never have the gratification of having a grandson.

After a few years, my father couldn't wait any longer. He was in his seventies; how long should he be expected to wait? He began to sound pathetic: "Without a grandson, how am I going to face my forebears in the underworld?"

"Don't you worry, *Baba*," Charley assured him. "You can tell them you fulfilled your duty; you had a son. It's not your fault that your son didn't produce any grandsons. Tell them to come to *me* to settle the score."

§

Charley's reaction to what happened after he left the reunion dinner was one of subdued resignation. Like me, he knew our father wouldn't agree with the welfare scheme. "Lining's head is hopelessly muddled" was his only comment.

When I told him that our father had accused me of suggesting that he take his money back from Charley, my brother simply let out a long *phooey*.

"He knows and I know it was Lining who drove the wedge," he said wearily. Lining was the only one who knew about the money and about Sandy's boys. She had never liked Sandy—or for that matter, Charley's first wife.

Before Charley returned the money, he showed the savings account book to our father. "Look, only interest went in and not a penny has been withdrawn."

Whether we attended the attorney's meeting the next day wouldn't make any difference. Charley shrugged, "They'll do what they want anyway."

Just the same, it occurred to me that Lining's outburst might have been a deliberate move to ensure that Sam and I would absent ourselves from the meeting. She succeeded, of course.

On the phone, my father told me I had to "make peace" with Lining before visiting him again: "We're a happy and harmonious family; we don't have grudges to bear. If you want to come and see me, you must go and shake hands with Lining."

"It's not a matter of shaking hands. How can we be together when every sentence of hers has a barb in it?"

"Oh, it's all her fault, is it? Does she hate you that much?"

"I don't know why she's like this. Why don't you ask her?"

"If she really hates you, has she shot you with a gun or stabbed you with a knife?"

"Sometimes words can hurt more than guns or knives, *Baba*."

"You'll be sorry one day! By that time it'll be too late to regret—

why didn't I listen to my father? When that day comes, you can go and cry in front of my tombstone!"

He hung up the phone.

After this exchange, I was terrified when it came time to visit them next. I felt as if I were about to enter a lion's den. To help with my anxiety, I made an appointment with the Knoxville psychologist who was teaching Sam biofeedback for his hypertension.

She opened the session by asking me about my childhood. As if her question opened a spigot, I started to cry and was unable to stop. Where did all those tears come from? Were they about my childhood or my whole life? I cried the whole session.

For the first time in my life, I realized something was seriously wrong.

Chapter 27

A Confession

When Sam was in graduate school in Iowa, he wore mismatched socks to classes one day, only to discover his mistake when he took them off at night. As a man oblivious to color, aesthetics, or fashion, he was content to leave matters of clothing to me after we were married. I bought all his clothes and decided what he would wear to face the world.

When the children were older and could fend for themselves, I took to indulging in the luxury of a little extra sleep on some mornings. Once in a while, however, I would crack open an eye to catch him tiptoeing out of the room. I would holler, horrified, "You can't go to the office wearing that!" Deflated, he would come back and change.

Sam's disregard for his appearance stemmed from his low self-image. His parents, neither of whom could have been accused of being attractive, would compete to "disown" him. His mother would say he resembled his father, while his father would retaliate and claim that Sam looked just like his mother. Thus, even as a small child, he knew he was ugly. He grew up uninterested in his appearance and never took a second look at his own image in photos. "Well, it just looks like me," he would say.

He was scrawny in his youth but filled out some during his late middle age. More importantly, he was becoming prominent at Oak Ridge National Lab—winning awards, being elected to the Executive Council of the American Physical Society, appointed a Fellow at the Laboratory—so that his large photo, among others so anointed, hung on the wall outside the Director's office. He was also given the extremely rare honor of delivering a laboratory-wide lecture.

All of the publicity made him a local celebrity of sorts and a magnet for female attention, especially for two young and pretty Chinese wives who worked at the Lab.

The more attractive and aggressive of the two, "P," would mysteriously appear at Sam's side at Chinese social gatherings whenever I was momentarily diverted elsewhere. In addition to exchanging pregnant glances, he would sometimes give her a ride home at her request. It didn't escape my notice that he had been paying more attention to his appearance and had even begun buying some of his own clothes, including a suit.

It was a gorgeous September day in 1992. President George H. W. Bush was running for re-election and having a rough time. In August, Barbara Bush had attended the Republican National Convention and declared at the podium that, among other virtues, her husband was "the most decent man" she had ever known. Her performance didn't go far in dispelling persistent rumors of his affairs, but it did inspire a satirical piece by Mike Royko, *Chicago Tribune*'s national syndicated columnist.

I was writing a satirical piece of my own, using Royko's column as a jumping-off point, when I took a break after dinner to shop at the local supermarket. I ran into P. Oddly, as she chatted with me, she had pity in her eyes. My latent suspicion was suddenly aroused—what had transpired that qualified me for her pity?

I put this question to Sam when I got home. He claimed he didn't know, but *I* had some inkling. He enjoyed her attention and—consciously or not—was being drawn gradually towards something more serious. Towards the verge of an affair. Enough feeling and interest suffused the air that P felt like a victor and, therefore, could afford to look down on me.

Sam was fifty-nine-years old. Back at Iowa State, the lucidity of his lectures in the most difficult graduate courses had consistently drawn the greatest number of students from not only physics but also other related disciplines. His colleagues marveled at how often he rendered an abstract and complex idea easily understandable. So it never ceased to amaze me how totally inept he was on emotional issues. All his clear thinking and analytical power seemed to elude him. He was quick to perceive an ordinary comment as a reproach and instantly turned defensive. Discussion became counterproductive.

I knew I had to take care of the problem without his help. At the same time, I felt I needed to consult someone and thought of Monica, Sam's oldest sister. A few days later she called and said bluntly, "You're barking up the wrong tree. It's your sister."

I was totally flummoxed. What did she mean, my sister? How had my sister gotten involved in this sorry affair?

"Sam told me you're making a mountain out of a molehill," she explained. "When the mountain was staring you in the face, you never saw it; right now you are taking a molehill for a mountain."

She might as well have been speaking in code. So P was a molehill and my sister had been a mountain? The implication took a while to sink in. It was as though I had swallowed something unexpectedly spicy. The burn started on my tongue, spread to my mouth, throat, esophagus, and head, setting off a series of small, slow explosions, until I needed to do whatever was possible to deaden the pain…

Right away I dialed Sam at his office. Before I had a chance to speak, he told me he needed to learn to use the new Macintosh computer that had just arrived and would come home later.

Coward! He was trying to delay the hour of reckoning.

Unbelievably, I was my usual acquiescent self. Even at this juncture, I couldn't say, "Come home this minute or else." Instead, I headed upstairs to search our photo albums for clues—clues from the time I thought my cup of happiness was running over, when I thought I had a devoted husband, a baby, and a sister who was my best friend…

How young we looked, how seemingly innocent they were—and how stupid I was! I wished I could wipe that foolish, complacent smile from my face. I wished I could tear up and burn the albums—the record of my stupidity and blindness.

But how could I tear and burn those years from my life?

When Sam returned home that afternoon, he didn't bother to

sit down. He just stood facing me and started to pour out his story. I stood, too, bug-eyed and slack-jawed, staring at this stranger, the father of my children, while he revealed the secret life that he had kept from me for the last thirty years.

Do I know this man at all? Why is he telling me this tale?

In his telling, he was so engrossed in his own misery and suffering that he had no room for feelings for me. There was no pity, not even an apology.

It took him several days to unburden himself. To this day, I'm still at a loss to recall how we went through this long ordeal. He would take breaks to rest, eat, and sleep before resuming his narrative. Being sickly, he had always taken meticulous care of himself, eating and sleeping on schedule. This time was no exception.

Perhaps shock was a powerful anesthetic. Many times I wanted to call out, "Please...don't say any more. It hurts too much," but shock and pride steeled me. Most of all, I listened because I had to know.

When he was done, all I could see around me was devastation and desolation. My thirty-one-year marriage had been a lie. I didn't know how to face that fact, and I couldn't run away from it.

His words still echo in my mind:

Yes, for thirty years, almost a third of a century, I've carried this secret in my heart. I wanted to tell you, but I was afraid. Many times words came to my mouth and I forced myself to swallow them. Sometimes I hoped you would ask me; I waited for you to ask, to force it out of me, leaving me with no choice but to come clean, but you never did.

All these years you really didn't know. You thought you were young, we were newly married, nothing could happen and nothing should happen, but you didn't know there was someone younger than you and...more attractive.

You trusted me completely, but you forgot that I'm made of flesh and blood. The fact of being married is not enough to turn flesh and blood into an inert piece of wood or stone, unresponsive to those around him.

My God! How could I not be attracted to her?! When I saw her beautiful, expressive eyes, I suddenly understood the meaning of the

Chinese expression, "soul-stealing eyes."

She was adept at throwing me a glance upward or sideways from the corner of her eyes. I could literally melt under that glance, and my soul became irretrievably hers.

She loved to tease me. She would insult me to the point that I was gritting my teeth. At the same time, I felt waves of sweetness in my heart.

She made me feel I was the most desirable man in the world.

You really should've been on guard. How could you not be on guard, simply because she was your sister? You even asked me, as if I never noticed: "Lining is pretty, isn't she? She's got long legs, a thin waist, and beautiful eyes."

Later, when we couldn't contain ourselves and made eyes right in front of you, you didn't even see it. You never realized what had happened.

In fact, you were the one who opened the door to welcome the person you should've guarded against the most—your own sister. You were the one who let the wolf inside our house and gave your husband away.

The first time I saw her was when she came from Peabody to New York during spring break. You were in early pregnancy, suffering from all kinds of problems, so your cousin Cecilia and her husband Ed hosted a dinner in their apartment.

All evening I felt her eyes on me. While talking with others, she never forgot to steal a glance at me. She clearly had no interest in Ed.

Someone asked her after dinner what she thought of her new brother- and cousin-in-law. She announced that it just so happened she had orders from her parents to send report cards home on Ed and me. She gave Ed ninety-five points.

"As for Sam..." she said with a naughty smile, glancing at me from the corner of her eyes, her voice like drops of honey, "he has failed. He'll be booted from our family, kicked out!" And she stamped her foot for emphasis.

I was stunned and turned red. I wanted to say, "Kick me out? What will your sister say?" but her words and the way she delivered them shocked me so much I couldn't strike back.

You are sisters and had grown up in the same family. I thought the two of you would be very much alike and had never imagined that while you were predictably well-behaved, she was a combination of both child and seductress. She was a spoiled little girl on her father's lap who could say or do whatever she pleased, and a mercilessly flirtatious temptress, all in one irresistible package. Her innocence was tinged with desire; her seemingly unintentional actions carried not so innocent designs, a blend of angel and devil.

Of course I couldn't analyze the situation at the time. I was simply astonished: She had just graduated from college—where had she learned these skills of attracting and tantalizing men? I was thrilled in her presence. My blood vessels seemed to dilate and my limbs tingled, almost as if I were making love. At the same time I sensed some faint signs of danger.

When she moved to Queens, she would come directly from work every Friday, carrying her overnight bag. Every Thursday, you would go shopping, stuffing the refrigerator full of her favorite foods.

I was also excited about her coming here, but my excitement was mixed with an element of unease and fear. I couldn't read her feelings or her attitude towards me. I often asked myself: Is she trying to seduce me, or am I overreacting? Maybe it was just the way she was; maybe she was like this with everybody.

I tried to drop a hint to you—"Lining is no longer a child. She should have her own life and meet other people. She shouldn't spend every weekend with us."

But you said, "She's new here. She has no friends and doesn't drive. What will she do on weekends if she doesn't come here? How can I let her be cooped up in her small apartment sleeping the hours away, without even a decent meal?"

And you added, "I'm cooped up here all week, exhausted from running after Andrea. I have no adult conversation during the day. Lining is my sister and my best friend. I look forward to her weekend visits. Don't you enjoy her company too?"

Aah! You were really blind! People say the most dangerous times in a marriage are when the wife is pregnant or the kids are young. That is so true. Andrea wasn't quite a year old, catching every bug that came along. When she wasn't sick, she was headstrong and rambunctious, getting into all sorts of trouble—she was not an easy baby to raise.

In fact, you really should bear part of the responsibility. Your attention was always on Andrea; you were deaf and blind to everything

Lining, 1963

Her inscription at the back of photo

else. You trusted me too much and didn't suspect Lining at all.

You worried that Lining would get bored, and you loathed leaving Andrea with a babysitter, so you suggested that I take Lining to the movies and ice-skating. You can't imagine how it affected me when she leaned on my shoulder during the movies and held on to my hand on the ice rink without letting go.

Do you remember? Although she was here every weekend, her most beautiful photo was sent to us by mail.

I found it in our mailbox when I got home one evening. You were busy feeding Andrea, who was still recovering from a bad case of bronchitis. When you saw me come in the door with the mail, you only had time to quickly glance at it before handing it back to me. You remarked, "She really looks beautiful in this picture," and returned to Andrea who had started fussing again.

In the photo, Lining's long raven hair is pulled back and swept up. Her face is on the verge of breaking into a smile, and her eyes radiate a rare tenderness. Not daring to let my eyes linger, I gently put the photo down and was struck by the words she had written on the back, "To the one I like very, very much, Lillian." (She signed it with her English name.)

Nine short words in English, in her uninhibited handwriting. My scalp turned numb and tingly, and my breathing stopped for a moment.

I quickly turned the photo face up and glimpsed at you. You hadn't noticed.

The photo came with two of her other graduation headshots, but no words were written on those.

All evening I felt disturbed, stealing a look at the photos once in a while, trying to figure out what she meant. I knew I couldn't ask Lining. There was no point. By that time I knew her better. I imagined she would reply with no hesitation, "Of course I mean my sister—don't you like your sister too? Ha! Ha! Ha!"

After getting me speechless and blushing, she would give me an innocent smile, her eyes imparting something not quite so innocent. My heart would start to pound, and I would feel like a fool.

The following weekend she was talking and laughing as usual. When you mentioned the photo, she simply shrugged, "Yeah, it was okay." She seemed her normal self, and I again suspected myself for reading too much into everything.

That summer, your brother Charley came to New York to visit us. The afternoon he left, Andrea had a fever and you decided to stay home. Lining and I took him to the airport. I had caught Andrea's bug, started sneezing, and taken two cold tablets before leaving the house. On the way home from the airport, I became so drowsy that I could hardly keep my eyes open.

Lining thought of a way to keep me awake. She used both of her hands to fold my right hand and occasionally scratch it lightly a couple of times. I drove home all the way with my right hand tucked between hers.

Lining and I had had hand contact during ice-skating, but this time seemed entirely different. "Flattered" is a far from adequate word to describe my state of mind. I was so shocked and thrilled that I lost all my drowsiness. At the same time, I was deeply perplexed. What did this mean? How could she be interested in me? Had she forgotten I was married to her sister?

You're extremely passive. When we were together, I always had to take the initiative. Now, for the first time in my life, I had such a lovely girl showing me time and again that she liked me—a lot. I was drunk with happiness.

For some reason that day she was wearing that dark green sleeveless dress of yours. It confused me. It was hard to tell whether the girl who was folding her hands over mine was you or your sister...

I tried to rationalize: she was just an emotionally immature girl; she probably thought of me as an older brother. I had no younger sister. Now I had one who cared about me, and I cared about her. What was wrong with that?

But I never dared to tell you about holding hands.

The famous Chinese adage warns, "One misstep can lead to regrets forever." I always visualized it as someone stepping over the edge of a cliff. I believed it couldn't happen to me. Now I know otherwise—you step over a cliff because you think you're far from the edge, and it's safe to keep going. Or you think you're stationary, just maintaining the status quo, but in reality you are going forward. That was what happened to me.

Every Friday I eagerly waited for her. When you were busy making dinner or attending to Andrea, she devoted all her attentions to me. She thought of all kinds of ways to tease me. While she was making fun of me, her eyes were telegraphing an opposite message. I was lost right there in our own living room, I was lost in her insouciant smiles and tender eyes, with you bustling around and Andrea underfoot.

Every Friday I went to meet her train and drive her to our apartment. It was the only time we were alone. I don't remember how it happened or when it began. She would get off the train; my left hand would reach out to take her overnight bag, while my right hand naturally grabbed hold of hers.

Hand in hand, her head leaning on my shoulder, it seemed to take only a minute to walk from the platform to the parking lot, but it also took so long that it seemed an eternity. I felt like a millionaire with the world's most beautiful girl on my arm. All my life I had never felt so proud, so rapturous, and—so guilty.

In the car I would squeeze her hand without a word, and she would squeeze mine. We communicated all our feelings, our love for each other, by squeezing hands. We had no need to speak.

But was that true? Can hand squeezing really represent everything? Years later, whenever I thought about those moments with her, they always appeared so short-lived, so tainted with suffering.

When we got home and you were so happy to see us, I felt even guiltier and more remorseful; my emotions churned so violently that I could hardly keep calm.

The two of you are so different! You're like an open book, whereas she kept all her emotions inside. She was as sweet and natural with you as ever, as if nothing had happened, as if she had been an entirely different person. I would start to question again—did I just dream up what had happened moments earlier? Had everything just been a hallucination?

But at some point, something did change: she and I began to avoid eye contact. When our eyes happened to meet, I would, as if it were a reflex, steal a look at you; I couldn't help it. I knew you—you were not going to put up with this. If you found out what was happening, you would leave me.

But you still didn't know. Sometimes, you obviously saw something fishy, but you didn't get it. You are a smart woman. How could your attention to Andrea have so thoroughly blinded you?

I became more and more uneasy. Outside our apartment door, she and I were a couple deeply in love, but inside we were in-laws. It didn't appear to bother her, but I was going crazy. I felt schizophrenic. More than feeling remorseful towards you, I was filled with disappointment and contempt with myself. Who was I? All my life I had fancied myself to be an honest, upstanding person, but now I had turned into a sneaky liar with plenty to hide. I had become a stranger, a stranger I didn't like and looked down upon—and that stranger was me!

Many times, I decided to stop this: no more holding hands or making eyes. But come Friday, as I looked into her expectant face or outstretched hand, my determination would instantly collapse. I finally had to admit to myself, I had fallen off the cliff. I was in love with her.

I asked myself, how had it happened? Had I been unguarded because she appeared to be ambivalent? The line between fondness and love was only a thread, and I obviously had crossed it without realizing.

It has been thirty years since I first fell for her, yet it's still hard for me to tell you because I couldn't admit it to myself. When I fell in love with her, I did want to take it a step further. In movies or novels, doesn't the protagonist always sleep with the third party?

It was different in our case, however—our relationship seemed to have a fixed boundary. Once we had progressed to that point, it became stationary.

Every time I suffered from a bad conscience and decided to stop holding hands, she would reach over to me. I was powerless to resist her. But when I threw all caution to the wind and tried to embrace her, she would immediately retreat. No, she didn't hesitate out of fear of censure from others or harm done to you; rather, it was a swift change of attitude. Instantly, her face would frost over, turn green, and her lips would turn white and form two straight lines. She was furious at me!

I was taken aback. I was chastened—no, frightened. All my romantic feelings went out the window. But when I stopped cold, she would encourage me by leaning on my shoulder again. It became a game of seesaw.

It is incredible that for almost a year, we repeated this game over and over again. We seemed to be sitting at opposite ends of an emotional teeter-totter, maintaining her required balance, neither going up nor going down.

Sometimes I felt she was expecting more from me, but I'd be damned if I knew what that was! I knew for certain that she didn't want to sleep with me, as is the usual progression between a man and a woman in love. She didn't allow me to do anything more than hold hands, but she wouldn't let me stop holding hands either.

Her feelings for me seemed to be fixed at a certain level, while mine were ever escalating. I couldn't stop, and I didn't know what to do. It hurt so much I thought I was going out of my mind. Besides, I had to think about you and Andrea.

Oh, it was excruciating! I fell in love with her, but didn't fall out of love with you. It was the first time in my life that I learned a man could be in love with two women simultaneously, and that it was not a good fortune but the worst misfortune. It could ruin all four of us, including our innocent baby.

I felt so lonely, so utterly helpless. I didn't have anyone to talk to or to ask for advice. Most importantly, I couldn't discuss this with you. Normally, you and I talk about everything; we were not just a couple who loved each other but also fellow soldiers in the trench fighting shoulder to shoulder against a cruel and pitiless world.

Now something had happened, something so serious that it could destroy our marriage, and I couldn't talk to you. I knew how much you loved your sister. I had the feeling that you were willing to cut your chest open to give her your heart. And you were not going to believe me. You were going to blame me for seducing your innocent sister. I was convinced that if things came into the open, Lining was going to deny everything, leaving me without a leg to stand on.

Basically, I couldn't understand or trust Lining. You and I, from our early dating days, were always wholehearted about our emotions. I never needed to hide my feelings towards you, and I didn't. I never had to guess how you felt about me. But Lining...after she had actively won my love, I still didn't know her heart.

I didn't know whether she really loved me, and I didn't dare ask. If she answered yes, I wouldn't know what to do; if she said no, I couldn't take the blow.

It wouldn't have been hard for a girl like her to find an excellent husband. Why was she wasting her time on me—a married man and her brother-in-law? If she really loved me, why was she so cold to me at times? If she didn't love me, why did she hold hands and make eyes with me?

Sometimes I suspected that she was interested in me precisely because I was your husband. But if it wasn't me she was after, what was it? If I made up my mind to leave you and declared my love for her, would she accept me? I didn't think so.

Besides, even if she truly loved me and wanted to marry me, could I leave you and our child and marry her? I couldn't! You trusted me so implicitly; how could I betray you? How could I abandon the child I fathered? If I did that, how could I face myself for the rest of my life?

I found that falling in love with Lining was the most thrilling, the most euphoric experience of my life, yet also the biggest catastrophe. Fate seemed to have played a cruel joke on me. I was happy and content to have married you; I didn't have any need for extramarital love. Who would've thought you'd have a sister? Who would've thought that in a huge country like America, your sister would come to work in New York? How could I have succumbed to temptation? I blamed myself for having been weak. I didn't know how to face the worst crisis of my life.

Meanwhile, her attitude changed. She stopped teasing and tantalizing me. She was no longer sweet to you; instead, she treated you like her maid. But you didn't notice and were still happy to do your best to please her. She became even more impatient with Andrea. She would hold her for a minute and start yelling, "How can this kid be so disgusting? Take her away! Take her away from me!"

She also became absent-minded, leaving her shoes, purse, clothes, half-eaten snacks, briefly read books, and newspapers everywhere. Our living room was littered with piles of her belongings.

After taking her to the train station on Monday mornings, you were exhausted. You told me that one time on the platform she realized she had left her return ticket in her purse in our living room. You ran to the ticket counter with Andrea in your arms and bought another ticket for her. She almost missed the train. You were a nervous wreck after her departure, and you were still oblivious.

But I was alarmed. Was she testing her power? Was she trying to force a showdown between you and me? Did she think that because I was under her spell, she could treat you like this? I started suspecting that maybe she was not as sweet and innocent as she appeared to be.

I realized I couldn't let things go on this way, but I didn't know what to do. I felt desperate, like an animal caught in a trap with no escape.

You also sensed that I was not my usual self. I used the excuse that my research wasn't going well. But in reality, in spite of my emotional turmoil, my research was progressing. Physicists outside the lab were recognizing my work, and I was given a substantial raise.

One weekend, Lining couldn't come. I felt as if a heavy weight had been lifted off my shoulders. I suggested that we pack a picnic and go to the park. It had been such a long time since the three of us had gone out together—a long time since we had felt so relaxed and happy. Even Andrea seemed to be particularly joyous as she ran, jumped, and even rolled on the grass. I suddenly realized that love should be like this: simple, open, and peaceful, not something conflicted and incomprehensible that left me bewildered, ashamed, and guilt-ridden.

The job offer from Iowa State came out of the blue, and I seized it like a drowning man grabbing hold of a life buoy.

I knew you would object to my taking the offer. I knew how much you loved New York City. To leave that stimulating metropolis to live in a small Iowa town? But to my astonishment, you didn't want to leave because of Lining!

"My sister came to New York because of us," you said. "She hasn't been here for even two years. How can we abandon her and move away? What would I say to my father? He really wants me to take care of her!"

I had to force myself to reply. "It might be good for her that we leave.

She is twenty-five but spends every weekend with us. How is she going to meet other people and get married?"

You must remember how hard I tried to persuade you to accept my rationale.

After you called to tell her we were leaving, you told me Lining was silent for the longest time. Then she started to cry. I felt my heart was being slashed into ten thousand pieces. She did love me after all! And I had hurt her!

I couldn't bear to tell her myself. I didn't have the courage to explain to her the real reason behind my leaving. Taking her to the train station for the last time, I held her hands tightly. "I'm so sorry I had to leave you. I shall miss you very, very much!"

She said, "You're going to be a big professor. You're not going to miss me."

I thought that would be the end of our short love affair.

You and I have been married for thirty-one years. During these years, you often complained that I always put my career first. You didn't know how hurt I felt every time you said that—how unjust your accusation was. I gave up my IBM career to save our marriage.

It was definitely not a wise career move. I will never forget my friends' and colleagues' faces when they heard my decision. Some of their expressions showed, "You ought to get your head examined," for a person in his right mind wouldn't give up his "golden rice bowl" for an iron one.

Although America is supposed to be a classless society, its professional structure is far from fluid. This may not be an appropriate analogy, but I find it like a wedding cake. I had been fortunate to make it from Iowa State to the up-and-coming IBM lab. If I had continued to do well, I would've had a shot at better, top-tier opportunities. Going back to Iowa meant that I would stay at the lower tier forever.

But I've never regretted that choice. I knew that if I had let this matter run its course, it would've burst open sooner or later, and it would've been an irrevocable tragedy for all four of us.

Although I felt fortunate to have escaped, I did pay the price: as far as my work and our living environments were concerned, I had dropped to a much lower level.

But all these were secondary compared to the pain of leaving Lining. We all know the Chinese proverb, "Use your knife of wisdom to cut silk threads of love." Alas! I learned that those threads are too tenacious to cut. Although my body had left New York, my love for her, like a faithful shadow, followed me to Iowa.

You must remember that I was extremely depressed in those days. I told you I had to adjust to teaching, my workload was too heavy, and I had gotten stuck on a knotty research project.

The truth was that when I was too busy or my research hit a snag, I could forget her for a little while. But when I had a moment alone or woke up in the middle of the night—that was when I missed her the most. The way she glanced at me, smiled at me, the jokes she made at my expense...

As terribly as I missed her, my feelings of guilt were worse.

In New York I had been filled with fear. I had been terrified of the inevitable showdown. Once I left, I was full of remorse for her.

Her crying on the phone convinced me that there was no one who loved me as much as she did, and that I had cruelly abandoned her. While I still had my family, she was alone, suffering the bitter fruit of unrequited love and desertion.

I had left without any explanation to her. I was afraid I wouldn't be able to control my emotions once I opened my mouth, and I would make things worse.

After I reached Iowa, I tried to write her countless times. I did finish two letters with great difficulty, but they were so inadequate that I tore them up. I found that some things can't be explained. I could only punish myself through profound self-blame.

If I had met her first, I would've married her without a moment's hesitation. Why had I met her after I was already married? Since I was no longer free, I had to make a choice. I chose to sacrifice her and the love between us. Only by doing so could I minimize the pain and damage for everyone involved.

The only thing that could've alleviated my guilt was for her to soon find a good husband. She'd have no problems in that regard—or at least, I really hoped so. I knew I'd be insanely jealous, but it would be my deserved punishment. I never thought of the possibility that she'd stay single all her life. She left Queens, moved to Albany, and was so miserable there that she told you she contemplated suicide.

Just think of how I felt! This punishment was far more severe than

I'd imagined, and I wasn't prepared for it psychologically. The resulting pain and suffering were unbearable. When I look back, I don't know how I endured those dark, horrendous years.

I never told you about my suicidal thoughts. For years, whenever I drove alone on a narrow, two-lane highway and a truck was coming toward me, a voice inside me would urge, "Hit it! Go ahead and hit it!" It was all I could do to not obey that inner voice. On an especially beautiful spring or fall day, I would think, "Such a gorgeous day! How nice it would be if I could die today!" The strange thing is, I only had those absurd, horrible thoughts when I was alone. They never appeared when we were together.

During the day, I tried hard to keep those thoughts at bay. But asleep, nightmares came often to torture me. Strangely, my nightmares were always the same: I'm solving a problem that has plagued me for months. Suddenly the doorknob turns, and someone barges in. He looks shocked and none-too-pleased, demanding, "Who are you? What are you doing in my office?" Ah, it was my IBM office that I had left long ago. I woke up from my dream, my face covered with tears.

The first time we went back East after moving, Clifton was nine months old and Andrea almost five. You stayed up all night talking with Lining after we had arrived in Albany. Afterward you told me you felt so guilty for having left her. I had to keep a blank face, but the pain and guilt I felt were indescribable...

She looked subdued and unhappy, a different person from the innocent and naughty girl that I had known when I first met her. She picked up Clifton, stared at him for a long time and seemed to think that if I hadn't deserted her, she and I might have had a child about the same age. I felt chilled all over.

I'm a straightforward person. My feelings for you have always been simple, but the way I felt about her was so complicated that I couldn't understand it myself.

All these years, she and I have had many opportunities to see each other. Although we both tried to avoid eye contact, it was sometimes impossible. I was afraid to look into her eyes. They made me want to cry, to pour out my heart and my remorse to her, no matter the consequences. Sometimes I couldn't help but search her face. I wanted to know whether she still loved me and whether she had really loved me then. Could it be that everything had just been an illusion, and I had suffered and ruined my career for nothing?

About ten years ago, my emotions for her started to subside. I was no longer the person I had been, and she was no longer the same, either. Gradually the soul-stealing girl faded away; instead, I now see a woman full of resentment, her eyes brimming with hatred for me and for you. Only pity and remorse remain, but my love for the young girl I left in New York will never die...

For twenty-eight years, I have buried this secret at the bottom of my heart. It's been like a wound that refused to heal, continuing to rot away. And I continued to endure the pain rather than tell you the truth because I was afraid to hurt you and destroy our marriage. I also didn't want to get between you and your sister. I knew only too well how much you loved each other. Unfortunately, all my efforts were in vain. Year after year, I watched helplessly as your relationship went from bad to worse to non-existent.

You didn't understand why she hated you so much, to the extent that she would deliberately badmouth you and drive a wedge between you and your cousins and friends. So many times I heard you sigh, "She used to be my best friend!" One time you even said, "I'm willing to give her everything, except you and my kids." That scared me. I thought you'd found out, but I was wrong. You still suspected nothing.

I came to the verge of confession when I saw how hurt you were by her ferocious outburst at me in the car three years ago. My impulse told me to come clean so that you would understand the problem, but I was afraid that telling you the truth would only devastate you more.

I thought, let me endure the pain in silence. After all these years, I've gotten used to the wound; the pain it causes has become a part of my body and my life. Let me carry it to my grave.

But before I knew it, I blurted it out to Monica. The dam I had built and maintained for twenty-eight years has broken at last.

Now that I've told you the truth, I hope you'll forgive me. My love for her lasted more than twenty years, and I paid a heavy price for it. I tried hard to hide it, but I have been constantly and deeply depressed by the pain and remorse. You may wonder how I could love you under these circumstances; you may think I stayed married to you all these years out of convenience or a sense of duty, not love. I have searched deep in my heart, asking myself the same question, and every time I've reached the same conclusion—I left her because I love you and Andrea. If it'd been only for obligation, I wouldn't have been able to endure all that suffering, I wouldn't have survived all these years.

I love you! I really, truly love you! There hasn't been one day I haven't loved you. Even when I was in love with Lining, I didn't stop loving you.

I was depressed early in life. Every time my mother yelled, "I wish you'd die! Go ahead and die!" I wanted to die. I seriously considered committing suicide when I was eight years old, but I couldn't carry it out. My survival instinct was too strong. I tried to approach my father but he seemed to live in his own world. I grew up knowing nobody loved me, but my urge to love and be loved was surprisingly strong.

The gate of heaven finally opened for me when I married you. They say in every couple, one party is usually more in love than the other. I didn't mind being the one who loved more. But before Lining, I had never been desired. That feeling was absolutely incomparable. She seemed to be the very answer to the innermost need that I hadn't even known I possessed.

Despite what happened, I feel that I've been faithful to you. I didn't do anything more than hold hands with her. No matter what standard you use to gauge our marriage, our lives together have been largely happy and harmonious, and we raised two good kids who are doing well.

I had to put in a lot of effort to pursue you, but she was interested in me from the beginning. How could I not think that she loved me more? But without her, I suffered great pain for many years; without you, I would've lost my will to live. You've become my mirror; only through this mirror can I validate myself.

At a crucial juncture twenty-eight years ago, I made a choice. I was not a hero, but I chose to cut off my limb to save my life, as the Chinese saying goes. As a husband, I might not have been one hundred percent faithful, but at least ninety-nine percent. You may feel that my love has been tainted, that it's no longer pristine or whole, but life is never perfect. I'm not a perfect husband, but I've tried my best.

Our marriage is like something precious and fragile. I treasured it and held it in the palm of my hands. Some outside forces caused me to drop it, but luckily, it didn't break. I picked it up and have been more careful ever since.

I learned an important lesson from this experience. From time to time, female students, secretaries, or colleagues showed their interest in me. Some were single, some were divorced, and others even had husbands and children. They knew that I have a wife. Some threw glances, while others came right out and tried to seduce me. A secretary even gave me a set of her bikini photos. As soon as she was out of my office, I threw them into my wastebasket. I was never tempted—not because I was a saint but because I know I'm no material for extramarital affairs. The price is much too high.

Besides, I learned that although this is a man's world and men frequently take advantage of women, some women, especially the pretty ones, also exploit men. They like to collect men as athletes love to win medals—the more the better. What the victims will suffer is not a consideration.

When I gained more of an understanding of this type of women, I did wonder at times about Lining's motives. She was probably fond of me, but it didn't seem like true love. The way she operated was very much like a cat catching a mouse, with no intention of swallowing it. She just wanted to play with it awhile. Sometimes she would pretend to let the mouse go so she could catch it again, just for her own amusement. What a cruel and dangerous game!

I'm six years older than she but was never her match; the more I think about it, the more I shudder at how close I came to disaster. I don't believe I could've survived it.

Years after we left New York, I suddenly realized that the way she looked at me—forlorn and full of longing—was always reserved for when you were present. However, twice when I was in D.C. for physics meetings, she was perfectly natural and treated me like an old friend. Did she purposely manipulate my feelings to wound you? You two didn't have any feud. Why would she go to such lengths to hurt you? I never dreamed that I was probably only a tool of hers!

In recent years, I did see she was two-faced. When she needed your help with her thesis and dissertation, her voice was sweet like honey. Afterward, she would quickly turn around and treat you as if you were nobody.

What chilled me the most was the episode three years ago, the fierceness with which she screamed at me to get out of her car. Her face turned green, and she was gritting her teeth to the point that her lips had retreated inside and turned white. I have no other way to describe it; she looked truly frightening. Sometimes you, too, get really angry, but I've never seen such a vicious expression on your face.

I was also offended that day by her total disregard of reason, by her refusal to see the situation from a different point of view; it was as though the world existed for her and no one else.

Maybe I was too inexperienced thirty years ago; maybe I idealized her in my memory; maybe she didn't show her true face when she was young; or maybe I don't want to believe that she never loved me and just used me. But I can't believe that the twenty-five-year-old Lining could've been so vicious and manipulative, setting out on purpose to destroy our family.

Oh, Lining is so complicated! Sometimes I feel that she's just like your father— two different people inside and out. She felt she was right about everything and justified to do anything.

Speaking of your father, I suspect that he had some inkling about Lining and me. During their first visit in 1965, when you and your mother were out shopping one day, your father suddenly said to me, "It'll be difficult for Lining to get married. Where will she find someone eloquent like Charley, kind like Paul, handsome like Ed, and most important of all, smart like you?"

I had been responding "Yes" and "You're right" to his idle talk, but his abrupt change of subject and comment about Lining's possible future mate were too close for comfort. I became very uneasy and stopped cold, while he watched me like a hawk. Fortunately he never mentioned her to me again.

He probably made these remarks to test me, but his comments also told me that he believed Lining deserved the best, someone with everything. With such expectations from her father, how could she ever get married? Nobody would be good enough. I certainly wasn't and never would be.

You may think you've been hurt, but if you look at the situation from that perspective, she's the biggest victim of us all!

Chapter 28

The Aftermath

While Sam was pouring his heart out, a distant memory suddenly jolted my consciousness with such shocking force that I momentarily stopped listening. It was my father's verdict, delivered when I was eleven:

"You will never be happy in life. No man will want you when you grow up. If you get married, your marriage will fail."

Gritting his teeth and his face green with rage, my father had delivered his words one at a time for emphasis, as if he had been spitting out bullets. It seemed like a curse at the time, but it was more a prophecy—a prophecy that had come true because his surrogate, my sister, had ably carried it out for him. My marriage had failed after its first year when Sam met her.

What provoked my father's fury was a childish offense.

On that morning, I had gotten up early, gone downstairs where Charley and our cousin Paul slept, and struck them lightly with my hand on each of their foreheads. Then, I had fled back to bed. I was resentful because I felt they favored Lining in their interpretation of the rules of our game, hide and seek. By hitting them, I meant to convey a message—"Don't treat me like this; it's not fair!" Then I did something worse. Scared out of my wits when my father, seething with anger, confronted me moments later, I denied it.

Even at eleven, I had sensed something wasn't quite right—what did hitting them on the forehead have to do with marriage or future happiness?

Since the incident had happened so long ago, I had never

235

thought of telling Sam. When I did bring it up days after his confession as a sardonic coincidence, he was baffled too and asked why my father became so angry for so trivial an offense.

We were taking a walk near a local dam when the answer came instantaneously to my mind: *my ninth aunt*.

Once the words came out of my mouth, I knew my answer was correct. In fact, I felt I had always known it in my subconscious and just hadn't admitted it.

Years earlier, my mother had told me the story of my father's two sisters, my fifth and ninth aunts, who had both been in love with the same man, outside of their respective marriages. Fifth Aunt, the pretty one and my father's favorite sister, married her lover after her husband died, while Ninth aunt, the plain and tactless one, was abandoned by her husband for her crime—the husband my father had chosen for her to cover up the scandal.

When I was growing up, I had overheard remarks about my strong resemblance to my ninth aunt. I didn't pay much attention to these comments for I assumed they were irrelevant. I never saw a photo of Ninth Aunt and was two years old when we left our ancestral home. I had no memory of her.

Nevertheless, could these tenuous threads be connected? Could they be one of the factors that have perpetuated my father's lifelong ill feelings towards me and precipitated his outburst when I was eleven? Was he speaking not to me that morning but to his estranged sister, my ninth aunt? If so, he probably didn't even realize it himself.

§

From somewhere deep in the top drawer of his bureau, Sam dug out the photo he had kept hidden. Over the years, I had looked for it a few times and thought I had misplaced it.

To the one I like very, very much, Lillian

Sam's previous behavior, particularly his phone-call marriage proposal back in Iowa, should have warned me that he was emotionally stunted. Liable to act on impulse for instant gratification, he was emotionally more a child than an adult. On my part, I had lacked the maturity to recognize it back then and had dismissed it carelessly later.

The way I saw it, much of his confession was rationalization and self-justification. My sister had set a trap for him, and he had fallen headlong into it—that part was true. From his description of their yearlong "tug of war," it was clear that if she had really wanted him, she could have had him ten times over. Yes, he had been conflicted, but he would have slept with her because the attraction was too strong. Only when she rejected him time and again and wouldn't allow him to retreat did he start to worry about his family.

For all his professed love for me, I saw very little evidence of it. Obviously, I paled next to his new love. Like a child, he had preferred his exciting new toy, but since he couldn't have it, he went back to his old toy, his marriage. It was better than nothing.

I marveled at his skill in lying throughout those thirty years of deceit. Still, his guilt and hopeless longing for her and the strain of living a double life had devastated his health, which had already been tenuous from his horrendous childhood. It was now obvious that many of his health problems had been largely psychosomatic—a form of self-punishment.

I found we had been in exile in small towns all those years, never returning to live in New York—courtesy of Lining. I, who had been so enamored of the city that I wanted to stay for the rest of my life. I gave it up for my marriage. I gave it up for a lie.

Now I was in a quandary. In addition to the pain, anger, humiliation, and sadness, I had to decide what to do about our marriage.

I remember an especially cold evening in the winter of 1961 before Sam and I married. We had just gotten back to the apartment I shared with my cousin Cecilia, when spontaneously, in front of the scandalized Cecilia and Ed, Sam took off my socks and shoes, rubbed his palms together, and massaged my feet. I was terribly embarrassed, but as the warmth from his hands spread over my feet, I told myself, "I shall remember this to eternity."

I was too young to know that although *I* might remember that moment forever, his feelings, real and sincere at the time, wouldn't last.

Perhaps it was the warmth I felt that night that fostered my illusion that his love would always be like a toasty warm coat against the world's cold arctic winds. I had no idea that the new coat had soon become riddled with holes from wanton bugs of desire. Shivering in the cold for thirty years, I had continued to wear it, unaware and unsuspecting, while the guilty party kept silent to save his own skin.

Now I was horrified to find it too painful, if not impossible, to cast off the coat. Over the years, it had fused to me and had become a part of me. How do you renounce and discard an integral part of yourself? Yet to live on with the knowledge of the holes would be equally excruciating and unbearable.

My sister had certainly relished her power. I remembered well her contemptuous words over the years: "I couldn't live your kind of life for a week!" "What do you have in Iowa? Birds wouldn't even bother to lay eggs there."

Sam said he hadn't betrayed me. But what else could he call his relationship with Lining and the later years of longing?

To use his analogy, he claimed he had treasured our marriage but dropped it on account of "outside forces," sidestepping his own participation. It didn't break because he had lied about it. But as far as I was concerned, our marriage had cracked. It would never be the same.

He accused me of being complicit. Maybe I had been—naïve, blind, and in denial. I must have sensed it at some level because I once dreamed about finding a letter in our mailbox from my father addressed to Sam and Lining. I attributed the dream to my being needlessly suspicious. I was so indoctrinated with our family narrative, and she appeared to be so sweet that I was incapable of suspecting her.

When Charley later learned about her exploits with Sam, he wasn't surprised: "Sure, she pulled that trick several times. Her best friend broke up with her for the same reason."

I knew life wasn't a rose garden. Neither was love small pox—one doesn't gain any sort of immunity. A man may love two women at the same time, but not with the same kind of love or the same intensity. Sam might have loved two women, but he succeeded in failing us both. I was offended when he kept repeating, "I had to think of you and Andrea." Did anyone need to take him by the hand and inform him that he should have thought of his wife and child *before* betraying them?

He also failed my sister because by escaping to Iowa, he had denied her the ultimate triumph she sought—an open declaration that he preferred her to me. After she had worked for two years to trap him and already begun to lose her patience, he had dodged. Was it surprising that she cried on the phone, stunned with disappointment? Idiotically, he took it as proof of her love.

He thought it was heroic of him to sacrifice his love, but no, he stayed with the marriage to save himself. If he had been sure that she wanted him, he might have left us.

He was right about one thing, however. If I had known about their relationship at the time, I would have left him.

Learning about it twenty-eight years later was a different matter. Now he was so emotionally and physically fragile that he was unlikely to survive on his own. While he had behaved abominably, he didn't deserve a death sentence—especially since it had been *my* sister who seduced him for the precise reason that he was *my* husband.

In his confession, he succeeded in painting an uncanny portrait of me as a patsy. I did feel like a patsy, for in the end I chose to pretend to the outside world that nothing had ever happened.

Nevertheless, I felt strongly that our children should be told. Understandably, Sam was against it but had to go along with it. Three months later, when our two children and son-in-law Doug were home for Christmas, we sat them down, and Sam told them the gist of the story. None of them had had any inkling before the revelation.

Confronted with such an intimate and secret dimension of their father, a dimension they hadn't known existed, they were shocked, felt awkward and didn't quite know how to react. Other than a couple of feeble jokes in a vain effort to leaven the air, they didn't have much to say and behaved afterward as though nothing had happened.

But as time went on, it appeared to be life-changing for Clifton, who had just gone back to school for his PhD studies, also in theoretical physics. Perhaps his father's revelation was so unsettling, he started his search to make sense of the world. For a while he became a vegetarian and began to meditate and visit temples, actively seeking some type of alternative answers. In addition to his studies and later, his successful career in engineering, he has been following a dual path of spirituality.

After they went upstairs to their bedrooms that day, Sam was visibly relieved that the ordeal was over. He declared, "I forgive you. You've been a good wife."

I was speechless. The chutzpah! Who was forgiving whom? That was when it dawned on me that something was missing from his long confession: he had been holding a grudge against me all this time—for being the impediment to his heart's desire.

I am convinced that on some level, Sam clung to the belief that Lining was in love with him once upon a time, a belief he never relinquished to his dying day. To be desired was such an exquisite pleasure that he was incapable of giving up hope. He had declared in his confession that his love for the young girl he left in New York would never die. It didn't. While preparing for his memorial service, our children found another photo of young Lining in his desk drawer.

It still astounds me that Sam, who was so clear-headed about physics, could be so muddle-headed about "love." Any psychologist could probably have solved in one session the riddle that plagued him for forty years.

Call it one-upmanship, sibling rivalry, or jealousy, but what Sam refused to grasp or was incapable of understanding was obvious to me. Lining always had to be the favored one, the one everybody loved more than others—just the way it had been at home, with our father. In doing so, she was probably motivated by something akin to craving. When

Lining, 1961; photo found in Sam's desk after his death

one is hungry, one looks for food; it was as basic as that.

Charley felt Lining had also tried to control him by other means. He saw it as power play—she knew she had the power and she used it. "She had no bottom line," he said. "People without a bottom line are dangerous."

The entitled, unapologetic Lining. Daring and willing me to discover their affair.

In psychoanalysis, her problem is called Electra complex, the female version of the Oedipal complex, originating from a girl's desire for her father. This would explain why she went straight for her brother-in-law and her best friend's husband.

In a way, I was partially responsible, since any man who had the misfortune of marrying me would have been put to the same egregious test. Sam happened to have failed miserably.

Sam and I went on living together amicably for thirteen years until he died one night of a massive stroke. I was bereft, and I genuinely mourned him as an integral part of myself and as an intellectual companion. However, since the day of his confession, some essential elements in our marriage had been irretrievably lost—including trust, respect, and affection.

The night he died, I woke in the middle of the night to his slurring words. In a little over an hour, he was on life support and declared brain dead. Clifton and his wife Tracy, who also lived in San Diego at the time, rushed to the hospital. After Andrea arrived from Philadelphia the following afternoon and before we stopped life support according to his living will, the two children each went to his bed and gave him a kiss. Then it was my turn.

I couldn't do it. Something in me rebelled against it. In the intensive care unit, just before his imminent death, I couldn't kiss him on the cheek and whisper a final goodbye. Andrea pushed me to do it. Later she asked me, "Aren't you glad you did?" No, as a matter of fact, I wasn't and still am not glad.

During that moment of truth, I realized I, too, was holding a grudge. My feelings for him were no longer, as he once put it, "simple and wholehearted." They were too complicated for me to fathom, and in the tangled mess was a strong element of pity—pity for him and for me.

Our problem stemmed from our pathetic but disparate need to believe. He yearned to believe my sister did find him desirable, and I needed to believe I could trust the man I married. Both of us were badly mistaken.

§

One day, as I approached the end of writing this memoir, I came face-to-face with a sudden insight. The powerful onslaught of emotions that followed made me recognize the truth my mind had refused to acknowledge all these years and that my consciousness had not yet been able to accept.

I have forever been that six-year-old abandoned by my mother during the war, defenseless and in shock. While my mind has successfully and permanently obliterated the memory of those six months among strangers, the horror stays in the depth of my soul. For the rest of my life, I have made decisions I thought were sensible and pragmatic, without realizing they were based on incapacitating fear, the fear of being abandoned and reliving that horror again.

More than fifty years ago, I convinced myself that K and I could not be compatible after such a long separation; therefore, I severed our relationship rather than put it to the test.

Now I realize that my decision was rooted in my fear of being abandoned, except that at the time, I didn't know I was afraid. In other words, I couldn't face the possibility of being abandoned by K, so I took the preemptive step of abandoning him.

That fear delivered me right into the arms of a seemingly safe prospect, one who fulfilled my worst fear without my realizing it. During my marriage, I willingly suffered the deprivation of living in small towns, Sam's health and emotional problems, and a mother-in-law from hell—all for that illusory safety.

Was it a real marriage? Yes, in many ways—except one. Sam represented himself to me as one person; in his heart he was another. Nothing can change the fact that I was lied to and I feel used. My marriage was the biggest and cruelest irony of my life.

Chapter 29

A Hunter for Love

Shortly after Sam finished his confession, I started writing what I thought would be a short story.

In 1992, the incident of Aron Ralston, who freed himself by severing his arm caught under a boulder in a mountain-climbing accident, was still eleven years in the future, but I had heard of a Soviet physician who had been compelled to perform a life-saving self-appendectomy.

While I can't compare my sufferings with the desperation and bravery of those men, I believe I have some idea of the pain they had to endure.

What I suffered, of course, was emotional pain—not physical pain. For me, I needed to face the facts, and the only way I knew how was to give words to them, even if I could only write the painful truth in fiction. Fiction would give everyone involved a measure of privacy and allow me the freedom to explore the minds and unknowable thoughts of others. I hoped to gain better understanding in the process.

It took nine months. When I was finished, the "short story" had become a novella, the longest piece I had ever written.

In the twenty years I wrote literary essays and short stories in Chinese, I had covered many subjects, but rarely touched upon my personal life. This was the first and only time I bared my soul to the public, albeit under the guise of fiction.

Understandably, Sam abhorred my writing the story even more than his having to reveal it to the children. He probably wished he could censor or forbid it. Short of that, he did come up with a way of coping with the situation. While I was occupied with writing, he spent evenings listening to one of his favorite operas—Verdi's *Othello*—identifying himself with Desdemona, who is wronged and murdered by the insanely jealous Othello. His extraordinary interpretation of his condition vis-à-vis the opera proved that he was a genius at conjuring up his own narrative to tailor-fit his behavior. Earlier, I had wondered how my sister could have lived with her actions. Now I realized she, too, must have had her own self-justifying narrative.

Writing the novella was so draining that immediately after, I suffered a fall, developed a severe knee infection, and was wheelchair-bound for months.

The next was to publish the novella. I had been a regular contributor to *World Journal*, the most respected and popular Chinese language newspaper in the United States, for more than eight years. However, my father was a faithful reader of the paper ever since he and my mother had moved to America. Just the thought of my father reading the story was enough to make me break out in a cold sweat; I intended to submit it to a newspaper in Taiwan instead.

Meanwhile, however, I had developed a close friendship with Qijun, the most venerable contemporary literary essayist and short story writer—whose works my father had used frequently to disparage mine.

We met at a literary conference, appeared on the same panel on several occasions, and once even roomed together for a week. She lived in New Jersey, and we developed the habit of speaking on the phone several times a week. Once we even joked about collaborating on a story. We also discussed our respective works in progress, and she asked to see a copy of my finished novella.

I had wanted to name it *The Hunter*—an unobtrusive title—but Qijun thought *A Hunter for Love* would be more enticing.

Qijun liked my novella so much she forwarded it, without my knowledge, to her good friend in Taiwan—the renowned poet Yaxuan, Editor in Chief of the literary sections of several papers of the same conglomerate. *World Journal's* literary section being under

Yaxuan's command, he gave my story to its fiction page editor.

I had hoped Qijun would give me a critique and some suggestions, not realizing that she would send it to Yaxuan out of sheer enthusiasm. Petrified, I lost no time faxing a frantic letter to the fiction page editor to retract the story, but was told it was already in production.

A Hunter for Love appeared the traditional way. It occupied most of the page and was accompanied by illustrations for the first three days to entice the readers, and was then relegated to the side with a smaller portion serialized every day. It took two months to publish the 65,000-word novella.

The structure of my story is a bit unusual, as it consists of five chapters—four of them told from the perspectives of different narrators. The first chapter opens with the husband's confession; the second chapter contains his wife's reaction; the third, his sister-in-law's session with her psychiatrist; and the fourth, his insomniac father-in-law's stream-of-consciousness thoughts before falling asleep. The fifth chapter is the old man's dream.

My father called me on the second day of the story's publication after he had read the first part of the opening chapter.

Unlike three years ago, when he thought Lining's "flirting" with her brother-in-law was acceptable and even cute, he protested that he knew nothing and would have disapproved of her behavior. His friends were all asking him whether it was true, he said. I insisted it was fiction, but of course he knew otherwise from the details. He never called me again.

But he phoned Charley four times. Deeply worried about a scandal, my father sought Charley's advice during the months *A Hunter for Love* was in publication. In the short four years my parents had resided in Chevy Chase, Maryland—an affluent D.C. suburb with a large Chinese population—my charismatic father had established a fine reputation as a successful patriarch and had even given talks in the community about how to have a happy family. He relished his standing in the community, and his bottom line, according to Charley, was never to lose face.

Now he was being put in the hateful position of seeing his family's dirty laundry aired in public. He had no idea what would come in the next day's paper, what more would be revealed, or how long the ordeal would last.

Although I tried to keep a low profile and didn't call him in the duration, I wasn't having an easy time of it either. Some days I tried to avoid the fiction page; other days I would brace myself, wondering about my father's possible reaction as he read those same words.

Because of Alzheimer's, my mother had long before lost her ability to read. My father told Charley that he had read my story to her and my mother had listened, weeping. When Charley told me this later, I burst into tears.

Oh, Muma, you've never said a word about my writing. I never knew whether you've ever read anything of mine. Now were you weeping for me or for yourself?

I have no idea how much of the novella my father read to her; it was probably only the first chapter. The rest would have been too close to home.

Although Charley made it clear that he wanted to stay out of it and that, in any case, there wasn't anything anyone could do, my father still wanted Charley to keep abreast of the problem and offer suggestions. Since Charley was not a *World Journal* reader, my father sent the clippings to him one batch at a time. He mailed Charley four batches over the two months, and Charley read them and returned them in one batch—with no comment. They never discussed the content, and my brother never called me to discuss the matter either.

Because it was fiction, and I published short stories from time to time, there was never any scandal. *A Hunter for Love* was reprinted in a newspaper in Taiwan and published as a book by the publisher of several of my other volumes. It received a great deal of attention from its readers. Discussion groups were held about the book, and curious readers frequently approached me with questions or comments.

My father died a year later, in December 1994, of congestive heart failure. Though Lining lived on a separate floor in the same building and dined with them in their apartment every night, my father never breathed a word to her about the story.

A couple of years after my father's death, during one of my visits to my mother, I was surprised to run into Lining in the nursing home one day. By then my sister and I were no longer on speaking terms, but she asked me for a copy of the novella. Someone must finally have alerted her to its existence. I mailed her a copy after I returned home. I didn't expect to hear from her, and I didn't.

A Hunter for Love in book form. Photo by Sylvia Durian.

The next and last time I spoke with Lining was on the phone; we discussed funeral matters after my mother's death. I had never confronted her about the affair and didn't plan to, but somehow the subject of the book came up. Lining claimed I had "connected the dots entirely wrong," and that I wronged her to protect my husband. It was Sam who had come on to her, and all those years she had tried her best to ward off his unwanted attention. She said she hadn't had the heart to tell me that I had a philandering husband.

Inexplicably, my hopes surged. All along I must have wished Sam had chased every skirt in sight, including my sister, rather than believe she had seduced him. Somehow on my mind's scale, to be betrayed by my own sister went much deeper—was a far more difficult pill to swallow than my husband's infidelity.

Sam was in his study next to the kitchen where I was on the phone. Instead of confronting him, I rushed upstairs and tore through the photos. The only pictures containing Lining after we left New York were taken when she came to Iowa for help with her master's thesis. I put aside everything and worked with her intensely for nearly three weeks, but we did take a break one afternoon when Sam and I gave her a tour of the Iowa State campus.

Lining teasing the man behind the lens; Iowa, 1969

I found the photo I had dimly remembered. There she was, under the sun, standing next to me, the adorable young Lining, sticking her tongue out at Sam, the photographer.

In this day and age, sticking your tongue out in a photo is considered no more than simply playful or childish. Even back then, forty years ago, my father would have interpreted it as "harmlessly flirtatious." Back then, when I saw the photo, I, too, thought nothing of it.

But now, knowing what had gone on between them in New York, and given Lining's counter accusation, the image burned before my eyes. Does she look like someone who is trying to ward off or to attract the attention of the photographer?

Chapter 30

THE ENDGAME

To this day I'm still incredulous—and ashamed, really—at how naïve I was when I set out for Maryland to visit my father on his deathbed. Clifton accompanied me on the trip to lend moral support. Sam had retired in 1994, and we had moved to San Diego two months before I learned that my father was seriously ill.

Though still wounded by Sam's revelation two years earlier, I vowed to set my feelings aside for the time being, for I had decided that this was no time to address grievances. I told myself I would be there to say goodbye to my father and help my mother through this difficult time.

My father was so deep in his morphine-induced sleep that he never knew we were there. He had lost weight, his skin was sallow, and he breathed heavily. When I had spoken to him by phone more than a week earlier, he had seemed his normal self—though he did complain about feeling unusually tired.

The hospital doctor explained to Charley and me that my father was suffering from congestive heart failure, which rendered his heart insufficient to support the other critical organs. He was on palliative care, and it was just a matter of days.

It was the last time I saw him alive.

In my parents' apartment, it was heartbreaking to see my mother surprised and overjoyed at the sight of us. Failing to grasp the purpose of our trip and having lost the concept of distance, she thought Clifton and I were just dropping in to pay her a visit.

My mother flickered in and out of lucidity. A lifelong tea

drinker, she had always been discerning about the choice and quality of her tea; now she pointed to her mug and complained that her tea had no taste. She didn't realize she was drinking hot water, according to my sister's orders.

As usual, I slept on a cot in my mother's bedroom. Unopened boxes of her belongings that Charley had painstakingly packed from her room in Taiwan were piled high in a row, leaning against the wall an arm's length away. They still smelled like my parents' apartment in Taiwan, slightly mildewed with a touch of smog.

As usual, my mother and I chatted side by side before falling asleep, and this time, she talked about Lining, who had stayed away since Clifton and I arrived.

Lining was my father's favorite; we all knew it, but we never spoke of it. In fact, we all—including my mother—did everything to pretend it was not so. Charley and I also knew that Lining could be very high-handed and had never gotten along well with our mother.

I remembered one day she had shouted at my mother at the top of her high-pitched voice, "I don't *allow* you to drink milk!" Shocked, I took her aside to remind her, "You can't talk to *Muma* like that! She still remembers the time when she was breastfeeding you and changing your diapers. You must show her some respect, especially when she's staying in your apartment." Lining had heard somewhere that milk was harmful to patients with rheumatoid arthritis. But my mother enjoyed drinking a cup of warm milk now and then, since tea had become a forbidden pleasure.

Always her taciturn self, my mother had never complained about Lining. Now things appeared to have taken a turn for the worse. She was suspicious of her.

Before going to the hospital, my father had entrusted all his keys to Lining. She had begun sleeping in his room, which contained the locked cabinet where my father kept his most important documents. My mother didn't think Lining should have free access to those documents.

Given my mother's current mental state, I wasn't sure how much I could rely on her judgment, so I tried to convince her that she should relax, trust Lining, and not worry unnecessarily.

In the morning I accompanied my mother to her weekly hair

appointment in the beauty salon downstairs. Afterward, while she was resting, I went to the lobby to fetch their mail and ran into Lining.

We had seen each other since her violent outburst at Sam, but we had never been alone or spoken together. I knew from the neatly folded and undisturbed pile of clippings in my father's glass cabinet that she hadn't read or been aware of the novella.

I had never confronted her about the affair or anything else. The truth is, all my life I have been uncomfortable with confrontations and avoid them at all cost. I could always find excuses. When Lining didn't acknowledge Andrea and me for help with her PhD dissertation, I was shocked and hurt, then I tried to rationalize: "What difference would it make anyway? None of the people who read them would notice our names whether they are on the page or not."

This time I had a different excuse. Looking into Lining's face, I was surprised to discover I felt no anger or bitterness—the family myth that I had been indoctrinated with since childhood must have instantly taken over and cast its powerful spell. I felt nothing, as if nothing untoward had happened between us.

But I did notice that *she* was hostile.

Lining immediately launched into a heated complaint about my mother's objection to paying their cleaning lady to clean Lining's apartment. I agreed with her that my mother was being unreasonable. Lining was spending time and effort overseeing our parents' daily lives—why quibble about the expenses of the cleaning lady? I promised to talk to my mother about that. (Only later did I learn from Charley that our parents were paying Lining's rent and had bought her a new Toyota.)

As I was turning to leave, she stopped me. "I see you just had your hair done. Did you pay your own bill?"

I was taken aback. As a matter of fact, I had not only paid my own bill but had tried to pay for my mother's as well. Her hairdresser told me she had a standing account, so I gave her an extra tip to thank her for taking care of my mother every week.

I told Lining this, but I was rattled. Was she trying to catch me in a possible infraction?

After lunch, Lining showed up at the apartment with Francene and her two daughters. Paul had passed away from lung cancer two years earlier. Years before his death, I had sensed that—under Lining's influence—our two cousins were becoming more and more unfriendly towards me. Gradually a battle line seemed to be drawn, with three of them on one side, and Charley and me on the other. That day, Francene and her daughters barely acknowledged my presence. The four of them went off with my mother to visit my father in the hospital. Clifton and I were not invited.

My father died early the next day, on Sunday morning. Lining insisted that we keep the news from our mother. I thought the idea was ludicrous. How could we keep this news from her, and why should we? Nevertheless, to keep the peace, I didn't challenge her.

Charley told me over the phone that we had all been given the power of attorney to manage the estate. It looked even-handed on the surface. Each of us had full power and could exercise it independently, but this setup came with an obvious loophole— what if the three of us didn't agree? Wouldn't the disagreement result in anarchy and chaos?

My father had known us well. He understood that Charley would be the first to bow out, since he was still bitter about not being trusted. I lived far away, had never been involved in the financial affairs of my parents, and therefore could not be expected to fulfill any power-of-attorney duties. Lining would be left with full and unchecked power. Whether any of us had veto power or the right to oversee what she might decide was left unspecified.

Lining had made a Monday appointment with my mother's physician—the very day after my father's death—and wanted me to accompany them. Once there, I realized that the objective was to confirm my mother's mental state. I was shocked to hear my sister relay to the doctor the news of our father's death in front of my mother, who sat meekly without understanding a word. Then my mother suffered the humiliation of failing every test, even after my translations.

Back home, I told my mother about my father's death. She cried, but the news seemed to temporarily jolt her out of her fog.

Before bed she told me that she wanted Charley to manage the estate, and for me to inform him first thing in the morning. She was adamant about not wanting Lining to have anything to do with their money or her affairs.

That was when I realized why Lining had wanted to keep my mother in the dark about my father's death. She had anticipated my mother's reaction and had rendered any of her possible actions futile with the afternoon's office visit—the doctor and I were unwitting witnesses to her mental deterioration and incompetence.

Charley said he appreciated my mother's sentiment, but it was too late.

Despite my father's professed fear that we would leave his body on the streets for the dogs, he had left clear instructions that he wished to be cremated and no funeral be held. But my mother insisted on a funeral before the cremation: "He was alive the last time I saw him; I need to see him again."

All of us were astonished that she displayed such strong emotions at the funeral. Only later did I realize that my mother was genuinely frightened to be left solely in the care of my sister, who seemed to sense her feelings and stayed away from her throughout the service.

Lining had arranged for all three of us to meet with the attorney after the funeral. Because Charley refused to attend, only she and I went. I can't explain what made me declare to the lawyer, "I'd trust Lining with my own money." To this day, when I think of what I said, I'm flooded with shame. What kind of imbecile was I? How could I have said this, knowing that I couldn't even trust my own husband with her? I have searched and searched in my mind and have been unable to find any defense for having made such an idiotic statement. With seven short words, I confirmed my status as the family patsy.

On the spot, the lawyer typed out a two-page memo giving Lining carte blanche to use our parental funds in anyway she saw fit. She didn't need to report to us, and we relinquished any right to oversee her actions. She would be given a monthly stipend for her trouble, the amount to be determined by her and her attorney. He gave me copies of the memo for Charley and me to sign.

Charley was furious. We agreed that we would not be able to overturn the setup without going to court, and we didn't want an ugly legal battle. Whether we signed the memo or not, it was a *fait accompli*, and we decided not to contest her on anything.

Next, Lining wanted me to go with her to the bank to verify that our parents' safe deposit box contained "nothing but certificates of deposit."

Had she forgotten that I was with them that day when my father carried a briefcase with "little gold fishes" and my mother's jewelry? Only Lining entered the vault with him, which meant only they had access to the safe deposit box contents. Why drag me to the bank now?

I refused. "If you say there's nothing except the certificates, why do I need to see the box? Besides, they won't let me in anyway." At that, she started yelling and crying. Charley had told me that these were her usual tactics when she failed to get her way, but I had never experienced them before because I had never refused her anything. Her theatrics were something to behold, but I stood my ground.

§

Whenever I think about those days after my father's death, the words "trench warfare" come to mind. Clueless, I didn't know what I was doing in the trench or where and when the next bullet would fly. Even having Clifton with me, I was foundering and unable to eat or sleep from the stress. In two weeks, I lost seven pounds. Although I was a comfort to my mother, who emphatically didn't want me to leave, I felt I had to go home.

The night before my departure, my mother tried to ease my mind, "Don't worry. I can always go home. I think I will go home, but first I must give some money to my sister-in-law…" My mouth fell open and my tears began to flow. She was thinking of her home in Hefei, a home that had been long lost, since the beginning of the Sino-Japanese War.

The next morning, Charley came to take Clifton and me to the airport, and my mother stood in the living room and delivered her last somewhat lucid speech: "He (pointing to Clifton) has you, and you have him; the two of you go and live a good life. I'm alone. I have no one."

It was all I could do to tear myself away.

To ease my conscience, I called her every day. A few times, she had her caregiver dial my number and announced happily, "I'm coming over to see you today."

"*Muma*," I said, knowing I was being cruel, "You'll have to have someone drive you to the airport to get on the plane, but don't worry, I'll come over to see you soon."

"Oh…"

I did visit her several times, but she was fast descending into oblivion.

To this day, I'm full of regrets when I think of my mother in her surviving years after my father's death.

I regret that we never told her she suffered from an incurable disease. In her lucid moments, she might have wondered why we didn't get her better medical help.

I regret that I had to leave her totally at the mercy of my sister. I inquired about moving her to San Diego, but her doctor said that any move from her familiar surroundings would only exacerbate her condition. My mother did not wish to move either—she wanted *me* to stay, to protect her and be her lifelong companion.

I regret, most of all, the way in which she was buried—with the urn containing my father's ashes on her chest. Since my mother did not wish to be cremated, Lining, without consulting us, decided to bury them in the same coffin.

In life, my father lorded over my mother. Thanks to my sister, he sits on her chest in death, for all of eternity.

§

Shortly after Clifton and I returned to San Diego, I received a copy of my father's handwritten will.

It was intriguing that after five years of exorbitantly-priced legal help, my father was never informed that handwritten wills were not legal in Maryland. My parents' estate, therefore, had to go through probate—which was executed by none other than Lining's attorney's firm.

The document itself was also peculiar. My father states that all his life he has treated his three children fairly and equally, and he is mystified why they have bickered bitterly and have never gotten along. He writes that he nevertheless wants his children to share the inheritance equally and help our cousins when necessary. He lists Charley's stepsons—whom he only met once—by name, expressing his loving concern, but he makes no mention of my children.

I felt this was his way of reaching from the grave to slap me for the unforgivable offense of writing and publishing my novella. Unlike the two burning slaps across my face as a child, those two icy slaps—one for each of my children—didn't hurt. His way of disowning my children was all right with me. I had felt like an orphan for some time; I guess I was used to it.

To be expected, Lining triumphed over Charley and me on the settling of our parents' estate. We did not contest her on anything, except that Charley did write a nineteen-page letter to the lawyer—for several years, he had kept a detailed journal—pointing out the irregularities Lining had committed.

There were several certificates of deposit earmarked POD (paid on death) to Charley, which she tried to get Charley legally disqualified from, but she didn't succeed.

Apparently, my father's "little gold fishes" turned up after all. Some time later, Lining offered them to Charley, but he refused.

I received a package of about thirty satin jewelry pouches from my sister. Most were empty. A few contained junk jewelry. Nothing I had seen my mother wear during her lifetime was in any of the pouches. Perhaps this was a taunt?

The last Charley and I heard from Lining was a letter via the lawyer, requesting that any further communication from us be sent through the office of her attorney.

§

It has been decades since our father's death and Lining's legal scheming, but I still don't believe she acted the way she did for money.

I think she needed power—power to triumph over her older siblings. She needed to justify my father's high expectations of her and repay us for all her years of feeling perplexed and inadequate because of us, despite enjoying our father's undivided love. We were much older and were stronger academically and otherwise. She probably felt threatened by us.

I'm sure she can recall many instances when we offended her. I still remember the time when she had failed an exam again, and Charley—seven years her senior and frustrated by her unwillingness to shape up—slapped her. My father wasn't home at the time.

Later when they lived near each other in Virginia, the fact that Charley vetoed many of her ideas certainly didn't endear him to her.

I remember her delight the first time she overtook me in height, cocking her head and looking down sideways at me, feigning surprise, "Oh my, that's how short you are!"

I also remember her pride in relating her first meeting with my mother-in-law Irene, who asked her hopefully, "Is your sister as tall and strong as you?"

I think about the Iowa photo in which she stuck her tongue out at Sam, the person behind the lens. How could she have seduced him as she did? How could she deny her part? What a betrayal to fly more than 1,000 miles and take three weeks of my time for help on her thesis, and at the same time, take every opportunity to attract my husband and sabotage my marriage! What kind of monster was she?

But now, in the cool twilight of my life, I begin to see what might have motivated her. How desperate, how excruciating it must have been for her to ask for my help. How galling to have to endure my unwitting remarks: "What do you mean by this?"

"Is this what you want to say? You need to say it plainly to get your point across," and "I think you should organize this section differently to make it clearer."

To me, she seemed muddle-headed, not knowing how to think and incapable of organizing or presenting her thoughts. Probably furious, she might have thought she was justified in flirting with my husband, to exact a modicum of revenge on me.

It took her seven years of hard work to earn a master's degree, then another seven years for a PhD in Russian history; each time she was waylaid by her thesis/dissertation. The second time she even needed the help of Andrea, whom she still remembered as a "disgusting" two-year-old. Andrea edited her aunt's PhD dissertation while writing her own. My sister's humiliation was complete. I was shocked and hurt that Andrea and I were not even mentioned in the acknowledgments page of her dissertation. Now I understand why.

And she could not abide anyone preferring me to her. The afternoon she went off to the hospital with my mother, Francene, and her daughters to visit my father, Clifton went to a bookstore, and I was left alone with the caregiver—a young Chinese woman from the mainland. I was curious about how she came to this country, and we had a nice talk. After they returned, Lining noticed her friendliness towards me and immediately started paying more attention to her in the remaining days I was there.

During those years, I gave several talks and participated in panel discussions in the D.C. area and met a reader in Silver Springs, Maryland. She became so fond of me that she went to the nursing home on weekends to sing to my mother, comb her hair, and comfort her. I was touched.

When Lining heard of those visits, she immediately went to the nursing home to meet her, and whatever she said convinced her. My friend never spoke to me again.

I asked Charley, "What could Lining possibly say to turn people against me? Why does everyone just listen to her version and not even give me a chance to defend myself?"

Charley, a fellow victim, replied, "I bet that with your friend and our relatives, she cried as she told *her* story. She is good at crying.

Once she cries, people believe her—*it must be true; she even cried.*"

For years those two brief, peripheral episodes have pained me, for I felt defenseless against her tactics and threatened by her thoroughness. She couldn't allow even a caregiver and a reader showing more friendliness toward me. But now I try to take comfort in the fact that I understand her better. I understand that we all have our weaknesses and we live by our own respective narratives; we are far more complicated than others give us credit for. Clinging to our narratives, we are caught in a Gordian knot we don't know how to escape.

But time—Old Man Time—has a way of resolving everything. Thanks to him, I feel freer than ever at last. Though still bearing my battle scars, I feel free.

EPILOGUE

The Chinese have a long tradition of speaking of their elders only with great respect, in glowing terms. Consequently, all the forebears come across in the family genealogies and elsewhere as saints or perfect specimens, with nary a wart or a blemish.

I know I am fortunate. While many people have unusual lives, not everyone has an opportunity to examine theirs and write about it. To honor my opportunity, when I began writing this memoir, I made a promise to myself to tell my story as is, not to whitewash or embellish.

My grandmother died when I was thirteen, the summer before we fled to Taiwan. She lived with us for almost two years before her death, and I remember her well.

She fell sick in July when my parents were away—my father in Shanghai, a four-hour train ride away, and my mother at her cousin's summer resort in faraway Lu Mountain. However, it was my mother who rushed back after learning by phone of her mother-in-law's illness. After her two-day journey, as soon as she took a look at the patient, she called an ambulance. My grandmother died in the hospital in the early morning.

I was taken to the hospital around noon and was shocked to find my father in the hospital room crying his heart out over his mother's dead body. His grief was genuine and profound, but I did wonder—what good would all his tears do my grandmother when she could no longer hear or feel?

Decades later, my father wrote two pages in memory of her to add to our family genealogy book. Failing to recognize my grandmother in those two pages, I wondered again. Why pile up generic praise and extoll banal virtues? How would that honor her life?

On the other hand, some Western memoirists are known to dramatize their prose for effect. I have no use for that either, as my life has already been too dramatic for my tastes.

For everyone concerned, particularly my children and grandchildren, I resolved to tell my story truly, the way I remember or see it, so that anyone perusing it will know what transpired in my life. Otherwise what I wrote would be meaningless.

My brother Charley is proud of the fact that he can shed his emotional baggage by refusing to dwell in the past. Yet, in our conversations, when the topic inevitably veers to the past, I see he is still bitter.

For me, the past is never past, for it informs my understanding of the present. It is, in fact, an important part of my present, and I have lived in its long shadow, from the old world to the new.

Freud's metaphor of the marriage bed is apt indeed. When Sam and I were married, how much of us were our so-called adult selves, and how much were hurt, angry, and bewildered children, liable to react to everything from that perspective?

I have characterized my father and my mother-in-law as two formidable forces of nature in our lives. When you have had a perpetual monsoon, year after year, joining forces with a tornado, you are lucky simply to have survived.

Without the benefit of self-knowledge or insight into our respective emotional baggage, I blundered through one event after another, always living at an arm's length from myself and everyone else.

In writing my story, I have come to realize that I have never completely given myself over to anyone, including Sam—although I was faithful and caring, a helpmate the best way I knew how.

Emotionally I might have been on the center stage of my life, giving what I thought was my all, yet a part of me remained crouching, hiding in the farthest corner of the second balcony, with my arms wrapped around myself.

Why? I don't understand it myself. I can't trace everything back to my father; many of my actions could have resulted from my nature or those months living as a defenseless six-year-old among strangers. Perhaps something in me died then.

My reserve plus Sam's vulnerability from his horrendous upbringing might have rendered him, like a moth, powerless to resist a brighter flame.

Two people, damaged in disparate ways and to different degrees, happened to meet on the dark ocean of life and embarked on a journey together. Was it happy? Was it sad? Who was right? Who was wrong?

What does it matter? It was what happened, in life, by chance.

ACKNOWLEDGMENTS

Throughout the process of writing this book, I have had numerous and invaluable discussions with my children, Andrea and Clifton. I have been blessed with their whole-hearted support, in addition to their reading of my first and last drafts and their computer expertise. It's not an exaggeration to say that the book would have died on the vine without Andrea, who devoted countless hours from her insanely busy life to refine my prose and help me in any way she could, including rescuing me many times from my computer incompetence.

It means a great deal to me that Andrea searched for and recovered my uncle's name in French. She found that a disease—Barré-Lieou syndrome—is named after his colleague and him. Andrea's timely discovery allowed me to use my uncle's correct French name as a small tribute to him, dead this past sixty-two years after suffering undue tragedies in his life.

Many thanks are also due to my granddaughter Sylvia Durian for taking two photos and converting nearly thirty original photos digitally, and to Andrea for safeguarding those photos in the first place and spending hours sorting through them with me.

I am indebted to my brother Charley for discussions of our shared past.

I wish to thank Dr. Barry Jacobs for planting the idea of writing a memoir in my mind so adroitly and unobtrusively, and Lynn DeMarco for being my physical first line of defense over these years.

Special gratitude goes to Jennifer Hu and Elizabeth Norwood for their expeditious, meticulous, and insightful editing; and to book designer Heidi Reed for her amazingly prompt and excellent work. This book also owes much to editorial advice from Greg Miller, Jun Suzuki, Philip Tseng, Megan Webster, Dante Fuoco, and Lucia Kearney.

My friend Jan Alessi deserves a medal for wading through my first draft with unwavering interest and understanding.

For obvious reasons, I stayed away from writing this memoir for years. But once I began, I wrote as if possessed. Many nights I went to bed convinced that I didn't have it in me to do it, and my health wouldn't allow me to finish it. Come morning, I was at it again. Now I feel incredibly fortunate and extremely grateful to have had the opportunity to bring this volume to its fruition.

Made in the USA
Charleston, SC
01 December 2014